Disclosing Man to Himself

DISCLOSING MAN TO HIMSELF

by

SIDNEY M. JOURARD

D. VAN NOSTRAND COMPANY, INC.

PRINCETON, NEW JERSEY

TORONTO   MELBOURNE   LONDON

Van Nostrand Regional Offices: *New York, Chicago, San Francisco*

D. Van Nostrand Company, Ltd., *London*

D. Van Nostrand Company, Ltd., *London*

D. Van Nostrand Australia Pty. Ltd., *Melbourne*

Published simultaneously in Canada by
D. Van Nostrand Company (Canada), Ltd.

Library of Congress Catalog Card No. 68-20920

Preface

This book continues themes I presented first in *The Transparent Self*. There, I explored the meaning of self-disclosure for wellness, growth, and personal relationships. Here, I have tried to develop a few steps further the "humanistic" approach in psychology. I have tried to show laymen and students and colleagues one view of what psychology might look like if psychologists tried more directly to show those whom they study what they have learned.

A lot of knowledge about a lot of men, if it is possessed by a few, gives these few power over the many. Psychologists seek knowledge about men. Men consent to be studied by psychologists. The question is, who is being helped when psychologists study men? If I have knowledge about you, I can use this to my advantage, and against yours. If I have knowledge about myself, I can increase my freedom and my power to live my life meaningfully. If you have knowledge about me, I would like you to enlighten me, not control me. And I would like to know you.

The book is an invitation to psychologists (and physicians, psychiatrists, teachers, clergymen, counselors, and psychotherapists) to disclose themselves to men, and man to himself, rather than to one's colleagues alone, or to institutional leaders. And it is an invitation to those laymen who are studied by or consult psychologists to ask for as much transparency as the professionals ask of them.

SIDNEY M. JOURARD

Contents

Disclosing Man to Himself

Part One

*A Humanistic Perspective
on Psychological Research*

1

A Humanistic Revolution in Psychology

If I complain I have no will of my own, that people are influencing me in subtle and mysterious ways, you'll accuse me of being paranoid, and direct me to a psychotherapist.

If I put on a white laboratory coat, and assert that you *have no will of your own, that your action and experience can be manipulated, predicted, and controlled, then I am recognized as a scientific psychologist, and honored.*

This is most peculiar.

A revolution is going on in psychology. A different image of man is being tried as a guide to research, theory, and application. Over the years, theorists have conceptualized man as a machine; as an organism comparable to rats, pigeons, and monkeys; as a communication system; as an hydraulic system; as a servo-mechanism; as a computer—in short, he has been viewed by psychologists as an analogue of *everything but what he is:* a person. Man is, indeed, like all those things; but first of all he is a free, intentional subject. The closest analogue we psychologists can find as a model for man is *ourselves.* The other man is more like me than he is like any machine, rat, or pigeon. We have found that the earlier models of man produced unintended consequences at the hands of those who apply psychology. The consumers of psychological writing tended to take our models too seriously and actually started to treat people as if they *were* the models that theorists used only as tentative guides to inquiry.

The disciplines of existentialism, phenomenology, humanism, and personalism are gradually being absorbed by workers in the field; and psychology is in process of being reworked, rewritten, and reapplied. Psychologists are using their experience of themselves as persons as a guide to exploring and understanding the experience of others. This is not the death of "objective," scientific psychology. Rather, it may prove to be the birth of a scientifically informed psychology of human persons—a *humanistic* psychology.

Humanistic psychology is a goal, not a doctrine. It owes its renaissance to the growing conviction that current and past approaches to the study of man have reached their limits in elucidating man's behavior and his "essence." It is a growing corpus of knowledge relating to the questions, "What is a human being, and what might man become?" Thus, humanistic psychology can be regarded in analogy with industrial psychology or the psychology of mental health or of advertising. These specialties are systems of knowledge bearing on particular families of questions: e.g., what variables affect morale, or the output of workers, or the maintenance of wellness, or the purchasing behavior of potential customers. Humanistic psychology asks, "What are the possibilities of man? And from among these possibilities, what is *optimum man,* and what conditions most probably account for his attainment and maintenance of these optima?" [39] *

The aim of science is to know, to gain understanding of some phenomenon which is in question. Sciences addressed to nature, the "natural sciences," seek understanding of natural phenomena in order to tame them, to bring them under control of human beings, for human purposes. Understanding of the processes and phenomena in nature enables man to predict, alter, and control them.

Psychology, the science addressed to man's being, likewise seeks to know and understand. But a sharp distinction must be drawn here between the science of psychology and the natural sciences. While psychologists and physicists seek to understand the phenomena they study, it is appropriate only for the physicists to aim at increased control of these phenomena. If psychologists aim to predict and control human behavior and experience, as in their textbooks they claim, they are assigning man to the same ontological status as weather, stars, minerals, or lower forms of animal life. We do not question anyone's right to seek understanding in order the better to control his physical environment and adapt it to his purposes. We properly

---

* Here and throughout this book superscript numbers refer to works listed in the Bibliography, beginning on page 233.

challenge any man's right to control the behavior and experience of his fellows. To the extent that psychologists illumine human existence to bring it under the deliberate control of someone other than the person himself, to that extent they are helping to undermine some person's freedom in order to enlarge the freedom of someone else. If psychologists reveal knowledge of "determiners" of human conduct to people other than the ones from whom they obtained this understanding, and if they conceal this knowledge from its source, the volunteer subjects (who have offered themselves up to the scientist's "Look"), they put the recipients of the knowledge in a privileged position. They grant them an opportunity to manipulate men without their knowledge or consent. Thus, advertisers, businessmen, military leaders, politicians, and salesmen all seek to learn more about the determiners of human conduct, in order to gain power and advantage. If they can sway human behavior by manipulating the conditions which mediate it, they can get large numbers of people to forfeit their own interests and serve the interests of the manipulator. Such secret manipulation of the masses or of an individual by some other person is possible only if the ones being manipulated are kept mystified as to what is going on, and if their experience of their own freedom is blunted.

Psychologists face a choice. We may elect to continue to treat our Ss as objects of study for the benefit of some elite; or we may choose to learn about determiners of the human condition in order to discover ways to overcome or subvert them, so as to enlarge the Ss'—that is, Everyman's—freedom. If we opt for the latter, our path is clear. Our ways of conducting psychological research will have to be altered. Our definition of the purpose of psychology will have to change. And our ways of reporting our findings, as well as the audiences to whom the reports are directed, will have to change. We shall have to state openly whether we are psychologists-for-institutions or psychologists-for-persons.

The trouble with scientific psychologists—among whom I number myself—is that we have, in a sense, been "bought." We have in our hands the incredible power to discover conditions for behavior or for ways of being in the world. We have catalogued many of the factors which have a determining effect on human behavior and on our condition. We know that, in every experiment that we analyze, there is always an error term, "residual variance"; and we seek to exhaust this residual variance to the best of our ability. We get better at it as we learn how to identify and measure more and more relevant variables. The trouble is, as I see it, that if we exhaust all the variance, the subject of our study will be not a man, a human person, but rather a robot.

Scientific psychology has actually sought means of artificially reducing variance—humanness—among men, so that they will be more manipulable. Our commendable efforts (from a technical viewpoint) in the fields of human engineering, teaching methods, motivation research (in advertising), and salesmanship have permitted practitioners in those realms to develop stereotyped methods that work at controlling outcomes—outcomes that are good for the businessman or politician, but not necessarily good for the victim. We have taught people how to shape man into a way of being that makes him useful. We have forgotten that an image of man as useful grows out of a more fundamental image of man as the being who can assume *many* modes of being, when it is of importance to him to do so.

I think that a scientific psychologist committed to the aims of humanistic psychology would utilize his talents for a different purpose. For example, if individuality and full flowering growth as a person were values, he would seek means of maximizing or increasing the odds for maximization of these ways of being. An example of the biased use of scientific know-how is brainwashing. The brainwasher, through scientific means, seeks to insure that the prisoner will behave and believe as his captors wish. The same psychologists who invented the means of brainwashing know how to prevent it from happening. The latter class of knowledge is more in keeping with the aims of humanistic psychology and should be more avidly sought and then applied in more realms than presently is the case, if humanistic psychology is to be furthered.

How odd it seems that psychology has learned more about man at his worst than at his best. How sad it seems that psychology has employed its powers of truth-finding to serve ignoble masters. I would like to propose that we don't wait until the scarcity of "full-functioning men" becomes a national emergency. Rather, I would propose that we psychologists reconcile our aims and commitment to truth and our adherence to the canons of scientific inquiry with our human concerns that man be free, that he grow. I propose that we commence an all-out program of investigation on many fronts to seek answers to the questions humanistic psychology is posing. For example, we need psychologists with the most informed imaginations and talent for ingenious experimentation to wrestle with such questions as, "What are the outer limits of human potential for *transcending* biological pressures, social pressures, and the impact on a person of his past conditioning?"; "What developmental and interpersonal and situational conditions conduce to courage, creativity, transcendent behavior, love, laughter, commitment to truth, beauty, justice, and virtue?" These questions themselves, and even my proposal that we address them, once struck me as less than manly, as tender-hearted and sentimental. I would never have dared pose them to most of my mentors during my undergraduate and graduate-student days. We were supposed to be tough and disciplined, which meant that we were only to study questions about some very limited class of behavior, not questions about larger human concerns. "Leave those to the philosophers, ministers, and politicians," we were told. Questions about the image of man smacked too much of philosophy and were not our proper concern. Actually, our teachers intended only that we learn the tools of our trade, not that we stifle our humanistic concerns; but they produced that outcome anyway.

Wilse B. Webb[108] has pointed out, in his paper "The Choice of the Problem," that there are many reasons entering into the selection of an area for scientific investigation. I am proposing that the quest for a more adequate image of man, for specification of peculiarly human optima, and the quest for the conditions which maximize or actualize these optima are worthwhile and important areas for study. I guess that, from another point of view altogether, I am inviting more of us to become educated men as we become trained psychologists. I suspect that psychologists who are educated men cannot help but be active humanistic psychologists. One measure of a man is the questions he raises, and another is the goals for which he uses his powers and talents. I am not making a plea for less rigorous inquiry. I am making a plea for the powers of rigorous inquiry to be devoted to questions, answers to which will inform a growing, more viable image of man as a human being with potentiality, not solely a biological or socially determined being.

When researchers are transparently pledged to further the freedom and self-actualizing of their subjects, rather than be unwitting servants of the leaders of institutions, then they will deserve to *be* and *to be seen* as recipients of the secrets of human being and possibility. I envision a time when psychologists will be the guardians of the most intimate secrets of human possibilities and experience and possessors of knowledge as to how man can create his destiny because man has showed him; and I hope that if we "sell" these secrets to advertisers, businessmen, politicians, mass educators, and the military, we shall not do so until *after* we have informed our subjects, after we have tried to "turn them on," to enlarge their awareness of being misled and manipulated. I hope, in short, that we turn out to be servants and guardians of individual freedom, growth, and fulfillment, and not spies for the institutions that pay our salaries and research costs in order to get a privileged peep at human grist. Indeed, we may have to function for a time as counterspies, or double spies—giving reports about our subjects to our colleagues and to institutions, and giving reports back to our subjects as to the ways in which institutions seek to control and predict their behavior for their (the institutions') ends.

2

A Letter from S to E

For some time now I have been talking to people who have served as subjects (Ss) in psychologists' experiments. They have told me of their experience, and it has troubled me. I want to share my concern with my colleagues. The letter that follows is my effort to consolidate the attitudes and feelings of the people to whom I talked.

Dear *E* (Experimenter):

My name is *S*. You don't know me. I have another name my friends call me by, but I drop it, and become *S* NO. 27 as soon as I take part in your research. I serve in your surveys and experiments. I answer your questions, fill out questionnaires, let you wire me up to various machines that record my physiological reactions. I pull levers, flip switches, track moving targets, trace mazes, learn nonsense syllables, tell you what I see in inkblots—do the whole barrage of things you ask me to do. I have started to wonder why I do these things for you. What's in it for me? Sometimes you pay me to serve. More often I have to serve, because I'm a student in a beginning psychology course, and I'm told that I won't receive a grade unless I take part in at least two studies; and if I take part in more, I'll get extra points on the final exam. I am part of the Department's "subject-pool."

When I've asked you what I'll get out of your studies, you tell me that, "It's for Science." When you are running some one particular study, you often lie to me about your purpose. You mislead me. It's getting so I find it difficult to trust you. I'm beginning to see you as a trickster, a manipulator. I don't like it.

In fact, I lie to you a lot of the time, even on anonymous questionnaires. When I don't lie, I will sometimes just answer at random, anything to get through with the hour, and back to my own affairs. Then, too, I can often figure out just what it is you are trying to do, what you'd like me to say or do; at those times, I decide to go along with your wishes if I like you, or foul you up if I don't. You don't actually say what your hopes or hypotheses are; but the very setup in your laboratory, the alternatives you give me, the instructions you offer, all work together to pressure me to say or do something in particular. It's as if you are whispering in my ear, "When the light comes on, pull the *left* switch," and then you forget or deny that you have whispered. But I get the message. And I pull the right or the left one, depending on how I feel toward you.

You know, even when you are not in the room—when you are just the printed instructions on the questionnaire or the voice on the tape recorder that tells me what I am supposed to do—I wonder about you. I wonder who you are, what you are *really* up to. I wonder what you are going to do with the "behavior" I give you. Who are you going to show my answers to? Who is going to see the marks I leave on your response-recorders? Do you have any interest at all in what I think, feel, and imagine as I make the marks you are so eager to study and analyze? Certainly, you never ask me what I mean by them. If you asked, I'd be glad to tell you. As a matter of fact, I do tell my roommate or my girl friend what I thought your experiment was about and what I meant when I did what I did. If my roommate could trust you, he could probably give you a better idea of what your data (my answers and responses) mean than the idea you presently have. God knows how much good psychology has gone down the drain, when my roommate and I discuss your experiment and my part in it, at the beer-joint.

As a matter of fact, I'm getting pretty tired of being S. It's too much like being a punched IBM card in the University registrar's office. I feel myself being pressured, bulldozed, tricked, manipulated everywhere I turn. Advertisements in magazines and commercials on TV, political speeches, salesmen, and con men of all kinds put pressure on me to get me to buy, say, or do things that I suspect are not for my good at all. Just for their good, the good of their pocketbooks. Do you sell your "expert knowledge" about me to these people? If that's true, then you're really not in good faith with me. You have told me that when I show myself to you and let you study me, that in the long run

it will be for my good. I'm not convinced. You really seem to be studying me in order to learn how to influence my attitudes and my actions
without my realizing it. I resent this more than *you* realize. It's not
fair for you to get me to show how I can be influenced and then for
you to pass this information along to the people who pay your salary,
or who give you the money to equip your laboratory. I feel used, and
I don't like it. But I protect myself by not showing you my whole self,
or by lying. Did you ever stop to think that your articles, and the
textbooks you write, the theories you spin—all based on your data (my
disclosures to you)—may actually be a tissue of lies and half-truths (my
lies and half-truths) or a joke I've played on you because I don't like
you or trust you? That should give you cause for some concern.

Now look, Mr. *E*, I'm not "paranoid," as you might say. Nor am I
stupid. And I do believe some good can come out of my serving in
your research. Even some good for me. I'm not entirely selfish, and I
would be glad to offer myself up for study, to help others. But some
things have to change first. Will you listen to me? Here is what I
would like from you researchers:

I'd like you to help me gain a better understanding of what has
made me the way I am today. I'd like to know this because I want to
be more free than I feel. I would like to discover more of my own
potentialities. I'd like to be more whole, more courageous, more enlightened. I'd like to be able to experience more, learn better, remember better, and express myself more fully. I'd like to learn how to
recognize and overcome the pressures of other people's influence, of
my background, that interfere with my going in the paths I choose.
Now, if you would promise to help me in these ways, I would gladly
come into your lab and virtually strip my body and soul naked. I
would be there *meaning* to show you everything I could that was relevant to your particular interest of the moment. And I can assure you,
that is different from what I have been showing you thus far, which
is as little as I can. In fact, I cross my fingers when I'm in your lab,
and say to myself, "What I've just said or done here *is not me*."
Wouldn't you like that to change?

If you'll trust me, I'll trust you, if you're trustworthy. I'd like you
to take the time and trouble to get acquainted with me as a person,

before we go through your experimental procedures. And I'd like to get to know you and what you are up to, to see if I would like to expose myself to you. Sometimes, you remind me of physicians. They look at me as the unimportant envelope that conceals the disease they are really interested in. You have looked at me as the unimportant package that contains "responses," and this is all I am for you. Let me tell you that when I feel this, I get back at you. I give you responses, all right; but you will never know what I meant by them. You know, I can speak, not just in words, but with my action. And when you have thought I was responding to a "stimulus" in your lab, my response was really directed at *you*; and what I meant by it was, "Take this, you unpleasant so-and-so." Does that surprise you? It shouldn't.

Another thing. Those tests of yours that have built-in gimmicks to see if I'm being consistent, or deliberately lying, or just answering at random—they don't fool me. Actually, they wouldn't be necessary if you would get on the level with me. There are enough con men in the world, without your joining their number. I would hope that psychologists would be more trustworthy than politicians or salesmen.

I'll make a bargain with you. You show me that you are doing your researches *for me*—to help me become freer, more self-understanding, better able to control *myself*—and I'll make myself available to you in any way you ask. And I won't play jokes and tricks on you. I don't want to *be controlled,* not by you or anyone else. And I don't want to control other people. I don't want you to help other people to understand how I am or can be "controlled," so that they can then control me. Show me that you are for me, and I will show *myself* to you.

You work for me, Mr. *E*, and I'll truly work for you. Between us, we may produce a psychology that is more authentic and more liberating.*

Yours sincerely,

S

---

* The following chapter describes an occasion when I served as *S* in an investigation I did not know was going on.—S.M.J.

3

An Experience of the Author in the Role of S

I would like to share with the reader an experience I had at being the unwitting object of the psychological scientist's "Look." I teach a large undergraduate course entitled "The Psychology of Healthy Personality." In the semester when the following occurred, there were three hundred students enrolled. I gave my lectures in the University Auditorium, speaking through a microphone up on a stage.

A few days after the results of the final examination had been posted, two young men* came to my office and said, "We thought you would be amused at this"; and they handed me a folder, with the title inscribed on it: "Observations concerning the technical jargon and course-specificity of a lecturer in the student-lecturer dyad of the Psychology 202 lecture environs." It was a report of observations these two men had made on my podium behavior throughout the semester. Neither of these undergraduates was a psychology major, but they had evidently been captivated by some of my more predictable and recurring behavior patterns; so every day they prepared rating-charts, and checked off the frequency with which I emitted certain classes of behavior. They carefully recorded my responses, and then wrote up a report, with their tongues obviously in their cheeks (they had read numerous psychological journals in order to grasp the style we might call "journalese").

Reading the report brought peals of laughter out of me. It was deadly accurate as well. And it gave me the uncanny feeling of having been looked at as an object *rather than as the subject I feel myself to be—a most salutary reminder to researchers of what their "Subjects"*

---

* R. B. Chumbley III and W. C. Haldin, Jr.

in psychological research might feel like. I append the report. Professional readers will have some idea of how their scientific jargon appears to young students.

Introduction

In the full interest of science and, more specifically, psychology in general, the authors have found this short study advantageous in order more fully to understand the bulwark of lecturer-student communication and disclosure. A rather basic tenet for the comprehension of the technical and otherwise epigrammatical data flung from the course structure and explanatory technique is the systematic compartmentalizing and statistical re-orientation of the jargon itself as apprehended by the student. A complete, volumatic apprehension is, of course, impossible. Therefore the authors, partly due to expediency and partly due to the superfluity of unnecessary and ambiguous data, have chosen what they have felt to be the twelve most appropriate categories of course-jargon necessary to the optimum understanding of the course itself.

Hypotheses

The hypotheses of this study are both very obscure and quite clear as was the raw data. Our purpose, aside from that described above, is to transcend the typical and construe in a new fashion the information released by the lecturer and to predict the volumes and types of verbiage issued by the lecturer on future occasion.

1. That the lecturer uses some words in varying degrees more than others.

2. That sometime during the term the lecturer will light his pipe during a lecture significantly more than ten (10) times.

3. That the lecturer will significantly exceed an experimental psychologist in number of categorized words per lecture.

4. That the use of the categorized words by the lecturer will correlate highly with the number of the same words used by another clinical psychologist.

5. That author-lecturers in general use to a high degree the words they themselves use most often.

Procedure

The basic procedure of this study was to collect the number of words falling into the categories displayed in the key of Figure I. Along with this data was collected a number of differentiated words falling into the category "most interesting words" and the number of what we termed "pipe-lights" per lecture. Tables of the latter two sets of data have been deleted due to their length and lack of necessity. A lecture was defined as the period of time falling between 9:50 o'clock A.M. and 10:45 o'clock A.M. on Mondays, Wednesdays, and Fridays during the Fall Trimester (1965) at the University of Florida.

Method

Two experimenters disguised as University of Florida PSY-202 students made check-marks on a data sheet during lectures (see definition above), as appropriate responses were produced by the lecturer. The data was recorded in graph form (see Fig. I).

Results and Conclusions

Hyp. 1 was validated (see Fig. I).

Hyp. 2 was validated to a certain extent, the qualification being that the sample obtained was one (1) and there is a certain degree of difficulty in accurately generalizing from such a small sample even on a t-distribution table. The number of "pipe-lights" however exceeded criterion by five (5) on 11/6/65.

Hyp. 3 was validated.

Hyp. 4 was validated.

Hyp. 5 was validated.

Extrapolation and Predictions

Although our results validated our hypotheses, much more research is necessary. Some of the relevant extrapolations are as follows:

Perfect word groups: 4,9,10,11,12.
Best weeks: 1&4.
Worst weeks: 7.
Average lecture: 9 words ±1.

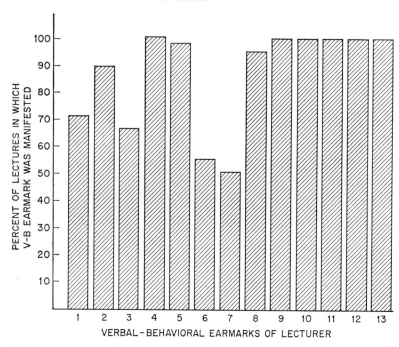

KEY:
1 *"authentic"*
2 *"modal"; "typical"*
3 *"transcends"*
4 *"suppress"; "repress"; "ego"; "id"; "superego"; i.e., any Freudian
    term*
5 *"healer"; "psychologist"; "psychotherapist"; "psychoanalyst"*
6 *"embodies"*
7 *"reality"*
8 *"mad"; "sick"; "check-out"*
9 *"healthy personality"*
10 *"experience"*
11 *any four adjectives used in succession*
12 *a reference to organized religion or a profane reference*
13 *ten or more pipe-lights*

Best month: October.
Worst month: November.
Most of one word used in a single lecture: "construe" (27x).
Perfect lectures (100% of words used): 10/3/65, 11/1/65.

Worst lectures: 11/11/65 (75%).

Most pipe-lights: 15 on 11/6/65.

Most interesting word: "opts-out" (present tense)
"opted-out" (past tense).

A perfect sentence would include: a Freudian term, four adjectives used in succession, a reference to organized religion or an obscene reference, "healthy personality," "transcend," and "experience."

e.g.: "Any damn fool should realize that a healthy personality transcends, discloses, and cannot suppress real, genuine, bona fide, authentic experience."

4

Experimenter-Subject Dialogue: Paradigm for a Humanistic Science of Psychology*

The image of man that emerges from traditional experimental psychology is of a "determined" being, subject to the controlling influences of assorted variables. This is not at all an image of man with which we can gladly identify. Indeed, one of the aims of a humanistic science of psychology is to liberate man from the constraining or inciting pressures of determiners. A humanistic psychologist, like his less humanistic colleague, is concerned to identify factors that affect man's experience and action; but his aim is not to render the man predictable to, and controllable by, somebody else. Rather, his aim is to understand how determining variables function in order that a man might be liberated from their impact as he pursues his own free projects.

In pursuing the project of developing a humanistic research methodology for psychology, the hypothesis occurred to me that the aspect which human subjects show to psychological experimenters may be an artifact of the typical relationship established by the researchers with their subjects. If people show only certain of their possibilities to investigators who relate to human subjects in a prescribed, impersonal way, it is possible that if a different and mutually revealing kind of relationship between experimenters and subjects were established, different facets of the latters' beings would be disclosed. Perhaps a more valid image of man might emerge if all research done in the past were repeated in the context of mutual knowledge and trust.

I have begun to explore the possibility of replicating typical psy-

* This chapter was first published in *Challenges of humanistic psychology*, J. Bugental (Ed.), and is reprinted here with the permission of the McGraw-Hill Book Company.

*chological experiments, first, in the impersonal way their designers
conducted the studies, and then, in the context of greater openness and
mutual knowing between the psychologist and his subjects. Some of
my students likewise are exploring in this vein. The remarks that
follow give a more detailed consideration of the rationale for such
replication, and an introduction to some preliminary findings. At this
stage we are only beginning a project that may take many years and
many collaborators to bring to fruition.*

Two Kinds of Encounter

Ultimately, we come to know something or somebody if that being
shows itself to us. If we are dealing with stones, animals, stars, or
viruses, the problem of knowing calls first for making contact with
the object of study, then devising means of getting it to disclose its
mysteries. Natural scientists have shown incredible ingenuity at this
task. They have devised gadgets that reveal previously inaccessible
aspects of the being of all kinds of phenomena: X-rays, telescopes and
microscopes, transducers, and recorders of light, sound, and movement.
This equipment has enabled scientists to find answers to questions
they pose about the being of things, objects, and processes in the
world.

To know the being of *man* is a different problem. Existentialists
have said that man is the being whose being is *in question,* not fixed.
Man chooses his projects and thereby produces his own being. He
chooses his ways to be in the world, and upon how he has chosen to
be will depend the aspects of his being that he will show to anyone
who happens to be looking. One choice open to him is whether he
will show himself at all or whether he will choose to hide in a cave.
Another option is whether he will aim to reveal his experience, his
"being-for-himself" [86] to another person, or whether he will seek to
conceal and misrepresent it.

If a man chooses to be fully known, he will show himself freely to
another man, in all possible ways. His behavior, which is the "outside"
of his being-for-himself (his experience), is unintelligible, however,
unless he provides the observer with the key. Behavior is actually a
code, or better, a cipher, analogous to Etruscan writing or Egyptian

hieroglyphics. It is the embodiment of a meaning assigned to it by the one who behaves. The observer can guess at this meaning, but the key rests with the behaver himself. For him, the behavior carries out his intentions, his goals, his projects. It is the goal of the action that gives meaning to the action. Yet it is precisely aims and goals that people tend most strongly to conceal from others, fearing that if the intentions were known, the other person might interfere. Machiavelli knew this when he advised his Prince to conceal his ultimate aims from his subjects. They were to be kept mystified. People will disclose their aims and the ways they construe the world only to those whom they have reason to trust. Without trust and goodwill, a person will conceal or misrepresent his experience, hoping thus to mystify the other and to get him to misconstrue the action that is visible.[41]

Encounters That Mystify

Suppose a young man is attracted to a pretty girl. At first, she is indifferent to his display of manly charms. He then tries to change her experience of him, in the hope that she will ultimately change her behavior toward him. What he does before her is the expression of his intent: "I want her to tumble for me." But he doesn't directly say this to her. If he did, it might frighten her away. Instead, he pretends he has no such wishes. He tries to appear as the kind of young man in whose physical presence she will want to stay. Once he wins her attention, he may start the next stage of his secret project. He will speak of jazz and Bach, philosophy and baseball. Then, he may remark about her lovely complexion and hair. His hand, apparently by accident, brushes against her shoulder; and she doesn't pull away. He suggests they go somewhere for a drink. There, he invites her to tell about herself; and he seems to listen to every word with rapt attention.

If a third person watched this relationship develop, he would infer that the young man is "on the make." This might be a possible meaning one could make of the sequence of his acts. Suppose the third person asks the young man point-blank, "Are you trying to seduce this girl?" The young man would probably deny such crass motivation. If he denies it, then his behavior, no matter how accurately it has been observed and recorded, is at odds with his words. It only becomes intelligible when he reveals his intention. Without this disclosure, we have only a string of responses that could mean anything. If we wish to understand the action, we must know *what it means to him*.

Viewed from an abstract perspective, this encounter between the boy and the girl is a mystifying one. He tries to mislead her as to his intentions. He is "on the make," and he tries to manipulate her experience and action so that she will behave in the service of *his* goals, not her own. When a person is thus "on the make," he will show aspects of himself that aim at persuading or influencing the other. The other person has been reduced from the status of person to the status of an object, a manipulandum, something to be used if it is useful and neutralized or changed if it is not.

There is another kind of encounter that people may undertake in order to fulfill different aims. This is *dialogue*.

Encounters That Reveal

In dialogue, as Buber[9,10,11] portrays it, each experiences the other as a person, as the origin and source of his intentional acts. Each participant aims to show his being to the other *as it is for him*. Transparency, not mystification, is one of the goals. It matters little whether the dialogue is nonverbal or verbal; whether it occurs between a philosopher and his pupil, a therapist and his patient, a parent and child, or two friends. The aim is to show oneself in willful honesty before the other and to respond to the other with an expression of one's experience as the other has affected it. Dialogue is like mutual unveiling, where each seeks to be experienced and confirmed by the other as the one he is for himself. Such dialogue is most likely to occur when the two people believe each is trustworthy and of goodwill. The threat that motivates people to conceal their intentions and experience in manipulative encounters is absent in dialogue. The aims that make the action of each intelligible to the other will be fully revealed.

Now, I'd like to examine the relationship between an experimenter and his subject in the light of those analyses of the two kinds of encounter.

Experimenter-Subject Relationship: Manipulation or Dialogue?

The usual encounter between a psychological researcher and his subject has more in common with the example of the young man "on the make" than it has with dialogue. The experimenter wants something from the subject, but he wants to keep him partly mystified as to what it is. Moreover, he doesn't want to frighten the subject away; so the psychological researcher often cloaks his intentions with camouflage. If he tips his hand, he may influence the subject and bias his findings. He tells the subject as little as he can when the latter appears in the laboratory.

Actually, in some ways a research psychologist tries to impersonate a machine by depersonalizing himself. He tries to be invisible or to be "constant." He seldom tries to find out from his subject just how that person experiences him, the researcher, either perceptually or in his fantasy.

Limits of the Impersonal Model

Increasingly, workers are finding that this effort to eliminate bias is failing. Rosenthal[85] and Orne[71] among others are showing that when a psychologist is there with a human subject he functions not unlike a subtle propagandist or attitude- and action-manipulator. They have shown that the data gotten from subjects (that is, the subjects' disclosures encoded in words or in nonverbal behavior) can be likened to expressions of compliance on the part of the subjects to confirm the psychologists' hypotheses about people of that sort. The psychologist perhaps aims to be "one-up" on those of his colleagues who claim that people are different. In fact, it seems to me that human subjects, to the extent that they are free, will please and confirm just about any researcher's hypotheses—witness the many confirmations of radically conflicting hypotheses. A person truly can choose a being, in the laboratory, that will uphold or refute his *experience* (fantasy or perceptual) of what the researcher wants him to show.

We researchers may be victims of the same myopia that has for long afflicted physicians, preventing them from realizing that many diseases are actually *iatrogenic*—outcomes of the doctor-patient relationship or the impact of certain environments on patients. Laing and

Esterson[56] have shown, for example, that schizophrenia—its symptoms as recorded in textbooks—is (at least in part and perhaps fully) a function of the disconfirming and mystifying behavior of relatives and physicians toward the patient's experience of his world, as well as a way of being which is evoked by the mental hospital milieu itself. It is known that instances of invalidism have occurred because a doctor implied to a patient, "Your heart is not as healthy as it might be."

In research, we have recognized the "social desirability"[14] variable. It has been investigated, and techniques have been proposed to bypass it or make allowances for it. We have recognized subjects' tendencies to misrepresent their experience, to produce some desired image of themselves in the mind of the investigator. So we have invented tests and traps to catch their conscious and unconscious deceptions (e.g., the "Lie" and "K" scales on the MMPI). We have utilized projective tests in the hope that a person will unwittingly reveal hidden aspects of himself. What we may not have realized is that a subject in a research project is no fool. He knows that many times his future career may be at stake, depending upon how he has appeared through test and experimental findings. So he has a vested interest in such misrepresentation. It is very sane for him to protect himself. He has no guarantee, at least in his experience, that his responses will help the psychologist to help *him* (the subject) fulfill himself more fully. Our commitments as experimenters and the settings in which we work sometimes make it insane for a person to uncloak himself.

The Dyadic Effect

Research in self-disclosure[41] has shown that what a person will disclose to another is a function of many variables, including the subject matter to be disclosed, characteristics of the person, the setting in which disclosure is to take place, and—more important—characteristics of the audience-person. The most powerful determiner of self-disclosure appears to be the willingness of the audience to disclose *himself* to the subject to the same extent that he expects the subject to confide his experience. I've termed this the "dyadic effect." It asserts, as a general principle, that "disclosure begets disclosure." Now this is not, by any means, the only condition under which a man might reveal his experience to another. He will often disclose himself unilaterally, without reciprocation, when he believes that it serves his interests to do so. This is what happens, for example, in much psychotherapeutic interviewing. The patient discloses much more about himself than the therapist does, on the implicit promise that if he does so his lot will be improved.

The question needs to be asked whether the relationship between the experimenter and his subject is anything like a setting for the dyadic effect to occur. Is it anything like dialogue? Do the laboratory setting and the typical relationship between an investigator and his human subject provide the conditions for the fullest, most authenticated disclosure of self by the latter, whether in words or writing or with action of unequivocal, revealed meaning? No!

In most psychological investigations, the psychologist is a stranger to the subject. It is hoped that the subject is naïve, unself-conscious, and willing to disclose himself verbally or behaviorally, with responses to stimuli to be recorded on objective machines. Now there may be some people who enter a laboratory in that spirit. Probably some infants and children are ready and willing to trust and show. However, I am convinced that the people who serve in psychological studies quickly become sophisticated and learn to play their parts. They are often taught what their part is by older, more experienced subjects, who have served in many studies. This is also what happens to newcomers to a prison or mental hospital. The "old pros" show the ropes to the novices. I have much reason to suspect that many subjects rattle off their performances before a researcher in a cynical way, giving him much "data" to carry off with him, away from people, to the calculating room. There the psychologist conducts complex analyses of variance, and writes up his findings as part of his dialogue with his colleagues. But the people he is arguing about—the subjects—may be out in the pubs telling their cronies about how they "put one over."

Not only do we not provide human subjects with a setting and a relationship within which authentic self-disclosure can take place; we limit their vocabulary also. We note only their GSR reading or their questionnaire responses or the marks they leave on an event-recorder. We ignore as irrelevant all the other possible means by which a person could show us what the laboratory conditions and the experimenter have meant to him. We appear not to be interested in grounding our psychology on his experience. Rather, we want only to account for variance in the one kind of message we got from him and his fellow subjects. This message is just a response: serialized, fragmented, quantified. We assume that such responses have the same experiential meanings for each of the subjects; we assume that whatever meanings the responses have for them are irrelevant. This is, I think, a mistake.

We can do something about it and, moreover, do it in the spirit of experimental inquiry. We can begin to change the status of the subject from that of an anonymous *object* of our study to the status of a *person,* a fellow seeker, a *collaborator* in our enterprise. We can let him tell the story of his experience in our studies in a variety of idioms. We can let him show what our stimuli have meant to him by his manipulations of our gadgetry; by responses to questionnaires; with drawings; with words. We can invite him to reveal his being. We can prepare ourselves so that he will want to produce a multi-faceted record of his experiencing in our laboratories. We can show him how we have recorded his responding and tell him what we have thought his responses mean. We can ask him to examine and then authenticate or revise our recorded version of the meaning-for-him of his experience. We can let him cross-examine us to get to know and trust us to find out what we are up to and to decide if he wishes to take part. Heaven knows what we might find. We might well emerge with richer images of man.

Preliminary Dialogue-Based Replications

My students and I have made a beginning in reperforming experiments in the kind of relationship climate I have been describing. However, I'd like to see it done on a larger scale by more workers to see which "classes of response" and which "psychological functions" are affected by the interpersonal context of dialogue and which are not.

Here is a progress report on what we have done so far toward discovering whether the dialogic quality of the relationship between researcher and subject makes a difference:

1. One of my students, W. R. Rivenbark,[83] varied the way in which he conducted interviews with subjects. In one of the conditions, he responded to the subjects' self-disclosures with disclosures of his own which reported true experiences of his that were comparable to those of his subjects. Compared with the other conditions, the subjects reported that they liked the interviewer and the interview more; they saw the interviewer as more human and more trustworthy; and they indicated that they would like to be interviewed by him again—as opposed to the conditions in which he was technically competent but impersonal and anonymous.

2. Rivenbark also conducted a simple word-association test, presenting words from the list given by Rapaport[76] in his *Diagnostic Psychological Testing*. His procedure was as follows: He gave some general, impersonal instructions to his subjects, letting them know what he expected from them. Then, he gave them one-half of the words from the list. Next, he gave them an opportunity to disclose themselves to him in writing, in response to questions or in mutually revealing dialogue. After this, he administered the rest of the words and secured the subjects' responses. Finally, he made a rating of the degree to which his relationship with each person felt to him like a good rapport and willingness to be open. He did not ask the subjects to do this. Then, he studied the reaction times of the subjects in response to the stimulus words. There were no differences in mean reaction time or in the kind of responses given between groups differentiated in terms of the way they disclosed themselves to the experimenter: that is, in writing, in response to spoken questions, or in dialogue. Rivenbark did find, however, that there was a significant correlation (rho of .68) between his ratings of "goodness of rapport" and the mean *increase* in reaction time between the first administration of stimulus words and the last.

We have no idea just now of what this finding means in terms of psychodynamics. It does show that somebody's experience of the relationship between experimenter and subject—in this case, the experimenter's experience—was related to differences in the objective outcome of the experiment. True, there is much wrong, from a methodological viewpoint about this study; but it is a beginning at the kind of replication discussed above.

Subject's Attitudes about Confiding

3. Rivenbark[83] conducted still another exploratory study, this time directed toward people's views as to how trustworthy psychologists and their tools are. He prepared a list of 15 possible confidants or settings within which one might reveal intimate and personal data about oneself. He asked 25 male and 30 female college students to rank these confidants or settings according to how willing they would be to confide fully under such circumstances. His findings, expressed as median ranks from least (1) to most willing to confide (15), are shown in Table A.

Significantly, the research psychologist was ranked seventh. Anonymous research questionnaires were ranked eleventh by women and ninth by men. This investigation may be thought of as similar to the work of public relations firms engaged to determine the "public image" of their clients. Though I dislike the term "image" in this context, I feel justified on the basis of these data in urging all research psychologists to seek to earn an authentically higher rank, as prospective recipients of the disclosures of our subjects.

Importance of Responsiveness

4. Another student, W. J. Powell, Jr.,[73] did a doctoral dissertation which was more carefully controlled than Rivenbark's exploratory study. He conducted interviews with college students, asking them to make themselves as fully known to him, the interviewer, as they cared to. He carefully controlled all extraneous variables and compared the increase in self-disclosure (using an operant-conditioning design) when, on the one hand, he responded to the students' disclosures with authentic disclosures of his own (in contrast to "reflecting" the feeling or content of their disclosures) or when, on the other hand, he responded with expressions of approval and support. He found that "approving-supporting" responses did not increase the students' disclosures at all. Reflection-restatement of their disclosures resulted in

TABLE A

Students' Readiness to Confide in Different Settings
(Taken from Rivenbark)[83]

Setting	Male Rank	Female Rank
Tell a radio or TV audience	1	1
Tell a stranger on a bus or train	2	2
Tell at a cocktail party with friends and strangers present	3	3
Write on an application for a job or club membership	4	4
Write in an autobiography for publication	5	5
Tell in a bull session with friends	6	6
Tell an interviewer for scientific purposes	7	7
Write in a letter to a friend	8	8
Write in an anonymous questionnaire for scientific purposes	9	11
Tell a priest or minister	10	10
Tell a psychotherapist	11	14
Write in a secret diary	12	9
Tell my closest parent	13	12
Tell my best same-sex friend	14	13
Tell my best opposite-sex friend or spouse	15	15

an increase in disclosures of negative self-statements but did not affect positive, self-enhancing expressions. Self-disclosure from the researcher was associated with significant increases in the subjects' disclosures of both positive and negative self-references.

5. Another student, Miss Lee Reifel,[80] conducted an interview with a girl whom she had never met before in the context of a game we invented, called "Invitations." The questions or topics for disclosure were typed on cards, and the rules were that the person could ask the interviewer any question that she was willing to answer herself, and vice versa. In this interview, the girl became incredibly involved and

literally revealed all she had to reveal. Miss Reifel disclosed much about herself too. By the end of the interview, which lasted several hours, they knew each other very well indeed. In another interview, Miss Reifel began by using the cards as a guide to "get acquainted" with a female student. However, for the first half of the session, she confined herself to asking questions only. The girl was to answer if she chose, but Miss Reifel would not explain or disclose more. Then Miss Reifel changed the rules and began to disclose herself truthfully regarding each question she next asked of the student. The transformation in openness and extent of self-disclosure on the part of the girl was remarkable.

6. Another effort we are making in this direction is the attempt to measure the degree to which a person serving as subject in an experiment trusts the investigator with confidential information about himself. I devised a kind of disclosure questionnaire listing 52 personal questions of varying degrees of intimacy. The person serving in a study was asked to write in answers only to those questions he was willing for the experimenter to know about him, leaving all other questions blank.

The number of completed items could be regarded as a rough measure of the subject's trust of the experimenter. We were interested in whether or not scores on this questionnaire would be correlated with the outcome of various experiments being conducted by graduate students and faculty researchers at the University of Florida. It is too soon to report more than some preliminary observations: split half reliability coefficients for the questionnaire are higher than .90 for men and women alike (N of 50 males and 50 females). Considering the questionnaire item-by-item, the numbers of males and females filling in a given item were correlated .92 (with $N = 52$ items). There were significant differences between experimenters in the mean number of items confided in them by their subjects. In Stratil's[97] study of remembering, persons who could be classified as "recallers" obtained disclosure-to-experimenter scores that were significantly ($P < .05$) higher than those obtained by "recognizers" (Stratil).[97] In a study of "conformity," Reitan and Lackey[81] failed to find differences in conformity scores as a function of the Ss' disclosure to the experi-

TABLE B

*A Questionnaire for Measuring Trust Between
Subjects and Experimenters*

INSTRUCTIONS

A series of questions are addressed to you on the following pages. They are concerned with features of your life that are generally regarded as intimate and personal, the kind of thing people will confide to another person *when they want that other person to know them.*

I have been studying patterns of self-disclosure for some years. Now I want to explore peoples' willingness to make themselves known to investigators carrying out all kinds of psychological research.

You will be serving in several studies conducted by research psychologists during this semester. I will be asking you to show the extent to which you are willing to let the experimenter know your personal characteristics.

After each experiment in which you serve, I will ask you to complete a copy of this questionnaire.

The questionnaire calls for writing in answers to those questions about yourself that you are willing to permit the researcher know about you. LEAVE BLANKS FOR THOSE QUESTIONS WHICH, *FOR ANY REASON*, YOU DO NOT WISH THE EXPERIMENTER TO KNOW. The amount you confide to the experimenter (and of course to me) is ENTIRELY UP TO YOU.

The researcher may find your disclosures of help to him in interpreting his experimental findings. And I will find your answers of help to me in my ongoing research in self-disclosure.

These questionnaires will be seen only by the experimenter and myself. After the data are entered on data sheets, the papers will be destroyed.

PLEASE REFRAIN FROM DISCLOSING ANYTHING YOU DO NOT WISH THE EXPERIMENTER TO KNOW. The research is meaningless unless you write in *only the truth,* and *only as much information about yourself as you feel comfortable in imparting.*

YOU MAY HAND IN THE QUESTIONNAIRE WITH NO ENTRIES, IF YOU WISH.

PERSONAL DATA

Your name _____ Male or Female _____ Age _____

Mo. Day Yr.

Date of birth _____ Marital status _____ Today's date _____

Name of Experiment just completed _____

Name of Experimenter _____

Items	enter checkmarks		Write the information you are willing for this experimenter to know.
	Willing to tell experimenter in private conversation	Have told to my closest confidant	
1. What is your religious denomination?			
2. Do you attend religious services?			
3. What features do you most dislike in your mother?			
4. What features do you most dislike in your father?			
5. How much money does your father earn?			
6. How much money do you get each month?			
7. What is your favorite hobby, or leisure interest?			
8. What do you feel most ashamed of in your past?			
9. What is your grade-point average at present?			
10. Have you cheated on any exams at U. of F.?			
11. Have you deliberately lied about a serious matter to either parent?			
12. What is the most serious lie you have told?			
13. Have you experienced sexual intercourse?			
14. Do you practice masturbation?			
15. Have you been arrested or fined for violating any law?			
16. Do you have any health problems? What are they?			
17. What do you regard as your chief fault in personality?			
18. Do you approve of segregation of Negroes?			
19. To which political party are you most inclined?			

	enter checkmarks		
20. What kind of music do you like best?			
21. What features of your appearance do you consider most attractive to the opposite sex?			
22. What do you regard as your least attractive features?			
23. How much money have you saved?			
24. To what clubs do you belong?			
25. Do you drink beer, wine or whiskey?			
26. Have you ever been drunk?			
27. What games (sports) do you play regularly?			
28. How often have you needed to see a doctor in the past year?			
29. What teacher here do you like best?			
30. Which teachers do you dislike most?			
31. Have you ever been tempted to kill yourself?			
32. What emotions do you find it most difficult to control?			
33. Is there any particular person you wish would be attracted to you? Who? (give name)			
34. What foods do you most dislike?			
35. What is your favorite dessert at meals?			
36. Is there any feature of your personality you are proud of? What is it?			
37. What was your worst failure in life, your biggest disappointment to yourself, or family?			
38. What is your favorite TV program(s)?			
39. What is the subject of the most serious quarrels you have with your parents?			
40. What is your most chronic problem at present?			
41. What is the subject of your most frequent daydreams?			
42. What are you intending to take up as your life work or career, after graduating?			
43. What annoys you most in your closest friend of the same sex?			
44. What annoys you most in your closest friend of the opposite sex? (or spouse, or the last person you dated)			
45. What do you feel the greatest need for help with?			

	enter checkmarks		
46. What were you most punished or criticized for when you were a child?			
47. What activities did you take part in in high school?			
48. How could you improve your present rooming arrangements?			
49. What is your main complaint about U. of F.?			
50. Have you ever engaged in homosexual activities?			
51. Do you like your first name? Last name?			
52. What is your nickname? Do you like it?			

menters, though the *S*s did disclose themselves significantly more to one researcher than the other. More work is under way. In none of the studies thus far conducted was the measure of disclosure obtained after the *E* and *S* first became acquainted, but *before* the conduct of the experiment. In due time, this will be done.

Toward Greater Experimental Validity

We are continuing with this kind of research, still in the spirit of exploration. There are many technical problems to solve in a replication project of the sort we have begun. We shall need to learn better how to rate or measure the subject's trust of the experimenter, and the degree to which mutually self-revealing dialogue is being attained in any given relationship between a researcher and his subject. But we can begin with a simple either-or discrimination between the impersonal researcher and the one who engages in a mutually revealing conversation before the experiment. More refined measures could evolve with experience.

It would be helpful, in attempting replications in dialogue of representative experiments, if experimenters were trained to be more versatile in interacting with human beings. Perhaps we could insist that they should be nice people, capable of entering into close, confiding relationships with a broad range of people. To be "nice" doesn't mean to be softheaded or unreliable in one's calculation of results. Training in experimental design, physiology, and statistics is no guarantee that one is qualified to interact in a confirming and evocative way with another person. I believe we can no longer afford to ignore the effect of the experimenter on the experience and behavior of the subject. We can no longer afford to divert nice, tender-hearted humanitarians into clinical work and leave the research for hard-nosed, hardhearted impersonal folk. If an experimental psychologist is unpleasant and threatening in the eyes of others, it might be better to confine him to the calculating room or else let him contact human subjects only when the design for the experiment calls for an impersonal investigator. If a person has gone into psychology to get away from people, let him design experiments, build equipment, analyze data, run computers, and so on. We need all the versatility we can get in psychology. However, when we want to find out how people behave and disclose themselves under more permissive interpersonal conditions, let the one who encounters the subjects be someone who, by training and by commitment, is able to enter into dialogue. How strange that good animal psychologists view their animal subjects like individual persons, worthy of respect, while experimental psychologists frequently treat their human subjects as if they were anonymous animal objects! It is already known that "gentled" tame animals show different behavioral and physiological characteristics from nongentled or "wild" ones (wild means, here, defensive and hostile in the presence of humans). Yet many of our subjects are assumed to be tame and trusting when, in fact, they are wild. Genuine dialogue may prove to be the appropriate context for research in *human* (free) beings. When the experimenter-subject relationship varies, we might expect the subjects' responses to stimuli to vary. It is appropriate to consider the question, "What will man prove to be like when he is studied by an investigator who consents to be studied by the subject?"

If we do no more than study the effect of various modes of experimenter-subject relationship on the outcome of psychological experiments, and we do this systematically, while including dialogue as one of the relationship modes, we shall have enriched our psychological knowledge considerably. Just as important, we may have taken a step toward reconciling the conflict between humanistic and nonhumanistic orientations to our discipline.

Part Two

Psychotherapy for Growing Persons

5

The Psychotherapist: "Trainer" or "Liberator" of Persons?

Personal counselors and psychotherapists specialize in helping individuals. Informed by knowledge about man in general, they seek to learn about the particular man who consults them, to help him overcome impasses in his life, fulfill more of his possibilities, and live more effectively.

It is time to look more carefully at this helping process. Whom does a therapist help? What does he help him do or be? How does he go about his helping project? Is he a technician, who simply applies the methods he learned, or is he a continually growing person himself? And whom is he for, anyway? For himself? For the social status quo? For the patient? For a new society?

In the first section of this book, I pointed out that scientific psychology aims at discovering laws of human behavior, so that man can be more fully predicted and controlled by somebody. This means that unless experimental psychologists are careful, they become the unwitting agents of society's leaders. They become psychologists-for-institutions. Their findings can be employed to reduce potentially free men to the status of puppets and manipulanda at the hands of businessmen, politicians, and others with a vested interest in "using" men. The personal counselor and the psychotherapist is, or can be, a psychologist-for-the-person. It is his task to learn about the determiners and limits in human existence and teach those who consult him how to understand, master, and transcend these limits—*then to pursue and enlarge their freedom.* At best, a psychotherapist is akin to a *guru,* a teacher who guides his patient toward liberation from the clutch of the past, from the impelling thrust of impulse and emotion, from the bewitching effects of social pressure, and from the "sleep" of repressed being.

At his worst, the psychotherapist is but one more agent of socialization, a "trainer" who adds his technical know-how to that of parents, educators, and propagandists, to insure that people will conform to institutional norms. It is necessary for everyone in society to learn and to conform to laws and customs, if for no other reason than to insure that society isn't disorganized into a mob of mutually destructive murderers, thieves, and rapists. But every society is organized such that some people enjoy higher status and more wealth and power than others. Every society is conservative. Change in the social order is resisted, often with brute force by those with the most privilege and freedom. They are quick to detect threats to their status from whatever source. The entire institutional structure of society is devoted to training people to conform to those ways that will keep the economic and political system in its present form. The family begins a socialization process, shaping children to the habits, values, and beliefs that will make the child "fit." The school system, far from educating, is actually an additional training institution, directing people to the ways in which they must go, else they will not reach minimally privileged status. The organized churches, instead of liberating men from the sometimes crushing grip of social conformity, actually collude with "Caesar," admonishing people to live in ways that prevent constructive social and political change.

People inevitably *sicken* as they live in the ways their society seems to demand. I have come to see sickness of all kinds, whether "physical" or "mental," *as a form of protest against a way of life that is not fit for the person who has been living it.*[41] Sickness is a way of "checking out" of one's usual roles and responsibilities in order to regain strength and perspective. I see sickness as an opportunity to meditate upon one's life, to examine values and goals, relationships with people, and one's usual practices, with the aim of understanding *how* one became sick and how one might live his life in a more fulfilling way (see Chapter 14). Indeed, the episodes of illness are actually the last and "loudest" protest of a violated organism against the destructive way of life that has been lived. If the ill person had been more sensitive to his own experience of himself, and more imaginative and courageous, he would have noted "all-is-not-well signals" long before he collapsed or broke down. The pain, fatigue, boredom, anxiety, depression, or feelings of futility would have caught his attention. He would have reflected upon them and sought to change his ways of living life so as to restore a sense of meaning, a feeling of zest and satisfaction. But change calls for courage. And it calls for imagination, to invent new ways to live that will not jeopardize other values crucial to one's existence. The courage, the imagination, and the capacity for reflective self-awareness, so necessary for the maintenance of health, are conspicuously lacking in the vast majority of people. These life-saving capacities are usually trained out of people during the period of their growing up. We are taught to believe that there is only one proper way for a person to be and to live. All other ways are deemed evil, illegal, or insane (cf. Laing,[53] Laing,[54] and Laing and Esterson[56]). Groping efforts to protest or to experiment are met by an onslaught that begins with parental criticism and may culminate with ostracism, imprisonment, or incarceration in a "mental hospital." *

If a person persists in the way of life that is dispiriting him, he will eventually break down with some form of physical complaint. The medical profession then springs to action and repairs the damage, so the person again can take his place in a system that is crushing him. He will sicken again. But he must not change his ways.

If the sufferer is called a "mental patient," he typically will be treated with tranquilizing drugs, electroshock, or a form of "psychotherapy" that persuades him to conform to existing patterns.

When we look at the psychotherapeutic professions and the physicians in this light, it becomes clear that practitioners of these arts are actually (though usually unwittingly) political agents. They are, in a real sense, counterrevolutionaries, opponents of those whose very sickness is a protest against prevailing ways to live.

Physicians especially are earning the criticism that they are un-

---

* One sociologist, Thomas Scheff,[91] has made a detailed study of the frequently casual way in which people are "railroaded" into mental hospitals. For many years, up to the time of his death in prison, Wilhelm Reich experienced and wrote of the way in which "little men" with large power invalidated those whose experience was not encapsulated in familiar categories. His *Listen, Little Man*[79] is a classic and should be read as such.

imaginative in their treatment of sickness, that they function like middlemen between the pharmaceutical houses and the consumer. They persist in treating symptoms of illness with a drug or knife, rather than exploring other methods, such as enlightened inquiry into the patient's way of living his life. Indeed, undue reliance upon drugs to treat symptoms *or* causes of illness is pernicious, for it diverts attention from the quest for causes and cures of disease *in the way a man lives!* Psychiatrists have followed the example of their medical colleagues and treat the miserable and the ineffective as if they were "sick," rather than the ineffective protestants against an unlivable life style that they are (cf. Szasz[100]).

Clinical psychologists, social workers, and even ministers have followed the medical view and emulate the psychiatrist's thinking and practice, excluding only the use of drugs.[67,68] It is time for this to change.

These remarks should come as no shock. Neither physicians nor psychologists are encouraged to become enlightened as to the structure of society, to possible ways of changing society so that more people can attain more freedom. Instead, they receive technical training in "healing arts" and leave politics to the politicians, philosophy to the philosophers, and religion to the ministers. The typical physician, psychiatrist, and clinical psychologist are middle-class citizens committed to the middle-class way of life and to a form of political and economic organization that will support such a way. They see themselves not as potential liberators of man and transformers of society, but as technicians whose job it is to repair breakdowns. Indeed, the very standards for adjudging whether a man is sane or "mentally ill" exclude anarchists, rebels, and revolutionaries from the ranks of the sane. If someone protests against the status quo, if he regards the system of monogamous marriage or life within the nuclear family as wrong, if he seeks to abort an unwanted child, he is likely to be viewed as neurotic, psychotic, or criminal. If he acts upon his convictions that there are better ways to live than those presently recognized, he will pay an immense price for it, even his life and freedom. There is growing reason to believe that psychologists and psychiatrists, through default, have truly become agents for the ruling classes. While Marx noted that religion in his time was the "opium of the masses," which consoled them for their suffering in this world, today we dispense the "opium" over the drugstore counter. The going way of life appears to be livable only with the help of billions of tranquilizing pills.

I am reminded of a story told me by a student who served in the Korean War. He met an old school chum during his mustering-out leave in Tokyo. His chum was much decorated for his courage and ferocity in combat against the North Korean and Red Chinese soldiers. He had been wounded twice. The soldier had been a used-car salesman during his civilian life. He was asked if he was glad to be going home. He replied, "Hell, I'm re-enlisting. I've never felt so alive as I have during combat. I wouldn't go back home to that way of life." The enormity of his confession is just this: from a patriot's point of view he was fighting for his country. But he was fighting, risking his life, to defend a way of life he had found unlivable! There must be better ways to live than those that can be endured only with the aid of sedatives, tranquilizers, or the dangerous thrills of war. But it would appear that conventional physicians and psychotherapists have not done much to search for these better ways. Rather, they devote their efforts to keeping people at the sickening ways. This need not be.

It is meaningful to speak of psychotherapists-for-the-person and physicians-for-the-person, as well as psychotherapists-for-society and physicians-for-the-status-quo. I think that the healing professions have not addressed themselves wholeheartedly to the task of healing, but rather to the task of repairing people for more bad use of themselves.

If psychotherapists have hitherto functioned as agents of socialization, as skilled persuaders who back up their efforts with the threat of hospitalization, they need not remain in this status. The personal counselor can function as an agent or champion for the individual client, helping him to *live* a new existence that is actually a miniature social revolution. Every time a timid husband or browbeaten wife is helped to fuller functioning and changed ways, a tiny sector of society has been changed. Every time a son is released from morbid dependency upon his mother or slavish conformity to his father's orders, a victory in the struggle for political freedom has been gained. If the father or mother can be enlightened, so much the better. In such cases, the tyrannical government exists in the home; but the home is a microcosm of society at large.

Every time a therapist meets his patient in the privacy of the consulting room, a secret society has just sprung into being. The purpose for which the society came into being is freedom, albeit *responsible* freedom. If the therapist is an unwitting agent of the status quo, he may well hinder his patient's struggle. If he is an educated man, one willing to help people find their own way to freedom, then some sectors of the population may actually regard therapists as dangerous subversives. I prefer to see psychotherapists as responsible anarchists, as the "loyal opposition," committed to an endless search for ways to live that foster growth, well-being, idiosyncrasy, freedom, and authenticity.

6

*Growing Personality, Not "Adjustment,"
Is the Goal in Counseling
and Psychotherapy*

People seek the help of a psychotherapist when their lives have reached an impasse. The symptoms of the impasse are diverse, including physical suffering, inability to concentrate, anxiety, depression, boredom or guilt, inability to love another or to make love, loneliness, obsessions, antisocial behavior—the entire gamut of psychopathology as we know it.

Diverse though the symptoms of misery might be, they share one feature. They are the inexorable outcome of "adjusting" to a way of life, a way of existing and behaving in the world, which an informed common sense would tell us *must* lead to a breakdown, to a "checking out" or a refusal to carry on further in that way. We know now that the elaborate schemes for classifying "symptoms" of mental "illness" into neat categories is unprofitable for would-be helpers of others. When we label someone "a schizophrenic" or "a neurotic," we lull ourselves into thinking that we understand him before we actually do. The impasses in existence are only superficially described as illness, a term which at best is a metaphor, not an explanation. We spent centuries regarding people who "don't fit," whose behavior we could neither understand nor accept as "evil," as "possessed by demons." It was indeed an advance toward greater compassion among men when the illness-metaphor was applied to the people who would not play the game of social existence as it was "supposed" to be played. But not all who, though physically intact, cannot play the game are sick. Perhaps none are. As Szasz[100] has graphically stated it, "mental illness" is a myth, one that had an historical purpose, but which no longer helps man regard and treat deviants as his brothers. Now, the persistent belief that people who "check out" are "mentally ill" and need to be "cured" of their disease symptoms beclouds understanding. Indeed, the belief that one's "patient" or "client" or "counselee" is an exemplar of some category of disapproved humanity—viz.: schizophrenic, delinquent, neurotic, etc.—leads the would-be helper to treat him as less than a full human being, less than a fellow traveler through this life. Anyone who has been treated by another, not as the very one he is, but as the embodiment of some category—a Negro, a Jew, a professor, a psychotic—knows that *he* is not being addressed by the person who so regards him. If I am regarded as "a patient" by "the doctor," and neither he nor I ever become acquainted with one another, we are doubtless both cheated; and it is questionable whether any enduring help can come out of so impersonal a transaction.

It is more apt to regard the one in need of help as a *fellow seeker*. He seeks relief from his suffering, to be sure, and more fundamentally (whether or not he can verbalize the ultimate goal of his quest), he is seeking a way to be in the world, a way to live with others, and a way of being for himself that is meaningful and rewarding; a way that produces satisfactions, hope, and meaning in expanding experience rather than pain, misery, stultification, and impotence. These latter outcomes are *cries for help*. They are, as well, proof that the seeker's way of life up to the point of breakdown was not compatible with wellness. It seems futile for a physician, psychotherapist, or "growth counselor" to "treat" a symptom by anesthetizing the person with assorted drugs, or by reducing him in some way, and then to send him back to the very way of life that was inimical to truly human being. What is called for in addition to cure is to help the seeker find some way that will permit him to function more fully, more authentically, with a more liberating focus to his existence. The counselor must aim to seek *with* his client and persist in the search until they jointly *discover* what changes in the client's self and world will permit him to live a life compatible with wellness. The helper, if he is to be more than a "first-aid technician," must grope with his client, to find healthy personality for him: that is, *a healthy way of being a person in the world* (the literal meaning of "personality").

What Is Healthy Personality?

Healthy personality is growing personality. It is a way for a person to function in his world, a way that yields growth without placing other important values in jeopardy.[39] People commit themselves to a repertoire of values; they live *for* them. One who is a healthy personality seeks to fulfill them, and he defends them when they are under threat. A healthy personality is to himself as a dedicated farmer is to his farm—he does everything in its time. The abundance of the crops, the state of his livestock, and the condition of his outbuildings are testimony to the farmer's alert and responsive care. The healthy personality likewise shows evidence, in his very being and presence, of his alert and responsive care for himself. He finds his life meaningful, with satisfactions and some accepted suffering; he loves and is loved; he can fulfill reasonable social demands upon him. And he is in no doubt as to who he is, what his feelings and convictions are. He does not apologize for being the very person he is. He can look out on the world and see it from the standpoint of how it presently *is* (according to social consensus); but he can also see himself, the world, and the people in it from the standpoint of *possibility*. He can regard the world as a place in which he can bring into being some possibilities that exist only in his imagination. The world, the other person, and himself—none of these are seen by a healthy personality as sclerosed, frozen, finished, or defined once for all.

Such a person has free access to a dimension of human being much neglected by the "square," the hyper-conformist, the modal personality. I am referring here to something that has been called "the unconscious," "experiencing."[24,25] "transcendental experiences," "mystic experience." This hidden dimension of the self, sought for centuries by men who have longed for personal fulfillment beyond rationalism, is usually dreaded by the average person. It could be called "experiencing *possibility*." It sometimes "peeps out" when one permits himself to be unfocused and aimless, unintegrated, not going anywhere or doing anything; but it is "tamped back" in anxious haste, for it is experienced like the contents of Pandora's box. When his unconscious threatens to speak, when direct experience of self or world invades his consciousness, he becomes overwhelmed with anxiety and may temporarily feel he is losing his mind and sanity. Indeed, he is on the point of "going out of his ego." His present self-concept and concepts of things and people are shattered by implosions and explosions of raw experience from within and without. He experiences his being in dimensions presently unfamiliar to him, hence frightening. But a healthier personality recognizes that his unconscious, this persistent but usually drowned out "dream," this source of new truth, is the voice of his true, real self—a statement of how he has mistreated himself (if the message is dysphoric) or an invitation to new possibilities of being for which he has become sufficiently grown and secretly, unconsciously prepared.

Wise men have always known that when the unconscious speaks, when fresh, transconceptual experience reaches awareness, it is better to pay attention. The breakdowns or check-outs that we have referred to are final outcomes of not listening. The symptoms and suffering are but the voice of the real self, the voice of human being protesting in a voice so loud it can no longer be neglected. Before the breakdown, the voice murmured softly from time to time; but its murmurings were in a code, a forgotten language[23] that could not be understood. And so the person persisted in the ways of behaving, the ways of construing himself and other people, that had become increasingly good neither for his own growth nor for his well-being. The healthier personality listens to his boredom, his anxiety, his dreams and fantasies and gropes for changes in ways of meeting the world that will permit greater realization of potential self.

Indeed, the healthier personality transcends the contradiction between conscious and unconscious, between being fully focused and grandly unfocused—he can oscillate between the extremes and push them further than the less healthy individual. When he focuses, he is fully focused; and when he "lets go," he really lets go. Healthy personality is manifested by a mode of being that we can call *authenticity,* or more simply, honesty. Less healthy personalities, people who function less than fully, who suffer recurrent breakdowns or chronic impasses, may usually be found to be *liars.* They say things they do not mean. Their disclosures have been chosen more for cosmetic value than for truth. The consequence of a lifetime of lying about oneself to others, of saying and doing things for their sound and appearance, is that ultimately the person loses contact with his real self.

The authentic being manifested by healthier personalities takes the form of unself-conscious disclosure of self in words, decisions, and actions. It is a risky way of being, especially in a social setting that punishes all forms of action and disclosure that depart from some current stereotype of the ideal or acceptable man. The healthier person will doubtless experience many a bruise for being and disclosing who he is, but he prefers to accept these blows rather than lose himself or sell himself (his authentic being) for short-run acceptability.

Indeed, there is much reason to suspect that authenticity before others is the same mode of being that permits a man to have access to the underground realm of experiencing, the unconscious. Defensiveness and concealment of self before others unfortunately are the same modes of being that screen off a man's unconscious, his preverbal experiencing from himself. The currents of feeling, fantasy, memory, and wish that would get a man criticism from others also produce anxiety in himself; so he blocks these from the view of self and others in the service of self-defense. In time, he succeeds in fooling himself as much as others into believing he *is* the man he is so expertly *seeming* to be. In truth he is an "invisible man." Whatever is authentic of him, whatever is most spontaneous and alive (his experience of his possibilities), is buried so deep not even he can cognize it. One of the reasons less healthy personalities are so self-conscious, so deliberate in their choice of word and action before others, is that they dread letting something slip out that truly expresses their being, something which will get them into trouble. They are, as it were, idolators of the state of artificial grace known as "staying out of trouble." In fact, they have sold their souls and possibilities for a good, but false name.

All this is not to say that healthier personalities are always fully visible, fully transparent, before the gaze of self and others. Such chronic self-revelation may be itself idolatrous, and is suicidal in certain circumstances. Certainly we would expect a healthier personality to have enough common sense, judgment, even cunning, to preserve himself in a hostile environment, dropping his guard only when he is among trusted and loving friends. And, in fact, a healthy personality will have been able to enter into and maintain relationships of trust and love with one or more people, people whom he has let know him and whom he knows and responds to.

Another dimension of healthy personality concerns the realm of values itself. Healthier personalities seek and find meaningful values and challenges in life, such that there is an element of direction, of focus, to their existence.[21] Less healthy personalities, estranged as they are from their real selves, usually pursue only clichéd goals and values current in their present social milieu. These latter goals frequently do not challenge or inspire the average person to the fullest integration and expression of his unique being; they do not "turn him on" or keep him going. The upshot is that he will often feel trapped or, worse, feel that he is "losing his mind." The latter fear is most likely to occur when a person looking at the externals of his present situation finds that he has accomplished or has been given "everything to make a man happy"—but that he, in honesty, is miserable, bored, and doesn't know what to do next. He has "loved ones," a family, material success, a nice house, car, and so on; but he finds his work increasingly boring, more like a treadmill, and his relationships with others empty, formal, and all too predictable; and he entertains fantasies of murdering his loved ones, chucking it all, and going to the South Seas, only to repress these ideas with the anxious thought, "I must be insane to harbor such notions." He might scurry into further "busy-work," commence drinking to excess, create excitement by treading along primrose paths at great risk, or do other searching in the outer world for some new meanings. He looks in the wrong place, the right place being within his own experience (see Chapter 9). The healthier personality, less estranged and less afraid of his real self, can look within and without and create or find new sources of value, new directions of commitment, even when these elicit some criticism from others in his world. He is freer to invest value in more aspects of the world than his less healthy counterpart.

A healthy personality lives in and with his body, he is an "embodied self."[54] He is not afraid or ashamed to touch his own body or the bodies of other people with whom he is on intimate terms (see Chapter 12). He is able freely to move his body, which has a look of grace, coordination, and relaxation. "He dances through life," to state this idea in its most extreme but essentially accurate form. By contrast, the less healthy personality is afraid to live in his body. He represses his bodily experiencing and feels his body alternately numb and dead or as a dangerous and stinking cesspool charged with explosive nitroglycerine. He must take care lest an urge, a feeling, an impulse, or a movement break through the tight control. For him, this would be disastrous. One of the most common evidences of disembodiment is muscular tension that reveals itself as stiffness in body posture, awkwardness in gait, the mouth a thin red line, the jaws clenched, and the face an immobile mask, frozen in false smile or anxious frown or counterfeit dignity; the voice emits sounds that are jerky, pressured, constricted. Touch such an average person on the arm or place one's arm around his shoulder, and he will instantly stiffen, experience panic, jump as if stabbed, and perhaps experience a mixture of sexual arousal and guilt or anxiety. The healthier person has a more fully lived and experienced body.[65, 77, 78] His face is mobile and expressive; he speaks in a voice that is free, not one which is fighting off an impulse to say something else at the same moment that the present speech is being emitted. It is no accident that average people receive psychotherapeutic benefit from instruction in vocalization or freely expressive dance and from massage and other forms of direct experience with their bodies. Indeed, the therapists of the future will without doubt be obliged to learn to live gracefully with their own bodies and to learn ways of inviting their clients to get back into theirs.

An important part of bodily experience is sex, the erotic impulse and feeling. Perhaps our puritanical avoidance of body-contact in everyday life expresses our mixed attitudes toward sexuality. A healthier personality is able to experience his erotic feelings without fear; and he is able to express them in a relationship with a chosen partner without needless inhibition, as part of the sexual dialogue. The less healthy person is usually so self-conscious that he cannot "let sexuality happen" in his attempts at loving transaction, and so he tries to force matters. The result may be premature climax, impotence, frigidity, inability to know and to attune oneself to the sexual being of the partner, and so on. Likely, the beginning at a cure of liberation from sexual difficulties is made outside the bedroom, but inside the self.

We alluded above to the ability of healthier personalities to find and maintain relationships of love and friendships in the world. This ability insures that a healthier person will have access to relief from the existential loneliness in which we all live. It will be noted that I used the term "relief." Loneliness is not a disease of which one can be cured; it is instead an inescapable fact of human existence. Less healthy personalities, cut off as they are from the fount of their real selves, find *themselves* terrible company. They cannot long tolerate solitude, and they run willy-nilly into busy-work, or superficial companionship with others. They do not, however, truly encounter another person and enter into dialogue with him. Hence, the feeling of loneliness, of not being known and understood, chronically nags at them like a boil on the buttocks or a stone in the shoe. The healthier personality, because he is less self-concealing and has readier access to his own fantasy, feelings, and memories, is less afraid of solitude when that is his lot; and when he is with others, he can feel secure enough in his own worth that he can let encounter and dialogue happen. During the process of such dialogue, the shell which encapsulates him as a separate, isolated being ruptures; and his inner world expands to include the received world of experience of the other. When the dialogue ends, he has experienced himself in the new dimensions evoked by the other person, and he has learned of the personal world of another—thus he is enlarged and changed. The less healthy personality defends himself against being so affected and changed in his contacts with others. He "rubs shells," or clinks his character armor against that of the other person, but does not meet the other. There is no encounter.

Just as a healthy personality dares to let himself be the one he is, so does he respect, even cherish and defend, the "suchness," the idiosyncrasy, of the other person in his world. He eschews sneaky efforts to manipulate the feelings, thoughts, and actions of the other; hence he truly experiences the other person as *an other,* as a source of being, different in some respects from himself and similar to him in other ways. The less healthy person dares neither to let himself be, nor to trust the being of the other when he is not trying to control that being. In his transactions, he seeks always to influence the other, if in no other modality than in the way in which he will be *seen* and experienced by the other. In the extreme instances of unhealthy personality, the individual actually (this can only be stated metaphorically) detaches his ego from his body and functions as a spectator and manipulator of his own depersonalized body as "it" transacts with the other person. This depersonalized body is then manipulated before the other, in the hope that the other's experience of and responses toward this counterfeit person can thus be controlled: robots performing before others who are perceived as robots.[54]

7

Psychotherapy as Invitation

The Invitation to Become Sick

Psychotherapy begins when a person cannot live his life further in the ways he has, and consults with somebody who intends to help him. The fact that a person would arrive at such an impasse should provoke wonder, since all of us are gifted with intelligence that could guide us out of existential culs-de-sac. But people arrive at this point, and there are those who would be of help. How does the sufferer reach his stalemate? *I believe he chooses it.*

I agree with the existentialist thinkers[29,86] that every man chooses his way of being in the world. But I would go further and assert that people choose their ways of being *for somebody*. A man chooses his way of being for himself, or for somebody else. His choices, naturally, yield consequences.

The way a person has chosen to exist was selected from possible alternative ways. It was selected because it seemed to be a way to fulfill or preserve *values*. These values include, for example, survival, identity, status, the love of another person, money, etc.

If we now look at some particular man's present condition, whether he be sick or well, we can ask, "Of what way of being is this condition an outcome? At whose invitation did the fellow choose this way of being and not some other? His own? His mother's? His teacher's?" And we can ask further, "What values were fulfilled, and which sacrificed, when the fellow chose and followed this way?"

Here are some examples of ways that a man might have followed: the *authentic* way, where he has been genuine in his transactions with people and true to his projects; and the *counterfeit* way, which seems to be the common, or all-American, way. And we can speak of the *involved* way—as in the case of one deeply committed to various

52

projects—and the *detached, uninvolved* way. There is the *personal* way of the man who enters into dialogue with his fellows; and there is the *anonymous* way of the one who neither knows, nor is ever known by, any single human being. All these ways are possible, and each can be viewed as a response to an invitation, a response that yields consequences for well or ill.

A "neurotic" person, for example, may be seen as one who has chosen a rigid, encapsulated existence. It is safe, but it happens also to be suffocating. He chose to be this way, not only to feel safe, but also to hang on to the love of his parents or spouse. But he pays a price for his choice. Of a sexually impotent man, we may say his mother invited him by word or gesture to follow the *eunuchoid* way. He accepted the invitation, and was rewarded with his mother's approval. Some reward! Some price! But one must pay for everything in this world!

If a man's present being is the outcome of his acceptance of an invitation to *be* in some way, we can ask, "What do we know about invitation? Under what conditions is an invitation accepted or declined? Who extends the effective invitations? And who are the ones who respond to them?" We actually know a great deal about invitation, though the knowledge appears under other rubrics. We know a great deal about the psychology of suggestion, of persuasion, of hypnosis, and of leadership. Anything written under those headings seems to me to be relevant to a psychology of invitation. A good psychotherapist or a good nurse, teacher, leader, or hypnotist—even a good salesman—all these are experts at extending invitations or challenges that will be accepted. An invitation to someone carries with it the implication that the other has the power to carry it out. It is a form of the "attribution of power," as Heider[30] has written of it. The successful inviters invite others to change some aspects of their being. They invite a person to change his ways of valuing, construing, striving, behaving, or buying; and the person accepts the invitation. The therapist invites his patient to eschew phoniness and to try authenticity. The teacher invites his pupil to abandon ignorance, his present ways of thinking and believing, and to expose himself to new experiences. The leader invites or challenges his follower to carry out a mission that the follower never imagined he could accomplish. The hypnotist invites his subject to recover previously inaccessible memories, and the subject does. The nurse or doctor invites a patient to take a pill or an operation, and the patient does.

The phenomena of invitation have so powerful an effect upon man that I have wondered about the extent to which they have affected our psychological research (see above, Chapters 1, 2, 4).[71] The "demand" (I would call them "invitational") characteristics of experimental settings in which psychological research is carried out have been pointed out by several workers. It is as if subjects are invited to confirm the experimenter's hypotheses, by responding in a certain way —and many do! [71,85]

In the field of medicine, we know that certain recognized sicknesses are the result of a physician's (witting or unwitting) invitation to consider oneself weak or sick. Such conditions are designated *iatrogenic* diseases. If we speak of iatrogenic illness, is it not just as meaningful to speak of iatrogenic *wellness?* Or "mother-o-genic" wellness; or "psychologist-o-genic" wellness? Could we classify some physicians as wellness-inviters, i.e., healers, and others as sickeners, who have a knack for persuading others that they are weak, helpless, and sick? There are some people in society who have a proven flair for transmitting powerful invitations to others to regard life as pointless and hopeless and to regard themselves as weak and worthless. There may be many in society who are gifted at getting people to "give up," to yield, to give in. Goffman[27] has shown how mental hospital personnel invite or shape patients so that they will conform to current conceptions of how a madman should appear. And a visit to any mental hospital will prompt this question: "What kind of behavior and attitude are invited by the hospital buildings themselves? By the social organization that prevails there?" Laing and Esterson[56] have shown how much of the traditional psychiatric symptomatology can be explained as the outcome of invalidating and disconfirming behavior from relatives and professional people toward anyone who experiences difficulty in living. In fact, it is warranted to wonder whether hospital personnel can *take* healthy behavior when it appears in the ones called "patients," or do they rather get terrified by it when it appears and persuade the patient (invite him) to stop this nonsensical autonomy and self-expression and step into line. Do hospital personnel invite "crazy" behavior, and punish healthy behavior? In Kesey's[49] novel, *One Flew Over the Cuckoo's Nest,* patients who became bumptious were sedated or electroshocked into their appropriate social roles. If that didn't work, they were lobotomized. I don't think the story told in that novel is far from truth, at least in then existing mental hospitals.

Psychotherapeutic Technique as Some Kind of Invitation

There certainly are technical aspects of being a psychotherapist, and every major approach to psychotherapy highlights some technical way of being that the novice is obliged to rehearse until he has mastered it. The assumption is made that if you master this technique, then the people on whom you practice it will respond and commence to function fully. A virtual plethora of specialized technical approaches to the conduct of psychotherapy is described in the literature of clinical psychiatry and psychology. One of the most recent, of course, is the emphasis on conditioning techniques. We can also mention Albert Ellis'[15] type of argumentative psychotherapy (that is what I would call his therapy—he calls it "Rational-Emotive" psychotherapy). There are the interpretative work of the good psychoanalyst, and the "reflection" technique described in Carl Rogers'[84] early writings, and so on. But now let us look at techniques within the framework that I have tried to build in the early part of this chapter.

Whenever any new technique is presented in the literature of clinical psychology or psychiatry, something happens that is akin to what transpires in medicine when the pharmacologist produces a new tranquilizer, a new antibiotic, a new pain killer, a new "wake-upper" or a new "put-to-sleeper." A wave of enthusiasm develops among practitioners, and the new technique or the new drug is used widely, with enthusiasm and with good results; then unforeseen side effects and limits are discovered. Some of the uncritical enthusiasm and widespread application gets tempered. These comments about drugs seem exactly relevant to operant conditioning techniques, psychoanalytic techniques and client-centered techniques, and others. In each case, some pioneer has been totally committed to fostering wellness in a disturbed person. This pioneer then reached an impasse in his efforts to promote fuller functioning in his patient. The techniques and insights afforded by his past training and experiences did not help him overcome the impasse. So he wrestled with the impasse in the spirit of total commitment. In the process, he obtained a new insight or invented a new technique that worked. This state of affairs, incidentally, resembles the situation of any creative artist or investigator. Creative potentials in a person, in this case the therapist, were evoked in the context of a problem that challenged him *wholly*. The solution for this particular problem was arrived at *creatively*. The therapist, being an ambitious fellow, proceeds to publicize, to teach, and to try it out in a wide array of other problems. If he is effective in publicizing and at winning disciples, this creative person will have evolved a "school." The disciples will seek to master the technique; and after practicing it for years, they may well become highly proficient at it. If they become sufficiently practiced, they can practice the repertoire of technical behavior almost automatically while their mind and heart are elsewhere. At this point they are not at all like the pioneer who developed the technique in the spirit of total commitment. These automatic technicians remind me of a nightclub pianist who can play up to one or two hundred pieces of music without thinking; his *hands* play while *he* is involved in flirting with the female patrons or in daydreaming. This common tendency, which I think I observe pretty reliably, to try to master a technique of interpersonal relating in much the same way as you master the technique of swimming, or piano, seems to me to illustrate the all-American idolatry of "having it made," the worship of automation. It is an effort so to master an interpersonal habit that one can *impersonate a totally involved individual* while one's mind and heart are on such things as, "Does she love me?", "How is my bank account?", "Gee, she's got a good shape!" —or whatever is meaningful to the person at the time he is practicing his technique.

Here is a curious phenomenon about human transactions: whenever the other person with whom you are dealing is self-conscious or contrived, whenever he is not fully present, when his "heart is not in it," when he is doing something, with his heart elsewhere and his true purpose concealed—then you sense this inevitably; if not right away, then in due time. When the other person is impersonating sincerity, wholeness, or full presence, his performance seldom convinces for long. Even professional actors, masters at impersonating the person whose role they perform on the stage, will drop this role when they are off stage. An impersonator's true aims may not be immediately apparent in his words or actions, but they will be transmitted or disclosed somehow. All of us have a vested interest in knowing what the other person is up to. What I'm saying here is that the suave, technical, well-rehearsed psychotherapist, like the suave salesman or suave minister, is impersonating someone who he is not. He is not fully committed to the *purpose* of his profession, and the people before whom he practices his automatized techniques inevitably arrive at the point where they do not take the practitioner seriously.

Psychotherapy is not so much a science or technique as it is a way of being with another person.[32] There are many reasons to be with another person and many ways to be with him. The psychotherapeutic way is the embodiment of an *intention*—the wish that the one who is Other for the therapist should experience his freedom, should be and become himself. The therapist's commitment to the value of the other's freedom, wholeness, and growth transcends his loyalty to some technique of "doing" therapy, or some theoretical orientation, e.g., psychoanalysis, client-centered therapy, or the Jungian, existentialist, or Adlerian viewpoints. The commitment to ultimate goals insures that the therapist will not become fixed on an automatized technique that reduces his patient to the status of "one of them" and which provides the therapist with a mask behind which he conceals his truer commitments. Yet this is not to say there is no place for technique in the art of psychotherapy. Technique, which must be learned from a teacher, is an *idiom* in which one expresses an initial therapeutic intent. The willingness to master techniques and to study theory is actually proof of the seriousness of purpose of the one who would become a therapist. This willingness separates the amateur from the professional.

Effective psychotherapists, who succeed in inviting sufferers to change their previous ways of being, are not technicians, though they will have mastered their techniques. How have they grown from therapeutic technicians into psychotherapists?

Some Dimensions of Growth for Psychotherapists

What is it about years of practice that makes a person a more effective therapist, if it is not increased suaveness and perfection of the techniques learned from some master? A novice psychotherapist who makes an interpretation may listen to what he has just said and wonder, "Did I say that well? Was it the right thing to say? Would my supervisor have said that?" He is chronically self-conscious. Unselfconscious mastery of beginning techniques in one's profession probably is a factor in increased effectiveness, but it certainly is not the only factor. Where, then, does a therapist grow? I shall turn to my own experience over the past ten or fifteen years for some possible answers.

Faith in the Other's Capacity for Transcendence

One change in me over the past five or ten years is the strength and basis in experience for my conviction about man's potential to transcend limits and determining forces that bear on him (see Chapter 17). I now believe there is no biological, geographical, social, economic, or psychological determiner of man's condition that he cannot transcend if he is suitably invited or challenged to do so. This conviction is scientific: it has grown out of experience and observation. Shaw[94] outlined a theory which offers promise to bring transcendence "under control." I believe there is no determiner which a man cannot get around, under, through, or over in order to pursue goals and values that have challenged him or that he has chosen to fulfill. Man's potentials for survival, for adaptation, for rehabilitation, for recovery from illness, and for growth seem barely to be scratched. Our concepts of man's limits have proven, century after century, to be too rigid. Man continually exceeds limits that science says are built into his tissue. He climbs Mt. Everest, he orbits the earth, he survives death camps, and he recovers from illnesses deemed fatal. Thus, whenever I encounter a patient who is suffering from confining and crippling effects of childhood privations and trauma and finds challenges in his present existence overpowering, rather than despair with him, and pursue all the roots of "pathology" in him, I immediately begin to wonder how it would be possible to mobilize his spirit or his capacity to transcend the present circumstances which he has let grind him down. Maybe over the years I've just become more effective at communicating my faith in their potentials to the patients themselves; or maybe I've become more effective at infecting patients with the seeds of faith in themselves. A patient will say, "You seem to have had faith in me, so I looked, and I found faith in myself." Maybe this is the factor in iatrogenic wellness—the strength of the *healer's* faith in the potentials of the sufferer to transcend the "limiting" conditions of his existence. If this is true, it raises a fascinating question: On what factors is one's faith in the *other person's* potential to transcend limiting conditions dependent? I think that question is answerable—I don't quite know how, just now; but I think as psychologists, we are duty bound to try to figure ways to measure the strength of a person's conviction *that the other fellow* has the capacity to transcend determining circumstances. It may be that bad "witches," or experts at producing iatrogenic illness, are the very ones who have either none of the faith that I am talking about, or the reverse faith. They may be absolutely convinced from their depths that people have no capacity for transcendence.

Capacity for Commitment

The second dimension of my growth as a therapist lies in increased capacity to commit myself to fostering growth or wellness in a patient. This capacity I experience as the capacity *to be there*—to be fully present to my patient, or honest enough to let him know when my thoughts are elsewhere. This capacity for commitment and full presence is experienced in the following way: I find myself accepting his pathology or growth restrictions as a *challenge,* one I continue to respond to after my present repertoire of conscious or habitual technique has been exhausted. This continued commitment in the face of failure of present techniques has resulted in innovation, in improvisation; it has elicited therapeutic creativity in me. I think that the correlate of commitment is this very increased creativity in the therapeutic encounter.

This observation prompts a digression. Something is fishy when a person practices a profession and cannot be creative in it, when he continues to practice something the same way year after year. Either the person has been brainwashed, or his creative potentials were leached from him as he received his training. Let me put it in still another way. A therapist's task is to promote wellness in another. He was trained for this task, and he begins it with a repertoire of techniques. He has learned to listen; that is very good. He has learned to make reflections of feeling and content. He has learned the art of relevant interpretation. This is his "bag of tricks," the kit of tools he utilizes in hope that they will invite a patient into growing. About 60 percent of a therapist's patients will accept his invitation to wellness, as he presents it. But what about the 40 percent of the case load that decline? It used to be that when my techniques (invitations) didn't "work," I would simply repeat them. I would reflect feelings more vigorously and interpret more incisively. Nothing happened. I was being most noncreative. I was showing a kind of character disorder, by persisting in behavior that was not effective. I was like the auto mechanic who knew how to do only three things—tighten nuts, turn screws, and connect wires. When someone brought in a car that wouldn't run, he would turn every screw, tighten every nut, and connect every wire. The car still wouldn't work. So he would find some more screws to turn, more nuts to tighten, and more wires to connect. At the least, we would want the mechanic to try something else or to return our money. One wants responsible creativity from a practitioner.

What is it about our methods of training therapists that seems so marvelously effective in drying up trainees' courage to be resourceful and creative in the arena of their commitment? Consider the ministry. Ministers seek to move people from a hellish existence to heaven on earth, to love their brothers and to end sinning. But clergymen use few means to embody their commitment and their invitations. Maybe this is a good thing, that they seek to invite people to wholeness and goodness solely through sermons, home visits, pastoral counseling, and hospital visits. But surely there are more ways than this that could be dreamed up. I'll raise this question: Where are the creative potentials in the ministerial profession? What other ways might a minister employ to carry out his vocation—since, clearly, his present ways have not been very effective at humanizing men.

We need to examine our training to see how it prevents us from being creative in carrying out our commitments. I think our training expresses a commitment, not to healing, but to loyal membership in a cult or élite. If we were trained for commitment to fostering wellness, then we couldn't help but become creative, because the know-how built into us in our training would carry us only to the point of the first therapeutic impasse. Here, at the therapeutic impasse, is where commitment is tested: is the therapist committed to his "school's" techniques—or to the patient's growth? If to the latter, then he will be creative[64] and inventive; he will display and embody the intentionality of which May has written. If to the former, he will function like a cracked phonograph record, uttering the same invitation over and over, oblivious to the fact that it has been declined.

Capacity for Dialogue

A third dimension of my own growth over the past five or ten years, which I believe is related to effective psychotherapy, is growth in capacity to enter into dialogue. This entails increased ability to establish contact, and sustain an I-thou relationship of mutual unreserve, *with a broader range of humanity.* I feel I am less afraid to let myself hear, feel, and then respond honestly to a more diversified array of people than was possible for me earlier. I am less afraid to let him and me be ourselves and reveal ourselves honestly. Maybe it is just a case of my having become more whole-hearted in my invitation to terrified, self-concealing people to disclose themselves as they are. I've come to believe, as I said earlier, that people choose a mode of being as a response to others' invitations or threats. They choose schizophrenic, or hysterical, or obsessional, or depressed being—for their parents, their spouse, or their friends. Part of this sick being is phoniness itself (cf. Mowrer [67,68]) and part of the sick being is the organism's response to a long career of inauthentic being. Now a therapist, himself a rehabilitated phony, invites the patient to try the frightening rigors of the authentic way, first with the therapist and then with others. Perhaps one grows in capacity for dialogue as a function of increased courage to be authentic with one's patient. This simple honesty functions as an invitation to him to be as he is at that moment. Certainly if one is not fully present with the patient and is not fully committed; if one is being a phony; if one is impersonating Sigmund Freud, or Carl Rogers, or Carl Whitaker and *isn't* one of these people—his effectiveness at dialogue will have been radically impaired.

A Core Stage in Psychotherapy

Successful therapeutic outcome is not a function of the techniques employed as such; rather it is an outcome of such matters as the therapist's faith in the patient's potential for fuller functioning. Faith in patients' potential may be pretty hard to hang on to. Certain patients, for example, in the back wards of state hospitals may put it to strenuous test. Here, the example set by early Christians may be relevant.—An early man of the Church replied, when asked why he believed the absurd message of Christianity: *Credo quam absurdum* ("I believe *because* it is absurd"). It may well be absurd to believe that some poor fellow has the potential to transcend a psychosis of 20 years' standing; but if you don't have some such fools in the world, nothing new is discovered.

The strength of the therapist's commitment to bringing about this transcending action on the part of the patient seems to be another factor, and the therapist's capacity for entering into dialogue seems to be the third factor beyond beginning techniques, that are involved in growing effectiveness at therapeutic work. These may also be factors in effective teaching, leadership, ministering, or anything else that involves two people, one of whom feels a responsibility to help bring about change, or a transcending state of affairs in the other.

Now let's assume that a therapist has been able to commit himself to his patient—to help this patient arrive at fuller functioning. Once this state of affairs has come into being (and it takes time to happen), the therapist and patient become a new unit. They form an I-thou "coupling." This term has a sexy sound, but it is not a sexual coupling. Nor is it without feeling, sexual or other kinds. In the limiting instance, such an I-thou unity can be depicted as a temporary linking of the receptors, central processes, and effectors of the therapist and the patient.

The approach to the ideal coupling is *gradual,* since many factors in both patient and therapist hinder its development. But let us note that when the coupling has been achieved, it is as if the patient's ego has been rendered effectively larger. Incoming information is received both by his ego and by that of his therapist. The coding of this information is likewise carried on by the new enlarged "double" ego. Decisions for action may be arrived at jointly, and the consequences of these actions are fed back, not to the patient alone, but also to the therapist. On the basis of this shared feedback, many decisions can be made and tried, with the consequence that new learning will occur in the patient. Since the therapist is committed to fuller functioning in the patient, he doesn't disengage, he doesn't undo the coupling until it becomes clear that the goal of fuller functioning is in process of being attained: the patient has improved at communication, he has increased courage, he has discovered meaningful goals, and so on. In short, he can get along in his existence without such a close coupling with his therapist.

Now let us turn to the establishment of the I-thou unity. It appears to be true that *only* within such a mutually open relationship can the therapist maximally present his therapeutic influence, at the risk, incidentally, of being demoralized or sickened by the patient. It is an open question when you get two people thus open one to the other— who is going to influence whom? I can attest that there have been therapeutic transactions where I have been sickened by the patient instead of his being ameliorated by me. When you are open, you take risks. This unity of I and thou in mutual openness, one before the other, appears to be the referent for what Fred Fiedler[17] called "the good interpersonal relationship" that he found to be a common denominator in experienced psychotherapists of different schools. This I-thou unity appears to be the medium within which brainwashing or "thought reform" goes on. It also appears to be a necessary condition for operant conditioning to occur, at least when the "reinforcement magazine" is another person. I think that it is the *sine qua non* for any kind of interpersonal influence that is not secret, where the influencer is as vulnerable and open as the one to be influenced. Any theory of therapy, any technique that embodies goodwill, is likely to be effective when the "coupling" has been attained.[19] And no technique will "work" when I and thou are not thus open.

How does a relationship evolve to that point where the therapist's intent to be helpful is likely to have maximal impact on the patient? How does he arrive at the point where he will be listened to, so that his utterances and actions will be maximally experienced by the patient? I include *actions* here because nonverbal behavior is also disclosure that conveys the therapist's intent to help the patient function more fully. Let me state this again. How does the relationship between you and me evolve to the point where what I say and do will have maximal impact on you? How does it come to pass that a patient will open himself up to be known and to be influenced? This really is the nub of psychotherapy, and teaching, and love, and leadership. How do you arrive in a relationship at the point where the other person is maximally open to you and will be affected by you? I now believe that *his* openness and vulnerability to influence and to good and to harm is a concomitant of *your openness before him,* so that you are also vulnerable.

This stage of mutual vulnerability, mutual acceptability, is gradually reached. It happens sooner with some patients than with others, assuming the therapist's commitment to the patient's fuller functioning remains constant. I have an informed suspicion, one consistent with a number of lines of experimental data that we do have, that *I* am a strong determiner of how open and trusting the other fellow is going to get. I suspect that he will become as open, trusting, and vulnerable as I am willing to be with him. If I want him to be maximally open, then I have to be prepared to be maximally open. If I want him to be only half-open, then I will only get half-open. If I want him to be maximally open, but I keep myself fully closed off, peeking at him through chinks in my own armor, trying to manipulate him from a distance, then in due time he will discover that I am not in that same mode; and he will then put his armor back on and peer at me through chinks in it, and he will try to manipulate me. I believe that the psychotherapist is the leader in the therapeutic dance, and the patient follows the leader. With some of my patients this maximum, mutual openness has occurred in the first three or four sessions while with others it has taken up to 150 or 300 meetings before the patient has experienced the desired degree of trust. I suspect that when it took 301 meetings for the patient to trust me, it was because I wasn't trustworthy for 300 meetings; on the 301st meeting, I may have felt enough confidence in myself and trust in the patient that I could be open before him. Then, in that very session we experienced this maximum, mutual openness—in short, an encounter. Then, I could give a lecture to the patient, give a reflection, give an interpretation, argue, do any technical thing that seemed relevant—and it would have maximum therapeutic benefit if I happened to be wise, or it would do maximum harm if I happened just then to be a fool.

The Psychotherapeutic Touch

I have found that some form of physical contact with patients expedites the arrival of this mutual openness and unreserve. So far, I have only held hands with a patient, put an arm around a shoulder, or given a hug—all in the context of an unfolding dialogue. I believe we are a nation of people who are starved for physical contact. In Chapters 8 and 12 I'll discuss this more fully but I believe the time to dispense with the touch-taboo in psychotherapy is now. Spitz's[96] and Ribble's[82] observations on the importance of mothering as a factor in optimum growth in infants are relevant here. Mothering is mediated, among other ways, by cuddling and holding. I suspect the need for such mothering is never completely lost. Harry Harlow's[28] experiments with monkeys, involving "mothers" made of wire or terry cloth, showed that physical contact with a wire mother was preferred by these little monkeys to no contact at all; and of course a nice, soft terry-cloth mother was preferred over one made of wire. Perhaps the need to feel something against his skin was the decisive factor that attracted the little monkey to a dummy mother, whether wire or terry cloth.

Physical contact, of course, is a mode of *knowing* a person, in the biblical sense. To "know" a woman, for example, certainly involves first of all her cooperation, her willingness to be known. She *lets* herself be known—that is, sexually touched and entered. More generally, and less erotically, a person lets himself be known by verbal disclosure of his experiencing; by permitting himself to be seen as he does things; and by letting another person touch him. When I ask someone, "How do you feel?", I am asking him to tell me what is going on in his experience; but I may also be asking for his permission to touch him so that I can find out what he feels like.

The most primitive mode of establishing contact with another person is to touch him—hold his hand, put an arm around his shoulder, or hug him. Words don't need to be exchanged in such a situation. Indeed, psychotherapists will often reveal their willingness to remain in contact with a patient by holding his hand when he will not or cannot communicate verbally.

The metaphor of "being turned on" describes the experience of physical contact. When part of your body is touched, you can't ignore that part of your body. It becomes "figure" in your perceptual field. You might say that that part of your body comes into being. One wonders about men or women who have never been touched or hugged, or have never been in intimate body contact with others. Could we say that their bodies have not come to life, that their bodies do not exist in the phenomenological sense? One wonders to what extent they feel that their bodies are alive. I suspect that the transformation from virginity or even preorgasmic existence to the experience of having a sexual climax is so radical as to be equivalent to a kind of rebirth.

The metaphor of "being touched," as in the expression "Your plight touches me," is relevant here. There are many touch-associations in our language and in our everyday experience, but actual touching is hemmed in by strict social taboos.

Chiropractors touch their patients and establish lasting doctor-patient relationships, as Sulzer[98] showed. I know it is easier to talk to someone when one is in physical contact with him, so long as the meaning of the contact is mutually known. Back rubs and body massage from nurses, masseurs, barbers, and hairdressers likely all serve to make the recipients of such contact more talkative—when they are not soothed into a blissful trance. I think we shall have to learn more about physical contact and its meaning as an expression of therapeutic intent.

One of the first things that ought to be done in any state mental hospital is to train a group of masseurs in the art of coping with terrified people who are being turned on. Good, loving massages on inaccessible patients may turn them on in a way that is terrifying to them and also terrifying to the person who has just awakened them. The therapist of the future ultimately will learn from that unheeded prophet, Reich,[77] and become less afraid to get into meaningful physical contact with his patient; and he will have to be able to cope therapeutically with whatever behavior and experience such contact evokes.

The Sound of Badges

Anything a therapist does or says in his relationship with a patient can be looked at as a redundant expression of a message about his *actual* commitment. Henry Winthrop has spoken of this as "acoustic badges," badges you can hear. Much of what anyone says or does has this badge function. The carrier of a fraternity pin thereby tells the viewer that he is a member of Sigma Sigma Sigma. Much of what one says in a therapy transaction, even when it appears that one is communicating many messages to the patient—that is, what actually gets across—is the single theme, "I am a psychologist, I am a psychologist." Perhaps one transmission of that message is all the patient needs. When one does repeat himself in this redundant way, he is revealing his actual commitment. This may be the desire to be seen as a member of some group of psychologists. The patient may not care. Reflections and interpretations may be experienced by the patient as expressions of the message, "I don't really care about you, I care about my fees, or my comfort, or the rightness of my theories or reflections or interpretations." Or, these same reflections and interpretations, whether awkward or apt, may be heard as repetitions of, "I want you to be healthier, I want to help you, I am trying to be helpful." If the therapist's behavior expresses a true therapeutic commitment to the patient, then the suaveness of his technique and his theory of therapy probably don't matter much. If he is genuinely committed, then anything he says and does in good faith will be seen by the patient as the expression of a man of goodwill. In the presence of a man of goodwill, patients drop their defenses. They begin to grow at that moment. When a patient experiences his therapist's sincere commitment to his well-being, he enters the core stage of trust and hope.

The Feel of Healing

I believe that trust and hope are not *contributors* to healing. Rather, they are the experienced aspect of a *total* organismic healing, or reintegration process. Trust and hope are indications that the healing or reintegration or transcendence process *has been set in motion.* Trust and hope don't cause healing. They *are* healing. We can look at healing from various perspectives. From a psychological standpoint, healing appears as a state of trust and hope. At a physiological level, it is revealed as changes in white-cell count or in some endocrinological changes. At a behavioral level, healing is manifested in growing vigor and relevance of "responding." Continued distrust and hopelessness in a patient undergoing any kind of therapy may be regarded as indications that the disintegration process is unremitting. The patient's acquiescence to determiners of his existence is persisting and may culminate in death or total withdrawal into psychosis. Anything a therapist does which invites a sick person to trust, to be self-revealing, and to have hope that a better life is possible is therapeutic. The onset of these psychological states signifies that the healing process or desirable personality reorganization has already begun.

Keeping the Growing Edge Growing

Now I shall speak of something neglected: opportunities to grow and to have one's growth confirmed for people in the healing, the helping, and the teaching professions. I have found them because I have needed them. I'll tell you some of the places where I found them and some of the barriers that I encountered in hunting, and trying to profit from, growth opportunities. The most valuable experience I have had beyond training, that has maintained my growing edge, is *contact with colleagues who are of goodwill* and before whom I have not been afraid to be myself; that is, be like a patient, a pupil, a teacher, or a groping, bungling, well-intentioned person trying to make sense of what he is doing and wanting to benefit from somebody else's experience. Out of informal friendships and informal workshop meetings, more formal workshops such as those held by the American Academy of Psychotherapists evolved. At Academy workshops 50 or 75 therapists spend five days and nights, *at* each other—liking one another, hating one another, reacting to one another, helping one another, experiencing one another, and sharing with one another what we do, what we don't do, why do we do it, and so on. I think therapists stultify if they don't have workshops of this sort available to them. If such are not available, then a therapist has to find someone he can trust, to tangle with, in order to avoid becoming smug, pompous, fat-bottomed and convinced that he has "the word." One of the greatest dangers of being a teacher, a psychotherapist, a nurse, a minister, or anybody else involved in trying to help others change is the delusion that one "has it made," that all-American fantasy. There is no one like a self-disclosing colleague to prod one out of such smug pomposity, and invite one back to the task.

8

Some Questions and Answers on Effective Psychotherapy

I presented the material in the last chapter in a lecture to the clinical psychology staff at Milledgeville State Hospital, during a consulting visit in 1964. After the lecture there was a question-and-answer period. The following are the questions and my answers to them. I present them with no further comment, in the belief that students and practitioners of psychotherapy may find something here to confirm or to challenge their present views and practices.

Question: Does a therapist enact a role?

Answer: When we commence a relationship with somebody for some purpose, we begin in a role, as teacher, or as customer, or as helper. In that sense each participant has a role to fulfill. A third party looking at this transaction can watch it and say, "You are fulfilling the role of the helper, and he is fulfilling the role of the helpee." I may be aware I am supposed to fulfill the role of helper, but I can do this in a way that expresses my genuine commitments and intentions and in my idiosyncratic way. Let me develop this, since it has important implications. It is the difference between *taking* a role and *playing* a role. To take a role is a commitment to a task; to play a role is a charade.

One reason a profession loses zest for its practitioners arises when the practitioner feels he can only work in a cut-and-dried, stereotyped way. In due time he outgrows that stereotyped way. If he feels he must stick to that stereotyped way, it makes him sick. This is why many nurses, psychotherapists, doctors, and teachers ultimately get fed up with their profession. They lose zest because they feel that they have got to keep up the appearance of the role of a teacher, a nurse, a doctor, a therapist in some stereotyped way. When they do that, what they are telling you is that they are more committed to imitating that role than they are to carrying out their professional commitment, that is, [to] bring about results. When your commitment is to goals and not means, you can't help but be eccentric, idiosyncratic, offbeat, oddball, and creative.

Question: What is a good therapist?

Answer: I think it is a matter of commitment. How do we define good practitioners? This raises the problem of evaluating. If you train teachers, or nurses, or psychotherapists, about all you can evaluate them for is the success with which they are impersonating the role model you provide for them in a textbook, or by the example of the living teachers. You are actually teaching them to be *imitators,* and you grade them an A, B, C, D, or "flunk" on the basis of how well they imitate. I think that is the way it should be. But trouble arises when the practitioner, who has successfully impersonated the role models, goes out of school to practice. He may continue to judge his "goodness" or "badness" on the basis of how well he conforms to his original impersonation. This is no longer appropriate. He should be evaluated and should evaluate himself on the basis of his results. If he is a salesman, then sales. If he is a teacher, by students who learn. If he is a therapist, with patients who get well. If she is a nurse, with patients who are comfortable and nonanxious during their recovery. The ways of producing these results must be more diversified than the role enactment which yielded a high grade in a training school.

I have seriously thought that training schools ought not to award a degree or diploma until two years after training. The graduate gets a provisional badge, if he has successfully imitated his teachers and followed their instructions. If in two years he still practices in the way he did when he left, that provisional badge is taken away. Unfortunately, there are many therapists who engage in a perpetual impersonation for the rest of their career. What makes it even more terrible, they feel self-righteous about it and condemn responsible explorers and pioneers. Some of our most creative psychotherapists have been vituperated, blasted, criticized, threatened with expulsion from their professional societies. They may have explored beyond the orthodox training they received, and so they should. But it calls for courage. Let us ask, "What do training schools or institutional settings do to our courage and creativity? Have they fostered them, or diminished them?"

Question: Will the professional associations like the American Psychological or American Psychiatric Association allow deviations and idiosyncrasies?

Answer: Yes, if it is carried out in a spirit of responsible commitment to the task of healing, and if procedures are shared with colleagues, for their testing and criticism. The freedom to explore, elbow-room, has always been there. In fact, not to grasp it is to neglect one's professional responsibilities. This raises the question, why don't more of us reach out and use it? I suppose a lot of the resistance to growth comes from within, but there may also be instances where it comes from without. A rule of thumb I always use in any setting where I work is, "Do I get headaches there?" If I get headaches, the resistance to my growth comes from without. If I get bored, the resistance to my own growth comes from within. But that rule of thumb may only be peculiar to me. It may not be relevant to you.

Question: If creative flexibility is the method of psychotherapy, how can you possibly train people to that way of practicing?

Answer: I think that when one is in training, one should be given a rigid way of being so that you have a model to wean yourself *to,* so you can wean yourself *from* the ways of being you learned from mother, father, Sunday school, your neighborhood, and so on. These ways won't necessarily be effective in a therapeutic interchange. But I think it is good to learn something orthodox to give you a sense of professional identity, a badge. But that is only half training. The other half is provided through supervision. Once a master is persuaded that the pupils have mastered basic discipline, then he must afford encouragement and challenge to his student. When the student is wrestling with a concrete problem presented by a real patient, he is, as it were, being tempted to break discipline. If it seems to him and his supervisor that something is called for, but that if he does it, he won't be a good Rogerian, then the supervisor must encourage his pupil to say, "To hell with Rogerianism. Full speed ahead." But in a responsible way, because he and his supervisor must deal with whatever happens next in the therapeutic dialogue.

Question: A sense of group identity, as is offered by some schools of therapy may have value, as you suggest; but won't it be difficult for a student to transcend his school's theories and techniques?

Answer: If the student in his postgraduate work-setting doesn't grow, the blame lies with the setting, his teachers, or the new practitioner himself. A teacher of some art presents beginning know-how to his students. But he knows that this is by no means the final answer to producing desired outcomes. The responsible teacher has two tasks. First, he must guide the pupil in the ways of basic discipline. But then, he mustn't be satisfied until he sees his pupil is ready, responsibly, to surpass his training in any responsible way that seems relevant in that moment to accomplish some therapeutic objective. I mentioned, the last time I was here, an occasion when I got down on the floor and competed with a patient in doing push-ups. At that point in our dialogue, it became very relevant for me to do five more push-ups than the patient did, because he was an out-of-condition "slob." It was important for this patient to do something physical. He asked me if I could do push-ups, and I said I could. He said, to prove he was in shape, "I'll match you push-up for push-up." He couldn't. That is not very Rogerian, and I wasn't doing it for the sake of doing it. It was an "emergent" from the relationship as it existed at that moment. A moment may come when the thing for a therapist to do is to hold his patient's hand, when he sits there in absolute despair. You may feel yourself called upon just to establish contact. Your impulse is to reach out and hold his hand, but your discipline and your training say, "There must be no body contact. To touch a patient is irresponsible acting-out. The patient may be a psychopath. You will get into a lawsuit and be sued for seduction or rape, and God knows what all." So you don't do it. Possibly, all those reasons for not holding your patient's hand are sound. But they may not be, at least not in all cases. The taboo on touching is one of those rules for conduct people seek. You know people are always looking for an absolute rule that will relieve them of the responsibility of evaluating each situation on its own unique merits, and then risking an action. Well, I think training should teach you rules, but then your trainer should encourage you or prod you to go beyond the rules in response to the call of the immediate therapeutic situation. This is where masters of the Zen way can teach psychotherapists and teachers of psychotherapy something. A Zen master presumably is an expert at getting someone to master some technique and then tricking him, bulldozing him, so he will forget technique and respond unself-consciously and spontaneously. The response is most likely then to be relevant and appropriate, with head and heart in congruence. This seems to apply to painting, archery, tea-ceremonial; and I don't see why it doesn't apply in psychotherapy.

Question: Psychotherapists are supposed to be "accepting" people. Do you accept your patients as they are?

Answer: I don't accept or reject a patient as he now is, because "acceptance" implies approval, and that isn't relevant. What I do is acknowledge to myself and to him that I confirm him as the one he is, and I invite him to take the freedom to reveal and be whoever and whatever he is—what he thinks, what he feels, and so on. I also grant myself the same freedom to be and to respond, to be this very person. What does this mean? It means I try to provide him with what I hope is a free milieu within which he can dare to express and disclose more of his being. This being that he discloses doesn't vanish into a swamp or quagmire; nor does it hit a mirror, then to bounce back. Rather, it is received by a real person—me—and responded to by a real person—me. I feel that an environment in which people can grow is one where both parties have the freedom, the responsibility, to be and to respond one to the other. I think Rogers, who is responsible for this formulation about providing the atmosphere in which a person can grow, has himself discovered and is reporting that it is not enough just to be a wonderfully permissive and "reflecting" individual. Most of the time a person wants some response from you *besides* "clarification" or a confirming "reflection." You can only clarify and confirm so long; then, the patient gets the idea you are understanding him. To go on beyond this point is redundant, even boring and ridiculous. There is more a therapist can say besides, "You feel...."

Question: What about the times when a patient expresses the wish for sexual contact with the therapist?

Answer: Many times, in the therapeutic dialogue, it becomes apparent the patient would like to climb into bed with you, or you might like to climb into bed with her. Fortunately or unfortunately, to do so is against the law, and it is against our professional ethics. It is probably wise we are restrained by our training from *acting out* a sexual wish, but there is nothing to stop us from *saying* we would like to.

Question: On the matter of physical contact, touching—what if you didn't feel comfortable, say, holding a patient's hand?

Answer: I wouldn't touch anybody if I couldn't feel comfortable about it.

Question: Should you acknowledge your discomfort about it?

Answer: I would think so. But then it is not enough only to acknowledge it. Suppose I discover I am a prude about touching, that I go into a panic everytime there is any body-contact between me and another person. Do I then sit back and say, "Well, this is the way I am, and I can never be different?" This is sort of a denial of one's whole professional conviction. If a patient suffers from a "touching taboo," you are implying to him that he can rise above it. What do you do when you discover these limitations in yourself? Sit back and say, "Well, I accept myself with these limitations, and I'll just hang on to them for the rest of my life?" Or do you struggle for ways of growing beyond them? This is where I think colleagues, professional workshops, and so on, can be very helpful in keeping one growing.

Question: Would you comment on the role of therapy for the therapist in line with this, as in the training of graduate students in psychology or residents in psychiatry?

Answer: The psychoanalysts were the first to insist that someone should go through a training analysis. Why did they insist on it? Part of their rationale was that it afforded insight and helped the trainee to grow. It helped make you more empathic and gave theory more experiential meaning. It afforded more faith in one's working procedures. But then, what seemed to evolve from this was the view that a therapist had to be, or have been, a severe psychoneurotic or character disorder or psychotic in order effectively to treat with severe neuroses or psychoses or character disorders. I don't think this was anywhere officially stated, but it was a sort of unspoken ideology around training departments that I was acquainted with. The real aristocrats among the trainees were those who had had nervous breakdowns. Everybody else was kind of "square." But I do believe that an experience as a patient can yield some benefits a learning therapist can get in few, if any, other ways. It can yield a fuller awareness of the extent to which one has been inauthentic in one's everyday existence, and some help and encouragement to dare to be genuine in one's everyday existence. This experience can also be gotten out of a good love affair, probably. There is more than one way to arrive at a "redemption" from phoniness. Such experience can enhance one's sensitivity to phoniness, to inauthenticity in another person; and it also gives one an opportunity to be a role model of authenticity for one's patient. Now, if you can get this courage to be authentic in some way other than therapy, so much the better; but I suspect it is rather difficult to. There may be some wise old men who have knocked around a lot, and who have worked in every kind of work—who have cheated, lied, stolen, and sinned. They have paid the consequences of all these things. Then on their own, they may have realized how they shortchanged themselves. They may have arrived at the "authentic way," and can be regarded as natural untrained psychotherapists. They can spot a phony since they have been one. They are experts. They are more expert at phoniness than the patient. They can help the patient grope for a way to be more genuine and at the same time be effective in life. They can help a person realize he doesn't have to be destroyed when he is genuine, that he won't inevitably be divorced, fired, or run out of town if he presents himself as he is. In 50 or 60 years, a man may discover authenticity and have some therapeutic capacity. But a "training analysis" or bout of therapy may expedite this.

Question: This is related to an earlier question about training, starting out with a definite set of techniques to learn. How can training as a therapist foster personal growth in the person who has mastered the techniques? Is this what therapy for a therapist is for?

Answer: I think that in a good training program, there should be two stages of training. The first stage we might call the "brainwashing stage." If it is to be brainwashing, the trainers should go at it whole hog. "Buster," you say to your trainee, "your job is to master the art of impersonating me, or Freud, or Carl Rogers. Master this, and we'll grade you on it." That is *stage one.* We might even guarantee that this impersonation practiced under supervision with patients is *harmless.* If it hurts anybody, it hurts the trainee. It gives him headaches if it is radically different from his usual way of being. *Stage two* might be viewed as a kind of shaping procedure too, but here you don't know what the final product is going to be. That is, as a supervisor, you go over the person's work; and whenever his indoctrination is binding him, you encourage him to dare to respond in a way that seems to him as a fully functioning person to be the appropriate way to respond. Such supervision is itself a kind of psychotherapy. The first stage of training resembles an experimentally produced character disorder, one which is of short duration and relatively easy to undo. Lifelong character disorders are terriby difficult to undo. We can hope stage one of training, the "impersonation stage," doesn't yield an inflexible character disorder.

Question: You spoke of giving provisional certificates or badges at the end of training, but if the trainer hasn't provided stage two of training, then it isn't he who has failed, it is the teacher. Maybe the teacher should have his certificate taken away by *his* trainers!

Answer: Yes, I agree, but in a sense he will be functionally unfrocked as a teacher; because if his trainees do lousy work, he won't get any new students. Let me play for a minute with the idea of training as "the experimental production of a character disorder." A character disorder, by definition, means automatic, well-rehearsed ways of being with people in the world. These ways aim at manipulation of other people and concealment of one's spontaneous experiencing from self and others. From the work of Wilham Reich on, we know that it is terribly difficult to conduct a "character analysis"; because while a "symptom" is very salient and ego-dystonic, it is another matter to regard one's automatic ways of being as symptoms. It is very difficult and very anxiety-provoking. But a "character disorder" produced in the lab, as it were, isn't of long duration. You produce it, and then you undo it. Whatever good there was in that experimental character disorder will presumably be integrated into your total being. A *trained* therapist certainly is radically different from an untrained person when you speak in terms of spontaneity. If I were your friend or relative, and I responded spontaneously and genuinely to you, in an effort to be helpful to you, and I hadn't been trained, my behavior would be quite different than if I had been through an indoctrination in Rogerian therapy or psychoanalytic therapy and then transcended this and was spontaneous with you. So there is *good* in the experimentally produced character disorder that we call training—provided you transcend it.

Question: Aren't such matters as a therapist's philosophy of life, values, and capacities for human relationship as important for therapists as study of anatomy or psychology?

Answer: Yes. I think it's possible for people even nitwits to go through a training program like a master of his techniques, but remain nitwits. There may be technically competent counselors and therapists who are yet uneducated boobs. They are master of some technique, as some engineers or doctors may be, but they are not *educated* in the sense of being enlarged and enlarging persons. Education, in the classical sense, implies being exposed to great questions that man has posed and seriously wrestling with answers that have been offered throughout history. Questions like, "What is man? What is good; what is true; what is just; what is beautiful?" This kind of education never ends. Out of it a fellow develops the kind of philosophy of life which seems to be a defining characteristic of a good therapist. Another defining characteristic of a therapist is that he should be a man continuously concerned about and open to his own personal growth. A trained nitwit doesn't grow any more. You don't have to have a good education to earn a living, or get results as a good engineer, because you limit what you do. If you are an engineer, and you are lousy with people, you get your secretary to do all the negotiating of contracts. You just deal with bridges and stones. There is room for technical training to improve competence in human transactions. But how elegant to have this technical training mediated by a growing, educated person, rather than by moral imbeciles.

Question: Doesn't effective therapy call for the ability to empathize with all kinds of people in all kinds of trouble? Where does a therapist get the experience to ground such empathy?

Answer: I think that a young therapist can have this capacity for empathy. What it entails is experiencing whatever you have experienced as fully as is possible. Let me illustrate. It is important for a patient to feel that he is being understood, or that you are trying to understand him. One means whereby you understand somebody is when you find you have experienced something similar to what he is struggling with. A patient may ask, "Do you know how I feel in this situation?" You say, "Yes, I think I do. I remember I was in a situation something like it. I think I know how you feel." But suppose a woman tells you, "My menstrual periods are agonizing. Can you understand how I feel?" Now I never menstruated, so far as I know, but I may have had experiences not unlike a period. A pain in my gut, or lower down; if I can acknowledge the breadth and depth of my own experiencing, I think my empathy has been enhanced and my chances of understanding and communicating my understanding are increased. This is why I say it is good to have been a phony and suffered from it, then [been] rehabilitated from it. It helps you to better understand the agonies of trying to become authentic that a patient is going through.

Question: Once you become authentic, do you stay that way?

Answer: One of the easiest things to do is to slide away from authenticity and to slide away from your commitment to be helpful to your patient. I'll cite you two examples of fouled up psychotherapy that I perpetrated. In each case it grew out of my own smugness and my own conviction that at last I [had] found "the way"—open disclosure to your patient: "Just tell this fellow what I think and feel as he relates to me." I did so in two separate cases and in each instance the therapy lasted three sessions, after which the patient said, "Thank you very much. You helped me a lot, but I have got to go now." In retrospect what I did was to fail to find out first of all whom I was dealing with. I was giving them rough medicine. They weren't strong enough to take it. Quitting was their way of letting me know I was being cruel, inconsiderate. Yet, I was practicing "my technique." That was the trouble with it. I was "practicing a technique." I was being authentic, you might say; but I didn't know the person I was being authentic with, and I wasn't seriously committed to the objective of being helpful to that fellow—because if I had been, I would have taken more trouble to find out who he was, and how strong he was. It's odd that I've done this more with men than with women—that is, misjudge their strength.

Question: But weren't you being authentic when you disclosed your experience to your patient?

Answer: Yes, I was being authentically blind. This may be a play on words, but you can be authentic and be stupid. I can see in retrospect what was going on between these men I failed and myself. One sort of expects a woman to be relatively weak. I am much more gentle with girls than with men at the beginning of psychotherapy. In an earlier stage of my training, I was indiscriminately gentle with people, no matter how strong they were. This also was a mistake. But going the other way and being that rough on a fellow—I was denying him the right to be weak, to feel as he felt. He quite properly left me. I wasn't doing him any good.

Question: Did you feel like a failure when they left you?

Answer: Let me tell you the kind of thinking I went through. "I lost these patients," I thought. "Fortunately, when you lose patients like this, it is not like a surgeon losing a patient; there are other sources of help those men can turn to." I referred them to other therapists, and I know they did follow up the referral. But then I wondered, "Why does it bother me?" And I thought, "Well, shoot, it is good they left, because if they stayed with me they couldn't have gotten any help. It is better to find it out sooner than later." Then I said, "No, I am not satisfied with that. I should have been able to keep them on. But why keep them on? You want to get rich off them. No, I don't want to get rich off them." I finally arrived at a formulation such as

I described with you. I really was not being my potential best with them because of the reasons I gave you. I was misjudging them out of pride. Pride in my own know-how. I just assumed these were strong fellows. "They are men after all, and they can take my straight talk." When you make an assumption and then act on it without checking, you are bound to bungle.

Question: You had a sensitivity to your own authentic being and not to theirs?

Answer: Yes, that's good. If I had not been so smug or blind, I would have kept my mouth shut for five or six sessions until I got to know who they were. I wasn't responding to who they were; I was responding to this *autistic image* I had of who they were. They very effectively told me, by leaving, that I wasn't treating *them* at all.

Question: What part does diagnostic testing play in your therapeutic work?

Answer: I don't do or ask for much testing now. When I do test, I feel duty-bound to tell him what the test leads me to think about him. If I give him a Rorschach, and he asks, "What do you find?", I'm likely to say, "Well, there is a lot of indication there that you are confused," or whatever is in keeping with the relationship that we have at the time. If I feel I can't share my thinking with him right now, I'll say, "I really can't tell you right now; but I will tell you later on." And I mean it. I will tell him, because I see this as part of our relationship from which I mustn't conceal anything from him unless in my honest judgment it would detract from our therapeutic goals. At this point I will withhold, and I will withhold vigorously. But even the withholding is part of the therapeutic interchange. It may boil down to something like this. He'll say, "Come on, you've got to tell me." I'll say, "No, I won't tell you." He'll say, "Here you go, doing all this talking about being honest, and I ask you for something and you won't tell me. Why do you conceal it?" I might say, "Because right now I feel it wouldn't be helpful." This is really a kind of test of his trust in me. He may say, "I don't trust you," and we can explore his mistrust and my trustworthiness. There is a principle to describe this; it is a mixture of judgment and honesty.

Question: It's a matter of relevant authenticity.

Answer: I like that way of phrasing it better than mine. What is relevant authenticity? Let me see if I can illustrate. A patient presents himself to me. As I examine and feel my own reaction to him, I find I don't like him very much. I don't burst out and say, "I don't like you." It is not relevant at that point. He may say this, that, and another thing, and ask, "What do you think, Dr. Jourard?" I'll say, "I have a lot of thoughts, but no conclusions right now. I must know you better." This is a true expression of where I am at that moment. But if he then says, "You know, nobody likes me. How do you feel about me?", I might say, "Well, just from the little sample, I find myself kind of angry at you. I don't really know why, I am curious to know why." That is authentic. And it's relevant. It is letting him know what I feel, but it is letting him know also something is equally true. Because I *am* genuinely wondering, "Why does he make me angry? What is it about him? Is he trying to keep people at a distance from him?" I'll reflect out loud. I'll say, "I find myself disliking you. I wonder, are you doing this because you are afraid to let people get close to you? Are you afraid to let me get close to you?" This becomes part of the ongoing conversation. But if I say, after he has been talking for five minutes, "You know I don't like you," he would quite properly say, "I didn't come here to be liked or disliked; good-bye!"

Question: Do you feel that the more authentic a person can be—relevant authenticity—the more a person can experience this, the better satisfied and happier he will be in life?

Answer: I didn't say anything about happiness. I don't think authenticity necessarily makes you happy; because when you are authentic, presumably, you are also open. You reveal yourself more and receive more consequences to this, some of which can be very hurtful. Also, in the mode of openness, you feel things more acutely, you feel the misery and the pain in the world. I suppose you just experience more fully, for whatever value there is in that. I suppose if there is something realistically there, to make you happy, then you will feel the happiness more vividly. As you will also feel the pain more keenly. It is a matter of choice. Which is it better to be, a zombie who doesn't feel anything very much, neither joy nor pain, or a poet, who feels great joy and great agony?

Question: Isn't it better to be safe and phony?

Answer: If one is an authentic coward, one shouldn't complain about the price one must pay for this safety. Neurotics complain about the price one must pay for safety. They withdraw from authenticity to be safe; but being withdrawn, they experience loneliness, boredom, or the dread of being found out. When a neurotic sufferer goes to a therapist to get help with his anxiety and loneliness, he calls them symptoms. The therapist says, in effect, "You don't like these symptoms. They seem to be connected with your withdrawal. You want to get rid of those symptoms. Then, stop withdrawing." The fellow says, "No, can't you give me some tranquilizers, so I can stay withdrawn and be anesthetized? I'll be glad to pay this additional price of being numb." Unfortunately too many therapists will give them a tranquilizer. That's one good thing about being a psychologist. You dare not use drugs. This puts you on your mettle. I have one instance where I "malpracticed medicine." I prescribed a "drug," Quik cocoa. A patient said he couldn't sleep. He had been getting sleeping pills. I thought I understood what was going on. I said, "I know how to get to sleep." I said it with great certainty, because I have great faith in it. "At bedtime, you get some milk and put it in a saucepan. You boil it over a very slow flame. (The slower the better.) You keep testing it with your finger until you can't stand it, short of boiling. Then, you put in two tablespoons of instant cocoa, Nestlé's Quik. Oh, any kind will do." I don't want to specialize in any one brand. "Then once you have mixed it up in a cup, you get vanilla wafers, and I specify any kind of vanilla wafers. You dip them in and eat them, and sip the hot cocoa. If you haven't got vanilla wafers, then get white or wheat toast, lightly toasted with butter melted in it and then spread apple jelly on it. (Grape jelly is too strong.) You take it and you will fall asleep practically before you finish it." I have never had a complaint from this. This has weaned a lot of people from sleeping pills and tranquilizers. I feel vaguely guilty about this because it is like a prescription. That's too much like practicing medicine.

Question: Do you ever allow them to leave off the vanilla wafers?
Answer: No.

Question: You mean they have to follow through?
Answer: Yes, because I am very interested in whether or not they trust me enough to do exactly as I say. Not that I want to make them obedient puppets; but there is a time you want to know—are you trusted, or aren't you? You know yourself that your aim is not to enslave them or to limit them. This is an expression of *care* really. You can call the prescription "Instant Mother."

Question: What was that phrase?
Answer: "Instant Mother."

Question: How many vanilla wafers?
Answer: NO MORE THAN THREE.

Question: How can you be sure a patient is being open with you?
Answer: I never know how open the other fellow is with me, in any final scientifically grounded way. I do know in certainty how open I am, let's say 80 percent of the time. In retrospect, I can find 20 or 30 percent of the time that I am play acting. Nobody is perfect. But you can never read another man's mind, unfortunately. No, fortunately. You can know when *you* are offering the truth and reality of your experiencing to the person. It is very interesting to see how the other person responds to your truth and reality. At the beginning he will respond with fakery, manipulation, and so on. In due time, I suppose, when he discovers it is all right, he will behave in ways that to him are more open. He will say that before, he was not leveling, but now he is leveling. About the only cue you have about his being on the level is his "congruency," the consistency of the messages that are coming to you—his verbal messages and his bodily messages. Here is an example of noncongruent communication from the patient. He says, with a smile, "I suffer an awful lot." His face tells you one thing, and his words are telling you another. When he starts saying, "I suffer an awful lot," and then he cries and can't talk, then probably he is being genuine, unless you have reason to suspect that it is crocodile tears. It seems to me when one is himself open, he is receptive to cues at a lot of levels. If these cues are dissonant, an open and

sensitive person will sense this dissonance. I can have someone cry, and I find myself not moved by his crying. Well, I don't berate myself and say, "You are hardhearted, Jourard." I say, "I find myself not moved by your tears. I wonder why?" So the question, "How do you tell when the other fellow is genuine," is answered by experiencing his impact on you.

Question: Is openness always good?

Answer: You can use openness in the service of defense, or hostility, as well as helpfulness. I've done it myself. It's a matter of your true commitment—what are you being open *for?*

Question: Is there any research on the therapeutic value of openness from a therapist to his patient?

Answer: We are working on ways of analyzing interviews, looking for self-references: "I feel," "I like," "I hope," "I fear," and so on, separated out from, "I did this, I did that." My own opinion is, that "myself" which I am to disclose to you is best defined as the *meaning* that things have for me. I am the only one who knows and can report the meaning that things have for me. You can watch me sinning. You can read accounts of my behavior. You will never know what these things mean to me. In interview transcripts, the phrases, "I believe," "I think," "I feel," "I like," "I dislike," as opposed to, "I did this and then I did that and then I did this and I did that," offer a research toehold we've been fiddling with, with some promise. And self-disclosure questionnaires, if they are answered honestly, presumably get at past openness of a person to significant people in his life. There are two possibilities.

Question: What and how does a therapist disclose?

Answer: Let me tell you anecdotally. A patient may ask, "Have you thought much about me and my situation since the last time we met?" I am obliged to say, if it is true, "No, you have not crossed my mind." With somebody else, I may find myself thinking about him so much I can't concentrate on other responsibilities or other patients. I don't know the answer to this question. But I do know that with a patient I am profoundly concerned about, I let him know that I am profoundly concerned. Among other things my telephone is open. I think

I mentioned it last time. I am a real patsy and a pushover. I can be manipulated. I get phone calls at three o'clock in the morning and do a certain amount of telephone therapy. I let the patient know that I can be manipulated. "I had rather not be manipulated, but if you call me, I'll assume you really needed to call me." In all genuineness I don't mind being disrupted. I have not minded having my poker disrupted. I love poker. I love bed, and bedtime has been disrupted. I have been at parties, and parties have been disrupted. I think, "What the hell, it's my profession. There are rewards associated with it, and I am in a sense being paid to be concerned." If I am not concerned, I let the person know that too.

Question: Shouldn't one see only a few people a day, in order to be effective as a therapist?

Answer: I don't believe there are any "shoulds" involved. You are in the situation that you are in. If you see fifteen people a day and I see five a week, in each case, one does what one can.

Question: Shouldn't you try to appear concerned about a patient, even when you aren't?

Answer: Why should you impersonate somebody who is thinking about this patient 40 hours a week, when in point of fact you not only are not but cannot? Let him know. When he is consulting you, he is consulting you as you are with your limitations, and he is entitled to that; and if he doesn't like it, he can go elsewhere.

Question: What do you say if you can't "get with a patient," can't feel with him?

Answer: I have found myself saying to a person I have been seeing regularly—if I find I can't get with him, I'll say—"I can't get with you." If I feel that it is my fault and not his, I'll put it to him, "Let's continue if you want," and I won't charge him for that hour; or I'll say, "Let's not meet today," if I figure he can take it. You know you weigh certain commonsense values, but I feel he is entitled to his money's worth, which is your genuine being. Now if I am not interested in him and it is his doing, then we have got to sweat out the whole hour.

Question: I was reading somewhere about a guy saying that the more fully he could be with a patient during the hour, the less he thought about it afterwards.

Answer: Like the Zeigarnik effect.

Question: The patient said he himself was just half there, and he felt guilty and thought about it the rest of the week.

Answer: That makes good sense to me.

Question: Should you take notes during the therapy hour? And how complete should they be?

Answer: I don't know what's good, bad, right, or wrong; but I will tell you what I do. Let's say between 1947, when I saw my first patient, and the last time I saw a patient, there is a decrease in the number of pages or words of notes I wrote. In 1947 I imitated the tape recorder; I tried to write down verbatim everything because we had to have verbatim notes to go over with our supervisors. Toronto couldn't afford tape recorders. That stuck with me, even to Emory University, where I looked over my Toronto notes. I was amazed. How did I write so much, and what was I doing besides writing? Now, I find I'll jot down a sentence at the end of the hour. Something or other, whatever hits me, and I never look at the note. I don't forget. The person comes in next time, and we pick up where we left off or wherever he is then. I don't see any value in compulsive continuation "where we left off last time."

Question: It implies the patient hasn't been living during that week.

Answer: Yes. Do you keep notes on your dear friend, whom you see three times a year at the national, state, and regional conventions? You don't jot down notes. In point of fact you are a therapist to your dear friend, whether you like it or not. You are important to his existence. He is enlarged because of his contact with you. He looks forward to seeing you these three times a year. You don't, or I don't, write down notes of the last meeting.

Question: Sometimes it may be valuable to have them.

Answer: That is only when somebody wants to use them, perhaps against you. Sometimes people can be malicious.

Question: How many patients can a person work with at one time?
Answer: I suspect there are a lot of interacting variables here, including your energy level and the need of the patient. It seems to me a patient is always competing for your attention against a whole lot of things including your own fantasy, your memory of other patients, your physical discomfort which is clamoring for attention, and so on. Still another thing is how much of your attention can *he* take? Sometimes too much attention destroys the thread of relationship that you have. He needs you to be just that inattentive. It sounds mystical; but I suspect that if you are committed to be as helpful as you can, that you give him as much attention as he needs. That is a suspicion. I don't know how you would test it.

Question: I keep wondering about this thing you referred to earlier. About the ingredients, the invitation to sickness or the invitation to wellness, and really what are the factors in this process? I can feel, I can sense this kind of invitation in me and in others all the time around me. Just what are the ingredients? Can you take us further on this?
Answer: Not much further. Let's translate what you are asking into a request for an operational definition of terms. Now, that is a good request. You invite me to be operational in my definitions of the invitation to wellness and the invitation to be sick. I think it would manifest itself in a multilevel way, but as expression of a fundamental commitment. Let's take the "witches" first of all, those who want to send out "sickness waves." They probably are operating on the following assumption: "Other people are no damn good. They are worthless, and life isn't worth living anyway." That is one way of trying to describe or infer their philosophy of life. This attitude permeates presumably all of their interpersonal transactions and their sickness-making manifests itself almost in operant conditioning terms. If every time the other person utters something that looks like joy or hope, they say, "Nay," they respond to joy or hope with negative reinforcement. And they disconfirm or punish any idiosyncratic expression from the other that reveals the other's identity. The sick-maker is a genius for making others feel worthless, like nobody, as not worthy of attention.

You see this in lots of mothers and fathers. And sometimes in those acquaintances that give you a pain in the neck. The "healers" seem to operate on the philosophy that life is good. People are good. Individuality and self-disclosure are good. There is hope. In interpersonal transactions they welcome diversity, strength, self-confidence, groping, trying. They confirm the other. When somebody is trying to do something impossible, they don't say, "It is impossible, why waste the effort?" They say, "Good, good; try it." If the person fails, rather than say, "I told you so," they pick him up, and say, "Never mind. Try again, try again." The "healers" and "witches" embody fundamental attitudes, what Freud termed "Eros" and "Thanatos."

Question: This implies some people are destructive to health.

Answer: Yes. If a person feels sick, hopeless, and worthless as long as he is involved with this person, and he feels better when he is away from him, what is to stop a therapist from saying, "Stay away from this person; he is a public-health menace to you"?

Question: What if the other person is a parent or spouse?

Answer: I don't know any magic solution. You and the patient wrestle with the dilemma. It is a conflict, but it is better to know what the conflict is and wrestle with it, than to deny it. Find out the cost of choosing this way or choosing that way. Then seek the guts to choose a way out or a way to live with the conflict. There is always the possibility, too, that somebody who lives with a "lethal" spouse or "lethal" parent may themselves have elicited this lethality. They may have invited the lethal one's lethality. It is they themselves that changed their way of being with that other person. For example, the patient may have repressed his anger and his strength. If he expressed them to spouse or parent, this might have shut off the lethality of the other. I've seen that happen. A therapist can ask, "Why don't you tell your mother to go to hell?" The person says, "I could never tell her that." But he may be helped to express his anger and find his strength. He gets the message across, and the mother stops having a lethal effect on him.

It is a fascinating thought that just as there are bubonic-plague carriers whom public-health officials want to corral, and syphilis carriers, and TB carriers—what about the "pain-in-the-neck-producers," the "psychosis-producers," the "disorganization-producers," who are, in a sense, a public-health menace, who spread misery wherever they go? Shouldn't these be identified and corralled? It is a possibility.

Question: I've been thinking about a similar situation, but I didn't really want to bring it up because I feel that it is going beyond what we have been talking about. I am not a child therapist, I'm a school teacher, but I see many children who are sick because they have sick parents. These are young children. Now, would you say something about that?

Answer: What is to stop a teacher, at great risk, from saying to the parents somehow, in a way that they will get the message, that "I really feel your child is having this difficulty in school because there is difficulty in the home"?

Question: Well, this we do, but then we run into the problem of referrals. Unless there is strength in the home, and a likelihood the parents are going to do something, nothing happens. We have no place to refer the problem to.

Answer: About the only comment that I can make is, "Man, that is a rough problem, and you have got to grope with it."

Question: We have to keep working with it.

Answer: Grope, that is my considered professional advice. Grope and don't give up.

Question: The main thing we can do is work with the child and hope that he can find himself and muster up enough strength to go beyond his difficulties.

Answer: Keep groping.

(POSTSCRIPT, 1967)

This discussion took place in 1964, and I found on rereading it that it still portrays my views on the conduct of psychotherapy. Especially my last comment, "Keep groping." That might be viewed as a worthwhile motto for any person involved with the arts of counseling, therapy, or teaching—where no techniques yet invented can be guaranteed to bring about successful attainment of aims. The therapist, like the artist, must continually grope for new ways to implement his objective, of bringing desirable human possibilities into being. A superb book has been published by Bugental[11] that offers a more systematic presentation of psychotherapy than my account.

9

Technique and Its Transcendence in Effective Psychotherapy

Technique

"Technique" is my action viewed from *outside,* not from the standpoint of my *experience* of it. As a psychotherapist, I experience myself as engaged in a project—actually, a variety of projects. In the consulting room, I seek to help another person understand and transcend the confining and determining factors that have culminated in his symptoms. I may also be pursuing numerous other projects: proving a theory, enhancing my reputation among my colleagues, avoiding anxiety, announcing my identity, seeking to get myself seen and experienced in some preferred way by my patient, seeking my own growth, etc. I do not experience my pursuit of these myriad goals as technique, unless I adopt the project of viewing myself from the standpoint of the other person. So long as I live my identity-for-myself (Laing,[54] p. 101), I experience my action as my very existence in the situation. My technique is simply what I am *seen* doing as I pursue my projects. If I watch my praxis as a psychotherapist, I at that moment abandon my aim of potentiating the growth and freedom of the other, and I pursue the goal of making my behavior resemble that of some model.

Psychotherapy, like any art, entails a process of "warming up." The warm-up, in terms of experience, calls for a rearrangement of my projects, so that listening to and responding to my patient and looking for ways to help him *become my existence* at that time. Other interests, at that time, do not exist. It entails a process of becoming com-

* This chapter was first published in *Explorations in human behavior,* Herbert Otto (editor), and is reprinted here with the permission of the Charles Thomas Publishing Co.

mitted to the therapeutic goal for this very patient, a sort of purification of the heart, a "willing one thing." One does not get warmed up to every patient, or in every meeting with the same patient. Nor does one stay with the commitment at every minute of the meeting hour without continuous reassertion of resolve.

From *my* perspective, as therapist, *I have no technique* when I am engaged in the therapeutic relationship. I am the embodiment of an intention, a thrust in a certain direction. My behavior feels free to me. I listen, and I respond in ways that have meaning to me as likely to mediate growth in my patient. My responses are not predictable to me or to my patient as I pursue my project. My being just then is as a therapist, a person with free intentionality. It is true that I begin to respond in ways that, seen from the outside, reflect my "programming"; but I surpass and transcend these ways throughout the interchange between me and my patient—if I am free, and if I am committed to my project of helping him. If I "fall" into some stereotyped way of behaving with my patient, it is because my project has changed at that time from helping him grow, to defending myself against some threat to my being that I have experienced.

Thus, as I see it, there is no *experience* of technique in the practice called "existential psychotherapy," or, better, "existing psychotherapy." Training in some theory and some approach is simply a way of proving to society that one's intent to insert oneself into the social system with the status, responsibilities, and privileges of a psychotherapist is *serious;* that one is willing to undergo sacrifices in order to gain qualifications; that one is trying to learn from his predecessors. But there is a limit to this learning. I can only be a psychotherapist in *my* way, not the ways of my mentors, unless my fundamental commitment is not to my patients, but to my mentors' ways (as if for some reason, mimicking their attitudes and behavior gives me some satisfaction, no matter how it is experienced by my patient). The training in this theory or that simply brings one to the therapeutic situation predisposed to construe and respond in certain ways. Seen from the outside, these ways may indeed be predictable and stereotyped, and describable as technique; but if the therapist who is beginning the journey to wholeness with a patient is committed to this project, he will not experience even this predictable, badgelike behavior as automatic. He will feel it as the embodiment of his intentionality. And, as the relationship unfolds, he will become less predictable, less identifiable as a member of this "school" or that, more creative and inspired, more spontaneous (Fiedler[17]).

Psychotherapy, then, is not technique; *it is commitment.* If the therapist, like any artist, maintains his commitment in full status as his *raison d'être* while he is with his patient, the commitment will evoke behavior from him that cannot be predicted or foreseen, that will be emergent and felt as spontaneous. Commitments to some prescribed "method" will be experienced as constraint, as barriers to the implementation of the project of healing. Just as any person discovers the determiners of his past and present being by experiencing them as obstacles to the attainment of newly chosen goals, so the therapist will feel his training to be a barrier when therapeutic impasses arise.

Impasses: The Limits of Technique

I was made aware of the ways in which my initial training and experience were obstructing my therapeutic work when I encountered impasses in relation to patients I was treating in the Southeastern United States. I received my training in an urban setting, in the North. The stilted, technical way of responding to patients, with carefully thought-out interpretations or polished reflections of feelings—which patients of the Psychological Clinic accepted readily enough and even thrived on—"cut no ice" with patients one generation away from a Georgia dirt farm. As one patient put it to me, "Doc, why do yew keep on a-tellin' me back what I jus' tol' y'all? Cain't yew talk lak folks ought to?" Reactions such as these, from patients I was supposed to be helping, gave me pause. I listened to tape recordings I had made of sessions with patients and to recordings of colleagues' sessions. I compared the way we sounded, the way we spoke when we were with patients, and the ways we were when we were among friends or colleagues. Heard from this vantage-point, it indeed seemed as if we were putting on our idioms the way a physician puts on a white coat—in our case, as a badge signifying we were "therapists on duty." Truly, such artifice, though practiced with the best of intention, was apparently functioning as an impasse-creator; in addition, such technical ways of being-with functioned so as to stifle spontaneity of experiencing and of responding in the therapeutic encounter. It is patients, then, who, if given the opportunity, will invite therapists to surpass their techniques, when therapeutic impasses arise.

Impasses provide an occasion for testing the therapist's motivation— he will show himself as committed to his technique and past training, to the ways of his "fathers," *or* as a free agent discovering new ways to foster healing. Each patient becomes a challenge to new possibilities of being in the therapist. To avoid this challenge by insisting on delimiting one's ways of behaving to a prescribed range is *not to be serious* about the therapeutic intent. In fact, it is to be in bad faith (Sartre[86]), because one is broadcasting an intent to be a psychotherapist by sitting in one's office awaiting patients—but if one has committed himself to appearing as a "psychoanalyst," or a "client-centered therapist," or a "behavior therapist," then one's dialogue with the patient will stop at the point when such a technician is called upon to surpass his technique by the meaning of the situation. If I am paying money to a therapist, I want him to be a *therapist* by free commitment, not a source of behavior in my presence that bespeaks his membership in a club from which he will be expelled if he behaves in some way not yet entered in the code of rules for members.

This view of therapy, as a commitment, does not preclude the possibility that an observer, whose project it is to discern regularities or departures in praxis, can study psychotherapy and point to technique. Indeed, such research in psychotherapeutic behavior is an invaluable source of new technique in which novices can be indoctrinated. The more diverse the techniques a novice is introduced to, the broader his initial range of helpfulness might be. Study of psychotherapeutic relationships has already provided us with the possibility of a "manual of psychotherapeutic technique," viz., interpretation, reflection, reassurance, fantasy-sharing, interrogation, up-ending patients' expectancies, etc. I have even introduced a technical response that I call "matching disclosure": when my aim is to show a patient that we are both fellow travelers in the ways of existence, I tell him how I have experienced and coped with some dilemma with which he is presently grappling. But, as I said, the "manual" must always be surpassed in pursuit of healing; at least it will be surpassed by an authentically committed therapist.

The therapist's project is to catalyze wholeness. The researcher's aim is to discern and describe techniques (therapists' action viewed from outside, that in context is seen to be associated with some desired outcome). The novice's job is to demonstrate to his mentors that he has mastered these techniques. The transition from novice technician to therapist is a leap across the gulf that separates commitments. Perhaps many do not make this leap. There are some who wish to be therapists without a period as an initiate or novice. The apprenticeship is necessary, because the period of training can actually empower a would-be therapist with a *broader* range of behavior than he might have acquired in his life up to that point. But I don't know of any proof that apprenticeship in one "school" of therapy, with a set of favored techniques, yields more effective and more committed therapists than training in another "school." There is no training in commitment; there are no schools for learning how to commit. Many people, however, become skilled at *impersonating* commitment. In time, their charade is discovered.

Transcending Technique

Anything I do—from swimming, to typing, to playing guitar, to "practicing" psychotherapy—can be looked at from a *technical point of view*. You can look at my "practice" to see "how I do it" (produce the outcomes I do—whether fast swimming, clear typing, beautiful music, or healed patients). I can reflect upon my action, separating myself from it and looking at it as if it were not-me, or as if I were some other person. But as soon as I become conscious of my technique, I change projects. I am no longer addressing the purpose for which my action was intended as means. I am, instead, querying about the extent to which my conduct resembles some model. The time to become self-conscious and to reflect upon one's praxis is when it fails to yield hoped-for outcomes. But so long as one is seriously addressing his task, one is a unified being; and effective action will emerge spontaneously, through trial-and-error in thought or deed.

Now in psychotherapy, I found myself for a long time trying to heal my patients by faithfully and self-consciously practicing technique as I learned it. It was only after reaching insurmountable impasses in my therapeutic work that I began to grow from novice technician into psychotherapist. It was as if I had been invited by my teachers and preceptors to be attentive to their example and to hue to it—to impersonate them, really. Grotesque situations arose with patients in which it was as if they weren't sitting with *me;* rather, they were speaking to an analogue of Carl Rogers, or Sigmund Freud, or—more immediately—my therapy supervisors. The sound of my voice, on tape recordings of sessions, was most unnatural, as if I were not myself, but "the therapist." In time, with fear and trembling, and as testimony to my resolve to be helpful to patients rather than to imitate the acts of someone who once had helped patients, I let my patients teach me how to be a therapist with them. I found myself transcending my technique. Here are some episodes which helped me discover that to be a psychotherapist means that one can be as flexible, inventive, and creative as law, ethics, and the dignity and integrity and well-being of oneself and one's patient will allow. And that leaves much elbow-room.

1. An attractive, even stunning, woman in her early twenties consulted me. She wore a tight yellow sweater and an equally tight skirt, both of which garments she filled exquisitely. She sat in the reclining chair in a most provocative way, telling her story. I was hardly listening. Suddenly, she asked me, "Would you like to go to bed with me?" I replied, taken aback, "You're wondering whether I want to be more intimate than a therapist." "No, I asked you if you'd like to go to bed with me," she insisted. I replied, in a panic, trying to get her back into what I then thought was the proper role for a patient, "The reason you ask this is because you aren't certain about your desirability." (In fact, both my comments, taken in context, were relevant and technically sound.) She said, "I keep asking you, and you won't answer." I said, in growing anxiety, "No, I couldn't go to bed with you, it's not ethical." "You couldn't?" she insisted. Finally, I blurted out, "Look, Miss X; I find you very attractive. But I don't want to go to bed with you." "Why not," she asked, "since you say I'm attractive?" I con-

tinued, "Because if I did, I'd be so scared and guilty I wouldn't enjoy it; and moreover, I'd run the risk of being disqualified in my profession." She breathed a huge sigh of relief, sat in a more prim posture, and proceeded to tell me of her experience with men whom she had enticed into situations she couldn't cope with, nor could they.

2. A man in his late twenties, very obsessed with his own manliness, consulted me for help when he found he couldn't finish a thesis on which he was working. We proceeded through the beginning stages of therapy swiftly enough—he told me about his present situation, his earlier life, his complicated relationship with his father—and then we reached an impasse of intellectualized chitchat. During one session, when the chitchat died out, there was a period of silence; and the patient sat there, with a look of desperation on his face. I felt an impulse to take his hand and hold it. In a split second, I pondered about the "countertransference" implications of such an act and debated whether I should do such a thing. I did it. I took his hand and gave it a firm squeeze. He grimaced; and with much effort not to do so, he burst into deep, racking sobs. The dialogue proceeded from there.

3. A nursing student was referred to me by her instructor. The girl became nauseous and faint whenever she approached a patient to give him an injection. None of the efforts of her teachers or fellow students to help her availed. She was in danger of being asked to leave the nursing program. She was obviously a tense young woman. I interviewed her and learned something of her family background and her experience at the University as a nursing student. She could be diagnosed as an hysteric, on the basis of her disclosures, but that thought was not very helpful in the urgency of the present situation. I pondered whether to take her on as a patient for intensive psychotherapy, but there was no time. I decided to try something different. In the third meeting, I asked her to get a hypodermic needle and show me how to use it. She could perform an injection on herself, in the arm or thigh, without fainting; and she could receive one from another. She filled a hypo with saline solution and showed me how to hold it; and with dispatch, I performed an injection in her forearm. I didn't do it at all badly, if I say so myself. Then I asked her to inject me. She

brought the needle to my upper arm, trembled, blanched, and said, "I can't do it."

In the next session, we were talking about her hobbies—she was a swimmer and kept herself physically fit. She prided herself on it. I asked her to do some setup exercises—touching her toes, deep-knee-bends, and push-ups. She thought I was crazy. I agreed, but asked her to proceed anyway. She did so. Then, as she stood beside my desk panting, I took up the hypodermic needle, handed it to her, and asked her to prepare it again for an injection. She filled it with solution; and when it was ready, I said firmly, "Now give me an injection." She came over to me, plunged the needle in, pressed the plunger, pulled the needle out—and then stood up, almost dazed, but not blanched, saying, "I did it. I did it. God damn it, I did it!" She showed up on the wards that day and gave injections wherever her instructor told her to. She continued effectively with her studies. I did not have further sessions with her, since she did not wish it. I am not sure one could call these four sessions "psychotherapy," though the outcome was evidently psychotherapeutic for her.

4. I was well into psychotherapy with a man whose complaint was his homosexual practices. He had been in therapy with several other psychotherapists before he consulted me, each of whom was "orthodox" in some way. He had successfully resisted the therapeutic impact of these other workers. I had begun, gradually, to depart from my own orthodoxy at the time that he was consulting me. About 40 sessions along, he narrated, with much reluctance and self-loathing, an account of "animal-contacts" he had had when he was an adolescent living on a farm. He had earlier spoken of his dread of intimacy with women. I felt an impulse to laugh as he spoke of his animal philandering. Again, in an instant, I debated whether to let go and laugh, and wondered what my mirth meant. I did let go and laugh, saying, "You mean you're afraid of a soft, tender woman, yet you 'made it' with a cow, a highly dangerous beast?"; and I narrated how as a schoolboy, I worked on a farm to help the war effort. The hired man had misinformed me as to the proper way to milk a cow. I approached the udder from behind, between the cow's rear legs, and the cow kicked

me into the gutter. His account of adolescent, bucolic love had reminded me of this. When I told him of my experience, he howled with laughter; and our nontechnical dialogue proceeded from there.

5. Again, a bout of laughter. A woman in her late forties, in about the twentieth session, told me something no one else knew of. When she was eighteen, reasonably sophisticated, she had been petting with a man on a date. As they became more impassioned, she permitted him to lie upon her, but denied him entry. The man engaged in interfemoral coitus. Some time later, she discovered she was pregnant, in spite of the fact that she was a virgin. At the time she told me this, we had been in an impasse for some sessions—an impasse characterized by self-loathing on her part. When she told, tearfully, about the abortion she underwent, I laughed. She asked, furiously, what was so funny. I replied, "All that trouble you had to go through, and you missed the delights of making love properly!" She burst out laughing, too, and the impasse was dissolved.

In each of these episodes, there was a departure from "appropriate" behavior from a psychotherapist, as I then had been trained to think of it. But in each incident, there was a therapeutic- or relationship-impasse that kept progress at a standstill. Following these "human" reactions, the therapy proceeded, in less technical vein, to fairly satisfactory conclusions—more like conversations between friends than between an impersonal but competent specialist and his patient. Perhaps other therapists have had comparable experiences.

Part Three

Experience:
A Neglected Dimension
in Psychology

Introduction to Part Three

Toward a Psychology of Experience

Scientific psychology began with the study of experience, in Wundt's laboratory in Leipzig, in 1879. Freud showed one of the limitations of the Wundtian approach to the analysis of human experience, pointing out that the psychology of his time addressed itself only to conscious experience, neglecting what he came to call "the unconscious." The Gestalt psychologists likewise assailed the Wundtian psychology, pointing out that the analysis of human experience into "elements" (as in chemistry) failed to do justice to experience as it was lived. Wertheimer, Koffka, Kohler, and Lewin were better phenomenologists than was Wundt and his followers. They studied experience in its meaningful forms and patterns (*gestalten*).

But in the 1920's, the study of experience fell into disrepute, largely because of the experimental success of the behavioristic researches of Pavlov in Russia and John B. Watson in the United States. Consciousness, mind, experience—these were regarded as extra-scientific realms, not suitable for study by hard-nosed, tough-minded investigators. Up to the present time, behavioristic approaches to the study of man, which view man as a determined and determinate being, enjoy intellectual hegemony in most graduate schools of psychology. The study of experience has been confined to investigations of perceptual behavior, thinking behavior, and remembering behavior. The emphasis has been on the visible, measurable behavioral pole of what a person experiences.

Together with the domination of the psychological scene by behaviorism has been the widespread adoption of psychoanalytic theory. According to the psychoanalytic view, man, while he can be free (or freer), is mostly a vessel driven by instinctual urges and irrational

103

super-ego prodding. And his conscious experiencing is not investigated for itself, but rather for the glimpses and hints it may afford of the subterranean unconscious mental life.

The upshot has been that the reporting and description of human experiencing has been shoved out of the realm of science, and relegated (or elevated) to the province of the arts and humanities. Novelists, poets, painters, playwrights, musicians—these have been the people who investigate human experience in its myriad forms. The only scientifically oriented people to take a serious interest in experience per se have been the philosophical phenomenologists, and a scattering of psychologists who began to read literature in the tradition of existentialism and phenomenology.

Now this is changing. As psychologists have moved in a humanistic direction, they have again begun to take an interest in experiencing. Not just in perception, but in total consciousness, that fascinating, complex refraction of being that assumes many incarnations—in the modes of imagination, remembering, fantasy, as well as perception. A new phenomenological psychology is in the making, one that, hopefully, will avoid some of the impasses of method and theory encountered by earlier students of consciousness. As examples of approaches to the study of consciousness, I can mention A. H. Maslow's[62] portrayals of "peak experiences"; my friend T. Landsman's as yet unpublished studies of "positive," "nadir," "turning point," and "transcendental" experiences; Gendlin's[24,25] portrayal of the creation of meaning; Laing's[53] work on modes of experiencing; and Heider's[30] work on interpersonal relations.

The chapters in the next section represent an effort of mine to reexamine certain realms of human life that have been studied from behavioristic and psychoanalytic perspectives. I have discussed learning, growth, and creativity from a phenomenological point of view.

10

Fascination and Learning-for-Oneself

In the fall of 1965, I attended an "Invitational Conference on Independent Learning" at Milwaukee, Wisconsin. The conference was organized to discuss scientific findings that bear upon the process of learning by and for oneself. It was hoped that such a conference might throw light on the growing problem faced by educators: more and more students are entering the university, with fewer and fewer teachers to guide them.

My assignment was to address the problem of independent learning from the standpoint of Personality Theory. I found that I couldn't say much from that viewpoint, except perhaps to report some of the research that had been done on "autonomy." Then, I became fascinated with the question itself, "What is independent learning? Why is it a problem?" And the chapter that follows was the result.

Learning for Others and Learning for Myself

The announcement for this conference states: "Recent insights from the behavioral sciences have expanded our conceptions of human potential through a re-casting of the image of man—from a passive, reactive recipient to an active, seeking, autonomous, and reflective being. What are the implications of this impelling new image for our concern with man the learner? Educators are giving increased attention to implementing in practice the recognition that the learner has both the capacity and the need to assume responsibility for his continuing learning."

How did man come to be conceived of as "a passive, reactive recipient?" By whom was he so conceived, and why? Who recast the image? The peculiar thing about man is that he is no-thing. No "image" can ever do full justice to his being. His being is a question to him. He lives his answers. He can be (as) a "passive, reactive recipient"; and he can also be an "active, seeking, autonomous and reflective being." Each way is a project, a choice, a decision. Another peculiarity of man is that he can let others answer the question of his being for him. If he appears to others and experiences himself as a "passive, reactive recipient," it is because he let himself be persuaded to be that way by and *for* that person. A man may live and show only his passive, reactive possibilities to his teacher, or to a researcher. In solitude or with some trusted other, he may experience and show his active, creative, or other unforeseen possibilities.*

Social intercourse resembles a contest between "definers" of my being. If I experience myself as passive and reactive rather than as active, seeking, autonomous and reflective; and if everyone sees me in this light, we may presume that such consensus is the outcome of a superb job of propaganda, brainwashing, or persuasion. I have yielded to others' definition of me, and thus I define and experience myself. I have a being-for-others, but not a being-for-myself.

If "authorities" are now beginning to say, "You know, we have been wrong, man does seem to have capacity to act, choose, and seek, autonomously," it is because some authorities suspended their preconceptions about man, and let some men disclose their experience of themselves to the authorities, who then *listened*.

Others' images of me are, at least in part, a reflection of what I have been invited or permitted to disclose of my experiencing to the Other who is forming an image. We might well wonder why it has taken men so long to disclose their active and creative potentials to the image-makers. And why have the image-makers been for so long blind and deaf to these possibilities that were always there? I suspect the "passive, reactive" image lasted so long because it served a useful purpose to somebody, and hence was imposed on man, who then

---

* This chapter is written from the point of view of "existential phenomenology." Readers interested in this branch of inquiry might consult Luijpen (1963) as an excellent introduction to the writings of Sartre (1956), Heidegger (1962), Merleau-Ponty (1962), and Husserl (1931), among others. For the relationship of existentialism and phenomenology to psychiatry and psychology, see Laing (1960, 1961, 1963), Van Kaam (1966), and May (1958).

This chapter also appears in Gleason, G. T., *The theory and nature of independent learning,* Scranton: International Textbook Co., 1967.

showed it to the image-makers. Indeed, passive, reactive men are predictable, manipulable, and controllable the very way they should be if they are to serve the interests of someone who can profit from the predicting, manipulating, and controlling.

Independent learning has now become a problem. I believe it is a *pedagogogenic* problem. We produced it, as physicians sometimes unintentionally produce iatrogenic illness. That independent learning is problematic is most peculiar, because man always and only learns by himself. The real question here is *what* does he learn and *for whom?* Learning is not a task; it is a way to be in the world. Man learns as he pursues goals and projects *that have meaning for him*. He is always learning something. Perhaps the key to the problem of independent learning lies in the phrase, ". . . the learner has the need and the capacity to assume responsibility for his own *continuing* learning." It may well be that those who train young people in the ways of their group (a most necessary task) have overshot the mark; they have trained youngsters to believe that they cannot, dare not, learn anything without a trainer close at hand. The only safe and good learning is learning-for-the-trainer. And the youngsters, being human, independently learned something meaningful to them; namely, that it is dangerous or futile to become *interested* in something, to learn for oneself. It is only safe to learn for the teacher's or for society's approval. One set of image-molders, the teachers, have been commissioned by social leaders to shape youngsters to the acquiescent mode. They implement this commission by invalidating a child's experience of spontaneous curiosity and fascination with aspects of the world. They insist he learn only when and what he is taught. He must learn for others. The teachers and parents have robbed children of their autonomy—their capacity to experience amazement, wonder, and fascination—by invalidating it whenever it appears. Then, they look at their product and find it wanting; they produced a Golem, a humanoid, a "dependent learner." Now we are asked to breathe life into it.

We are caught on the horns of a dilemma. Children must be shown the ways of their group; they must be taught and trained. *But they must also be able to transcend this training* and learn for themselves, if they are to experience their lives as meaningful, and if the society in which they live is to grow and change. The question is, how is it possible to reconcile the contradiction between teaching children for society and letting them learn for themselves, such that children can serve their society without loss of freedom and capacity to go *beyond* what they have been taught? This is the same problem, writ large, that every serious teacher—of piano, of art, of psychotherapy, or even of teaching—faces: how can one teach a pupil in the fundamental techniques of this art without producing a mere technician? In any of these arts, we wish the learner to commit himself, to be willing to struggle for objectives *beyond* mastery of exercises and technique (learning experienced as "for-the-teacher") and even beyond current goals. We hope he will seek to make actual *his own image* (not his teacher's image) of beautiful music, pictures, healthy personalities, or independent learners. If the teacher has been effective, he will have shown his pupil that techniques are no more than a beginner's set of tools, to be used up to the point that an impasse is reached. Then, the true artist, the involved therapist, the committed teacher (committed to *his own image* of ultimate goals, not means), gropes and leaps into the unknown, "exercising that courage that is not devoid of fear and trembling," to invent or discover new means to further his project of actualizing the image. If the old versions of ultimate goals have lost meaning, the pupil will envision new embodiments of them.

The Guru and the Commissar*

Every man must come to terms with what now is. He must learn to speak, move, and even experience the world in the given ways, those deemed right and sane where he lives. It is not easy. It takes a long time. The temptation to stray is strong. "Commissars" stand close, to insure each person conforms to his prescribed position and role. Once a man masters the rules of the social "games," what then? He plays the games so long as they yield meaningful rewards and the rewards of meaning. Ultimately, the games become confining, boring, even strangling. The man may then wish to opt out, but he cannot—

* With apologies to Koestler whose book *The yogi and the commissar* suggested the title for this section.

there are no other games to play. So he may become sick. Then, he is patched up by doctors who pronounce him healed, and they send him back into the game. If he seeks to transcend the given, for new realms of experience, he threatens the sleep of the unawakened. They condemn and invalidate him. So he gives up and becomes "normal," or else seeks a richer experience in private, the while impersonating a typical person.

Since time immemorial, each society has secretly harbored "gurus." These wise men have been sought by sufferers, who may have been rich in goods but poor in spirit. The gurus have taught the seekers to let go their attachments in this world, the better to concentrate on spiritual purification. The intimated rewards have not been wealth, fame, or power; but rather enlightenment and liberation, an enriched, more meaningful experience of oneself and one's world. The gurus have helped seekers attain liberation from entrapment in their culture. They have invited the experience and disclosure of individuality that had hitherto been concealed under the trappings of conformity to roles.

The society that would not fall must locate and treasure its gurus, protect them, and not deny seekers access to them. The gurus and their ways are not for everyone. Gurus cannot be hired or bought; they can only be *deserved!* A society without gurus is stagnant, and will perish as did the dinosaurs, unable to change ways to cope with changing conditions.

In America, I think we are experiencing an absence in our midst, an absence of gurus. We have myriad commissars, but no one to lead beyond their ways. The commissars insure that everyone conforms to existing ways, to the image of man that is current, that is synonymous with goodness and sanity. Commissars use bribery, guile, and threats of force to get people to follow the prescribed ways, the ways that keep the society and its existing power-structure intact. Who are the commissars? Most of our teachers are commissars. So are our parents. And our policemen, our psychiatrists and psychologists, and even our neighbors. Radio, TV, and the press function as commissars. All commissars collude with one another to keep us wanting what we are supposed to want and doing what we are supposed to do. Conform, and be rewarded. Dissent, and be damned—or unpopular, our current synonym for damnation. If someone begins to depart from the ways deemed sane or good, he meets a graduated barrage of pressure aiming to bring him back in line. First, the person will experience twinges of guilt and anxiety if he even *thinks* of stepping out of line. If this built-in regulation fails, there is the threat of graded punishment from without. If the person will not yield to parental or family criticism, rejection, or threats, the solid wall of community invalidation will confront him, to threaten exile or imprisonment. If the dissenter—who embodies a protest against ways to live that he *cannot* live—persists in his dissent, he may finally be condemned as mad and be banished to a mental hospital where he is shocked, drugged, frozen, or operated upon, to get him in line or out of the way. And so, the majority of people, young and old, stay in the roles to which they have been trained. The commissars win out. In the ultimate victory of the commissar, each man becomes the unchallenged commissar over himself! I think this time is close at hand.*

Behavioral scientists help commissars at their task. Teachers, parents, and psychiatrists are all informed about ever new, more effortless and automatic ways to bring people into line. School curricula are scientifically broken down into units. These are administered in palatable doses by scientifically informed trainers, who employ the latest form of programmed instructions (see the postscript to this chapter, Ch. 11). Counseling centers, audio-visual aid depots, and a barrage of books and pamphlets are all available to help commissars carry out their assigned task of turning pupils *off* themselves and on to ways they are supposed to follow. The result is that we turn out more graduates from our training institutes than has ever before been true in human history. But we are discovering, we who have graduated from such institutes, that something is missing. The something is *ourselves.* Somewhere along the line, we have lost ourselves, our capacity to *experience* in new modes and qualities. If we are at all sensitive, we notice the absence and become concerned. We start to seek ourselves and our lost capacity for experiencing. I hope we find us.

* See H. Marcuse, *One-dimensional man* (London: Routledge and Kegan Paul, 1964) for an account of the ways in which dissent is invalidated.

If present trends in American training continue, the existing gurus, wherever they are, may become extinct, like Dodos; or, if they are cunning, they will hide underground. Then, a giant manhunt will be mounted as soon as the Public Health Service and the Department of Health, Education, and Welfare discover that they are having to cope with a nation of ninnies. Gurus, true teachers who challenge and stretch men's imaginations and souls, will be asked to preside over universities and kindergartens. If this doesn't happen, then one day the Red Chinese will short-circuit our electric power stations; the air-conditioning will break down and so will the computers and the teaching-machines. Our nation will sit stunned, the people having forgotten how to live for themselves, knowing only how to live for the system and for things. An era will have ended. Then, it will be the turn of the Asiatics and Africans to follow the American Way, until they too reach the end of their tether. Finally, men of Mars will land on earth and have their turn.

Beyond the Tether

We *created* the problem of independent learning by the way we taught and trained people to the social roles awaiting them in a social structure that resists change. Pedagogues, parents, people in general, invalidated the experience of learners and shut down their capacity to experience wonder and fascination. We created the problem, and it haunts us, not because "behavioral scientists have expanded our conceptions of human potential by recasting the image of man"; no, the problem haunts us because we find ourselves *at the end of our tether*. We are running in circles at its limit. The tether is firmly fixed to a peculiar debasement of a once magnificent image—the American Way of Life. Originally revolutionary and dynamic in conception, the American Way of Life is now a design for living that more and more Americans cannot live, without the aid of tranquilizers and the threats of the ubiquitous commissars. Yet, all the time, we advertise this way of life abroad, and try to sell it as we sell toilet paper and Buicks, with "hidden persuaders."

What is independent learning? No authoritative definitions are available, and so I shall offer a provisional specification. I shall look at this phenomenon from the standpoint of the learner. What an observer might call independent learning—learning for oneself—the learner experiences as fascination with some aspect of the world, envisioned in the mode of possibility, that is in *imagination* (cf. Sartre[88]). Independent learning is the embodiment and implementation of imaginative fascination. Some aspect of the world discloses itself to a person. He "flips" from the experiential mode of perception to an imaginative consciousness; and he experiences himself as beckoned, challenged, invited, fascinated, by the possibility. The transmutation of this possibility into an actuality then becomes the dominant project of his life. He lives it, and he lives for it.

The person in whom fascination has been turned on, or awakened, suffers a divine discontent, a magnificent obsession (Shaw[94]). He will wallow in his obsession if others leave him alone. He will forget to eat, sleep, play, socialize, or do anything else until he has brought his image of possibility into actuality, or lies nurturing the wounds from his fumbling, awaiting recovery to renew the onslaught. Then, he may again show an interest in other kinds of doing. But, in the midst of his learning rampage, he is far from being "well-rounded," "socially adjusted"; in fact he departs hugely from current images of how people should be. Indeed, the "turned-on learner" *needs to be protected from other people,* from self-consciousness, from the need to conform to images, from distraction, and from serious self-destruction as he contemplates and absorbs himself in the encounter with his fetish —the mystery or the missing skill. When he is thus turned on, no badly-written text, no stuttering teacher can be an obstacle or a deterrent, so long as they embody some of the knowledge that has become the life quest just then. "This book or that teacher has something I want just now. I'll get it out of them somehow!"

Independent learning arises when our present existence has reached an impasse, when our experience has gone stale. The project of "staying the same" has lost its meaning, and so the person seeks "a new interest in life." If he finds one, and he lets himself be addressed by it, he becomes possessed of the divine madness. The burden and dilemma that were his existence have now been thrown off. His existence is now *the quest.* He is turned on. He will not be diverted.

He may appear ruthless as he pursues his quest. He cannot be bored by it though he may bore others by his talk of it.

This state of being, of being involved, of experiencing new possibilities of meaning for one's life, and being engaged in their fulfillment—this is what I am construing as independent learning. It entails transcending the past—past involvements and interests, social pressure; in short, it is a matter of detachment and liberation from the momentum and inertia of previous ways of being, behaving, and experiencing.

The fascinated questing of which I speak can be evoked in a number of ways. It may occur of itself in someone who is desperate enough (like the illumination of the Buddha), whose life has been like a Zen *Koan* that he has broken through. *It seems to occur spontaneously in young children before they have been socialized.* More commonly, when it does occur, it happens through a relationship between an entrapped person and some other who functions as his guru and exemplar—someone who releases his imagination, who expands his consciousness; someone who offers a "psychedelic encounter."

Indeed, the guru may aid the process of liberation from previous attachments by helping the person experience more keenly the degree to which he feels trapped. The capacity to become fascinated may be impossible until some level of disengagement from usual concerns, ways, and commitments has been reached.

Or, the one who is to be the guru may function as a tempter—his way of life may excite envy and admiration. His serenity or his enthusiasm may evoke curiosity. He may appear to be having more fun, living more fully, experiencing more. Or he may disclose images of possibility that attract the attention of the bored, unfulfilled seeker, who then becomes fascinated and subsequently experiences his previous involvements as obstacles to his pursuit of new meaning and experience.

Whatever the occasion for being thus turned on, it is this fascinated engagement with an image of possibility that I define as independent learning. We might call it "awakening" or "inspiration," but it is always *intentional* (Husserl,[34] pp. 36, 84; May,[64])—that is, it is always related to something in the world; it is always awakening *to something,* being inspirited *by* and *for something,* fascinated *with some-*

thing. And it is embodied;[54] that is, the person lives and acts his experience of awakening. In principle, the turned-on state, which is experienced by the person as different from his usual, repetitive experience, should appear different *to the other person.* We thus have the possibility of a psychology, a physiology, even an epidemiology and sociology, of "being turned on." It is to part of this possibility, an exploration of relationships between personality factors and being turned on, that I shall now turn.

Personality: Procrustean Bed or "To-Be-Transcended"

Now I no longer believe that there are dimensions of personality that exist "in-themselves." Id, ego, super-ego; self-concept, self-ideal, public selves; traits; drives and needs—these are the terms in which we have long thought of and described "personality": "This individual is highly authoritarian or egalitarian; he has a strong ego or a weak one; his MMPI scores are thus and such, etc." This way of conceptualizing a person, whether as a whole or just some part of him, is no longer relevant or valid for me. After having tried out psychoanalytic, trait-theory, self-theory, and other kinds of theoretical models of man, I have opted for a model that is no model, or is a meta-model. It is one implicit in the philosophical tradition of existential phenomenology (Luijpen[59]). According to this perspective, man is the being such that in his being, his being is in question. His being is inextricably linked with the world he experiences as real. Other people are part of this world. The being he discloses, shows to me, when I am in one mode of my being—impersonality, formality, and distant, reserved, playing the role of hard-nosed scientist—is different from the being he will show me when I am with him in the mode of invitational dialogue. In short, his experience of his being and the being that he discloses will differ with the context. His being-for-me will differ from his being-for-himself, his being-for-his-dog, his teacher, his mother, the experimenter who studies him, and the guru whose help he may seek to transcend his personality traits or structure. There is a problem here: to dimensionalize and discover hierarchy here, a hierarchy of being. I suspect it is measurable objectively and subjectively in terms of "degrees of freedom." That is, a person may experience his being-for-his-dog as a freer, more authentic and expressive being than his being-for-his-boss, or his wife.

In the last analysis, a person chooses all modes and manifestations of his being. He cannot choose the initial impact on his experiential field of a shout, a blow, a promise, a sunset, a caress—all these things just affect him. But he can effect various actions upon his experience once it has happened. He can blot it out, reconstrue it, project it, distort it, try to preserve it, or let it flow. His personality-for-others and his personality-for-himself can embody a resolve to confine his experience and action to the limits of a procrustean mold. He can regard his experience as being without value and importance or as rich in value. If so, he is impersonating a robot; and he may experience himself as such.

A person can choose *what* of his experience he will disclose in words or behavior (behavior is meaningful disclosure, too) to whoever is nearby. Indeed, we have begun to explore what he chooses to disclose to others, in words, behavior, or even in physiological messages; under what conditions; and to which others (Jourard[41]). In light of this research, I now suspect and challenge the validity (or at least generalizability) of all published psychology, including the psychology of human learning and of human personality. I suspect their validity, because the original data (which after all are disclosures) may have been gathered under conditions in which the person being studied neither knew nor trusted the experimenter to whom he showed his learning or his traits. The experimenter doesn't know what experience of the subjects is embodied in the subjects' behavior. What the psychological scientist calls "data" is actually one mode in which the subjects disclose part of their being. There is a growing body of empirical data now to confirm the assertion that a person's being for psychologist A may differ from his being for psychologist B (cf. Ch. 3; Rosenthal[85]). Perhaps we should subtitle each report of a research: "Ss' disclosure of learning, of traits, etc., for Dr. So-and-So."

In what follows, we shall actually be talking more about *interpersonal* conditions of independent learning, than about personality factors. The capacity to "go out of one's mind" (to transcend one's personality) seems to be one of the necessary conditions for independent learning, for learning-for-oneself. And so we are interested in *who* is able to invite a person out of his mind: who are the "psychedelic people," and who is willing to accept the invitation? There may well be a stable trait that could be isolated, that we might call "transcendence-readiness," or "readiness to leave one's personality." Perhaps it persists in people, beyond childhood, through failures on the part of the commissars to get the child fully socialized. Maslow[62] referred, in this connection, to "resistance to enculturation" as one of the general traits of his "self-actualizing" subjects, in whom "peak experiences" were not a rare occurrence. The peak experience, of course, entails a leaving of one's mind, one's usual personality.

A Kind of Death and a Kind of Rebirth

Now, a hypothesis. I believe that independent learning, the embodiment of the state of being fascinated, involves six stages. The first is the experience of the impasse. The next stage we will provisionally call the stage of detachment, a kind of dying. The third is immersion in oneself—an entry into one's center, one's source of experiencing. Next is an emergence, or rebirth. Fifth is the experience of new possibilities. Sixth is the selection and pursuit of one of these. I shall attempt to illustrate this hypothesis with examples from several realms: religious conversion, brainwashing, research in psychedelic drugs, psychotherapy, and dialogue.

I base my hypothesis upon personal experience, buttressed by reading that has seemed related, and the reported experience of others. It appears to me that fascination-with-something, the process of being turned on, has a certain "natural" history in adults. It is the natural state with healthy children who have not yet been "turned off." The "turning off" begins with the experience of despair, boredom, or meaninglessness as one continues his habitual way of life—acting in one's roles, doing one's work, being one's public self. Friendships grow stale. Work becomes meaningless and pointless. One feels dead, or deadened. The world looks stale, and music loses its savor. Nothing changes. *Plus ça change, plus c'est la même chose.* I'm doing something for everybody, and nothing for me. One feels trapped. No way out seems apparent. Each step out of the circle encounters dread or a sense of hopelessness and futility. One tries new hobbies, new friends, new work, changes of scenery; but it's just a case of changing the ambience within which one feels like a robot. The depression deepens. One becomes afraid he is losing his mind. It is at this point that one's friends, family, conventional psychiatry, and religion may enter. They try, and too often they succeed in halting a natural growth process. The person in this state gradually "loses interest," "stops caring about things." He is regarded as sick, in need of "treatment" to stop him from going out of his mind. Actually, the "not-caring" is a self-initiated process of detachment from previous concerns, a phase in the death-rebirth process we are concerned with. If nothing stops the process, the person gradually enters his own experience more and more. His self-structure dissolves. He detaches himself from his image of himself, from previous friendships—which, after all, have been stabilizing him, keeping him in sameness, which is not the same as sanity. The person may become panicky, as the process of detachment continues; and he finds himself experiencing emotions, fantasies and memories, that ordinarily have been repressed. He surely needs reassurance here, to let the process unfold rather than shut it off. He is encountering his possibilities. *If he lets go enough,* he will fully enter the realm of experiencing that mystics have described as "transcendental," like a homecoming, a visit to the source, rather than a hell to be avoided. It is, in fact, the way of experiencing that we all shared as children, before we were wholly engulfed by the culture.

One cannot, and does not long stay in this realm. One re-enters his ego, but with a new perspective. The self-structure is redefined. I choose a new identity for myself and present it to others who may confirm it or not. The world doesn't look the same now. It is not the same because I am not the same, and it is my world. I look at the old things and the old people; and new features, new possibilities disclose themselves to me. I commit myself to some of these, and I am renewed, until some later time; when the new fascinations, values, and projects go stale, I must begin the process again. When I am reborn and awakened, I experience the world and the people in it as a constant and varied *calling,* a constant source of invitations to become involved. The calls and invitations that were always there, but I never heard them before. The sky called to be looked at. A person clamored for love and attention but I did not hear. Mysteries whispered their presence, but I didn't notice; I thought what was mysterious was actually known and understood. In short, I begin once again to *encounter* the world, and the people in it. In the encounter, I let myself experience the varied reality of the world, a reality that I did not experience so richly, or in so many dimensions, as I now do. Renewed by the plunge into the depths of my own experiencing, I survey the world that I am encountering. Some invitation, some call, some challenge, fascinates me more than the others. Nobody can predict what will now fascinate or repel me, not even me. I commit myself to this one, and off I go until I become deadened once again by a new set of habits.

It has just occurred to me, after completing a year of sabbatical leave in England, that the process I just described is a sabbatical leave of one's mind, of one's personality structure. The academic sabbatical is a removal from one's usual surroundings, but I discovered it is easier to get out of one's surroundings than to get them out of oneself so that new surroundings can invite one into encounter. Many of my American colleagues in England successfully shielded themselves from fascination with and involvement in the English experience, because of the panic they felt when invited to let go their usual preoccupations. They carried America with them. Indeed, the phenomenon of "culture shock," long noted by anthropologists, is another dimension of the experience of leaving, not just one's country, but one's mind. One has to let the American in one die in order to become a participant in a new experience, to be reborn.

Indeed, initiation ceremonies of all kinds recognize this, like fraternity initiation rites or Marine boot-camp training. The hazing, in whatever form, is a symbolic killing-off of a previous incarnation, to abet the reincarnation in the new way of being.

But we are as afraid of dying as we are of leaving our minds. We equate habitual ways of valuing, construing, and acting with life itself. Therefore, to stop these, even when they cease to yield satisfaction and meaning, is experienced as the end of life. It is equated with death. We are afraid to explore the possible experience beyond the tether.

In the act of love, the climax is frequently experienced as a "dying." And after the successful act of love, a person feels himself reborn, ready to respond anew to new dimensions of the world that suddenly, magically, have disclosed themselves to the person. But many acts of love are climaxed not by ego-shattering orgasm; but only by localized, pleasurable twitching. Evidently one has to be ready to go out of one's mind to make love, the love that renews and revivifies.

In the psychedelic-drug experience a person ingests a substance; and then, if he lets go, he commences a voyage into depths of experiencing of which he never would have dreamed himself capable. Later he will re-enter his ego, but again with the experience of being reborn. He will experience the world as if, hitherto, he had looked at it through a fogged-up window, with only a tiny spot wiped clear. With the rebirth, the whole window is wiped clean; and the world stands forth. The world will disclose itself to him in different dimensions than it had disclosed itself hitherto, and he will select some aspect of it with which to involve himself.[58] (In a later chapter [Ch. 13, pp. 167–169] I report on an experience with LSD.)

Brainwashing is a corruption of the death and rebirth theme. There, the commissars, who know what they want a person to do and be, convince him that he (his old self) is dead. Under the regime of torture, a person may indeed enter the transcendental realm, but he re-enters a new "robot," into new roles that have been ready-made for him. Doubtless, they seem as real and meaningful to the brainwashee as did his previous incarnation which had been made untenable and unlivable for him by his captors.

In religious conversion, the common denominator seems to be the despair at continuing in the old way.[36] The person enters his experience after leaving the world. If his background and present associates are appropriate, then, like the brainwashee, he enters a new way of being that is more or less ready-made for him.

In good psychotherapy, the therapist lets his patient enter his experience deeply. He remains present to help the patient cope with the terrors that arise as he lets go and experiences feelings, memories, and the like that have been long suppressed. With his interpretations, the therapist may aid the process of symbolic dying and facilitate the onset of the therapeutic despair, or the therapeutic psychosis which is part of every effective psychotherapy sequence.[111] Then the person is reborn, and he faces the world with the capacity to respond to its invitations in new ways.

In good teaching, after the fashion of Socrates, the skilled and compassionate dialectician will challenge every assertion and belief of his pupil until the pupil feels he is going to go out of his mind. He may balk at this point. But he may also flip into a realization of infinite possibility, and be thus turned on.

This is my hypothesis restated: independent learning entails the experience of fascination. Fascination is a response to an invitation or challenge disclosed by the world. The invitation and challenge were always there, but the person could not experience them so long as he remained "hung up" or fixated in his usual roles, self-structure, and preoccupations. It is necessary that the usual attachments be suspended, and raw experiencing be turned on.[24] This disengagement from usual concerns is fostered by entrapment and despair (it can be fostered in dialogue); and it may be experienced with dread, as a going out of one's mind, or a dying, followed by rebirth or re-entry into an enlarged self-structure. In the reborn state, the person is now more open to his experience of the world. While he is in this "open" condition, a challenge appears, and the person responds. He may or may not be confirmed by others in his new being. I would propose that something like this happens repeatedly in those healthier personalities for whom independent learning is no problem. I would propose further that a variety of factors militate against this complete process of death and rebirth. I shall classify these under two headings, the social and the personal. Then I shall discuss some factors that foster independent learning.

Social Deterrents to Independent Learning

Each society has a vested interest in maintaining a status quo; or, at the least, it will tolerate only a slow rate of social change. The entire socialization and training process, which includes our schools and universities, aims at producing a modal personality of some specified kind. This is a programmed person, interchangeable, a "behavior package"; one who is stable, predictable, and wants what he must want and does what he must do to keep the social system functioning. Once the person is ensconced in some group, everyone in the group "gets used to him" and constrains him to keep to the ways of being that identify him for *them*. If his identity is an alienated one, if the only being he and they recognize is his being-for-others, he will not likely change. Any challenges or fascinations likely to jeopardize his identity-for-others will be experienced by him as a threat to his status, and even to his existence.[54] So long as a person remains in his group, he is likely to accede to the pressures to conform to others' definitions of his being.

If the "well-adjusted" group member experiences in himself a protest against his identity-for-others and attempts to change it, he encounters the barrage of resistance I mentioned earlier. It takes courage of heroic proportions to redefine oneself in the face of such invalidation, and such courage is rare. So, apparently, is independent learning.

Personality Deterrents to Independent Learning

I have spoken before of the commissars. In a sense, we can regard the existing personality structure of the individual as an internalized commissar. The introjected family, teachers, and others comprise a kind of portable Big Brother who watches what I do; and when I experience anything counter to his rules, I feel guilt and dread. These affects are unpleasant enough to steer me back into sameness so that I can again recognize myself as the person I had always (desperately) believed, or at least hoped, I was. If I ignore my guilt and anxiety and persist in experiencing in the forbidden ways, I may feel, with horror, that I am becoming insane. The incipient birth of my unique possibilities is dreaded more than death itself, and so I kill myself (my possibilities) in order to live as a robot. I cling more desperately to my roles, my self-structure, and try to impersonate to myself and to others the one we thought I was. But I hope I have made it clear that, unless I let go, unless I follow my experiencing and enter right into it, I shall remain the same person, the one who has found his goals and values meaningless, his life a charade and a gesture.

Mystification and the Destruction of Autonomous Being: A Dyadic Deterrent

When the Other is in "bad faith" in his relationship to me, he confuses me. I never know what he is up to, because he does not mean what he says, and his actions belie his stated intentions. That same Other, if he is in a position of power over me, as a parent or teacher, may disconfirm my expressions of interest, of feelings, of intentions: "You don't really like to do that, now do you?", or, "I know you *must* be glad to be here," etc. If a child has been unsure of his own experience and its meaning, he may allow his being to be thus construed for him. He will eventually be mystified [56] as to who he is and what his true interests are. These are replaced by a pseudo-self, a set of interests and habits and experiencings which may serve *someone's* interests and freedom, but not his. Such a mystified person is hardly likely to discover the fascinations which proclaim the beginning of independent learning.

When a teacher, parent, or therapist is unaware of being a servant of some ideology or some social system, or when they deny that this is what in fact they are: when they insist that what they do to and with the child is "for your own good," they confuse and mystify the child. They contribute to his sense of ontological insecurity,[54] and certainly thereby impede independent learning.

Some Factors That Facilitate Independent Learning

The capacity to become fascinated anew, after old fascinations have worn out, is abetted by numerous factors; but it is the *interpersonal* factor I shall focus upon. Since each of us is an Other to somebody, we can perhaps do something to foster independent learning in the others for whom we are the Other. The basic factors in fostering independent learning, including the processes that underlie it and make it emerge as a response to invitation and challenge, are the human responses of challenge and invitations, stimulation of imagination, confirmation, "letting be," honest disclosure, and willingness to enter into dialogue.

Confirmation

Buber has said that each man wishes to be confirmed by his fellow, and each has the capacity to confirm his fellow. To confirm the other in his being means to stand back and let his being "happen," let it disclose itself, and to view it with respect, to acknowledge its reality and authenticity. Confirmation does not mean wishy-washy, insincere permissiveness; because often the most direct confirmation is to take a stand in opposition to the disclosure of the other. But the confirmation, the meeting, even in opposition, confirms for the other that he is the one he is. It lets him know that he exists. Confirmation means that I recognize the other *person* as the author of his acts and his utterances. I attribute them to him and his freedom. I confirm him as a free agent who chooses his existence and is responsible for it. The opposite of confirmation is invalidation and disconfirmation. There are many ways to invalidate another person, and they all have the net effect of weakening his sense of his own identity and worth, his sense of being a source of experience and action. One can ignore the other—pretend he doesn't exist, except as a doll, a thing, a nobody, or just another body. One can attribute his actions and utterances to some source other than his free intentionality; e.g., "You don't mean that; it's your illness that is speaking, not you." One can disconfirm all action and utterances save those that are compatible with one's concept of the other. Everything else that doesn't fit these expectations "is not him." Under a sufficiently sustained regime of such disconfirmation, a person will indeed come to doubt his own existence, lose his identity-for-himself, and try to confine his experience and conduct only to that range consistent with his identity-for-the-other.

Confirmation is, in a sense, an act of love. One is acknowledging that other as one who exists in his own peculiar form, with the right to do so. One recognizes that one's *concept* of his being *is only that*— a concept, and not his being. One recognizes that it is *for him* to reveal and define himself to us in this way, at his pace, thus reinforming and altering our experience and concept of him. It is not only not our duty, it is an outright sin to define another's being. Our concept of each other is always out of date. Yet, if he has a weak sense of his identity for himself, if he is ontologically insecure, he may let us do this, or even ask us to.

When I let the other person be and confirm him in his being as he discloses it to me, I am creating an ambience within which he can dare to *let go of his previous concepts and presentations of himself*. They are not binding upon him. My suspension of my preconceptions of his being invites him to let go while he is in my presence. He can drop yesterday's self-presentations, commitments, interests and goals, and explore the possibilities of new ones. He can weep, regress, enter into himself while he is with me, and feel assured that I am waiting, perhaps with a hand holding his, until he emerges to tell me who he is. And I confirm him, at each instant of the journey, as being the one he is—John searching; John in despair; John emerged, with new goals and values.

Disclosure and Dialogue

After a person has abandoned his previous incarnation, entered his experiencing, and then emerged, he experiences the world as disclosing new possibilities, new dimensions of its being for him. But I am a part of his world, and I have the capacity to disclose myself to him even while he is embodied in his usual fixed roles and self-definitions. When I am with him, I can disclose to him how I experience him. I can enter into dialogue with him; and with each of his utterances or acts, I can respond out of my experience and disclose to him what it is that I am experiencing. If I remain in contact with him, consistently in dialogue, I may actually lead him to the edge of going out of his mind, thus clearing the way for the emergence of a new self. I ask you to consider dialogue. You say something from your being— let us employ a jazz combo to illustrate. I blow a phrase on my trumpet, and you respond with a passage on your saxophone. Your response is both a reply and a question and a challenge, and so I reply. And so it goes until one of us loses his nerve and dares not let spontaneous, true disclosure out. Dialogue has ended for the time. Now switch to the dialogue in psychotherapy. The patient says something to me. I reply, in honesty. My reply evokes experiencing in him, and he utters this. This evokes a reply from me. We continue in this way until one of us has tripped off panic in the other; at this point, insincerity, dissemblance intrudes, and dialogue has ceased. One of the participants does not wish to be known, and he holds back. In dialogue at its best, the participants remain in contact and let their reciprocal disclosures affect one another. If the dialogue occurs in the context of letting be and confirmation, then the weaker of the two may indeed flip into raw experiencing, find it safe, and emerge in a more awakened state.

Authentic disclosure of self is a likely factor in the promotion of awakening, of authentication and validation of the other, and the emergence of independent learning. But authentic disclosure is rare. More common is semblance, role-playing, impersonation of the other one wishes to *seem* to the Other. Hence, the other person seldom truly encounters a person-in-process. He meets a pledge of consistency, a world of people who do not invite him into new possibilities. If I am in your world, and I do not grow and change, then you are in a world that obstructs and impedes your growth! In true encounter, there is a collapse of roles and self-concepts. No one emerges from an encounter the same as he entered. My willingness to disclose myself to you, to drop my mask, is a factor in your trusting me and daring then to disclose yourself to me. This disclosure of yourself to me aids the process of your disengagement from your previous ways of being. And as I disclose myself to you, I am your world, and this world discloses new possibilities to you—it evokes new challenges and invitations that may stir you and enliven your imagination.

Challenge: Turning on Other's Imagination

If independent learning is the implementation of fascination with imagined possibilities, then we must be concerned with the imaginative mode of experiencing. We already know much about the perceptual mode of experiencing, but imagining, the "imaginative consciousness," is less fully understood. To imagine means to transcend the here-and-now, to shut off the perceptual mode and invent new possibilities that thus far cannot be *perceived* by anyone.[88] The possibilities exist in the imaginative consciousness of the experiencer, and it is for him to "real-ize" these and make it possible for him and others to perceive in actuality what before existed only as his image.* The free imagination, like freedom itself, is a threat to all status quo. The free imagination appears to make intentional learning (rather than passive, associative conditioning) possible. The learner, even in a schoolroom, is animated by an image of a future, possible being that is not yet attained. A good pedagogue will seek to vivify and intensify this image—the image of what it will be like when one can read, or count, or play the piano. "Can you see yourself as the life of the party? Would you like to be? Then enroll now. . . ." The dull child, the

* See Chapter 14 for a fuller discussion of imagination.

one who resists teacher's efforts to teach, is often the one whose imagination has been turned off because the possible being it could disclose is frightening. Or his world is so threatening he must stay in the mode of perception, lest a danger appear. Imagining is dangerous because it means a cessation of vigilant scanning. The teacher who turns on the dull pupil, the coach who elicits a magnificent performance from someone of whom it could not have been expected, are people who *themselves* have an image of the *pupils' possibilities;* and they are effective in realizing their images. Good leaders, who have a vivid image of possibility, produce followers in whom this image is awakened; and the followers achieve remarkable feats, on their own. The art of challenge needs to be better understood, but it does seem to entail the ability to awaken a sleeping imagination to fascinating possibility and the possibility of becoming fascinated. Good pornographers are able to awaken the erotic consciousness with images of sexual possibilities. Good gurus are able to awaken the imagination of possibilities in the experience of their followers. Beyond awakening the image of the possibility, the good guru is effective at challenging a person to commit himself to realizing the possibility.

Encouragement

It is often a long and discouraging voyage, to make an envisioned possibility actual. A friend, parent, teacher, or guru may help the independent learner make his way by offering courage, encouragement, and support in the face of blind alleys, setbacks and failures. Many people have the capacity to imagine possibilities, even fascinating possibilities; but they stop their pursuit after a failure or two. The helper will offer the support which keeps the seeker seeking and trying. The seeking is what is applauded, not solely the "successful attainment."* Many people will neither imagine nor try, because they cannot be guaranteed a visible success.

Where Are the Gurus?

People who relate to others in a confirming, authentic, challenging, and encouraging way seem to be agents in fostering independent

---

* In Kazantzakis' [47] *Odyssey, a modern sequel* Odysseus says, "Your voyages, O my soul, are my native land."

learning in others. Likely, too, they are themselves independent learners, animated by images of possibility that they are themselves actualizing. Imitation of admired role-models (hero worship) is certainly an influential factor in everyone's development, and we shouldn't underrate the importance of this in our deliberations. Indeed, how admirable, heroic, growing, and seeking in fascination are the available Others in society? Who wants to be like his father? His mother? His schoolteacher? If the young people of today are any illustration, they seem to be hell-bent on pursuing an image of a possible being that is portrayed for them by the publisher of *Playboy*. The man who plays with the Bunnies and the Bunnies who are the playmates of the playboys seem more to inspire independent learning (of how to look like one and behave like one) than do the professors of introductory psychology, or the teachers of third-grade social studies. The playboy jack-rabbit is a false messiah, a corrupt kind of guru; but he turns people on. So, of course, did Hitler—but Jesus awakened people too! [78]

I wonder if the Establishments in society can tolerate gurus? I wonder if schools, homes, industry, politics, and business will permit people to be turned on to projects of their choosing? Independent learners rock the boat. True education, as opposed to training (which is essential), is by definition subversive. Education liberates individuality: it frees and strengthens autonomy. Training constricts: it reduces variance; it diminishes freedom and lessens autonomy. We cannot ignore the fact that education is a political act, or, better, the embodiment of the political stance of the anarchist.

Yet, every society needs its anarchists, its gurus; or it will shatter from its own rigidity. Do we have any? Do we have enough? And are they honest?

The Psychophysics of Being Turned On (or Off)
—Each Man His Own Scale

How might we conduct research into the phenomenon of independent learning; or fascination; or being turned on, to or by something? A method exists, one that has a history as long as that of experimental psychology—the psychophysical method, or an adaptation of it. In the psychophysical methods, a subject is asked to report his experience of a difference in weight, or size, or odor. This is the being of the phenomenon for the person. The experimenter then looks at the stimuli and notes their being-for-him or their being-for-his-measuring-devices. Systematic research into independent learning might proceed by devising schemes for self-rating and ratings by an experimenter as to when a person has been turned on, or fascinated. Then, one inquires into the structure of that turned-on person's world, as it exists for him and as it may be "objectively" recorded by the E—how he experiences certain other people in his world, himself, his body, etc. The relationship of these other people with the S can be explored by interviews with these others—how they experience the S, what they wish for him, how they implement their wishes for him, etc. The techniques employed by Ronald Laing and Aaron Esterson[56] in their magnificent studies of the families of schizophrenics are quite germane here. They were able to show, with incredible vividness, how the "symptoms" of the patient made sense as intelligible reactions to the behavior of the others in the patient's world. They would interview the patient alone; then the patient with mother, with father, with mother and father; then mother alone, father alone, and mother with father. The interviewers were skilled. The interviewees revealed, dramatically, how they changed their being in each context; and overall, it became clear how the one designated as the patient could do little else than go mad. Duplicity, disconfirmation, annihilation of the patient's autonomy—all were lucidly disclosed in these interviews, together with mystification of the patient as to what was going on. Why would it not be possible to study the significant people in the world of a turned-on person in similar ways? We might find that both the turned-off, dependent-learning state and the turned-on, fascinated, autonomous questing become quite intelligible as the reasonable and intelligible praxis of a person *in the world that exists for him.* And since all of the participants in such studies would *be* personalities, ample opportunity would be afforded for shedding more light on the facilitating or inhibiting effects of various personality structures on independent learning.

11

Postscript: About Teaching Machines, an Opinion

As the population explodes, hordes of students are knocking at the gates of our educational facilities, at all levels from kindergarten to graduate and professional schools. Educators are alarmed, since there simply are not enough teachers available to approach the educational ideal of a pupil at one end of a log, his mentor at the other. Classrooms increase in size; lecturers expand their vocal range with the microphone and television camera; but still that does not serve the learners' need, nor the teachers' ideals. On the scene has arrived what at first blush looks like a savior, the man who develops "programmed instruction" materials—so-called teaching machines—that permit an independent learner to master a syllabus or a skill by himself, at his own pace, even to the point of examining himself to see how well he is doing. Programmed instruction is a technique whereby a finished product, like a skill or a body of knowledge, is scientifically partitioned into incremental steps; and the learner masters these piecemeal, from a simple beginning up to the final, complex behavioral performance. It was originated about 30 years ago by a Midwestern American psychologist, Sidney Pressey, and perfected by B. F. Skinner in the 1950s, serving as a kind of proving-ground for the theory of behavior that Skinner evolved. Teaching-programs have been lauded by enthusiasts as a boon to business and industry, serving as efficient means for training workers in such skills as assembling electronic gadgets, or acquiring complex but stereotyped ways to behave. At the present time, programmed materials have been developed and are in use for teaching people to learn languages, the beginnings of mathematical skill, knowledge of human anatomy, and other subject-matter that must be memorized in professional training programs. But there are those who see reason for less enthusiasm about the teaching-machine approach to education. Indeed, some men have inveighed against them, seeing them as the epitome of the dehumanization of education. I think a considered view is possible, one that reconciles the enthusiasm of the proponents, with the legitimate objections of the opponents. I wrote the following as an attempt at such a considered view, some weeks after the conference at which I presented the paper on "Fascination."

The "air-conditioned nightmare," which Henry Miller[66] saw developing in 1941, now is more fully upon us. The idols we still worship are ease, effortlessness, being similar to others (i.e., avoiding criticism), and hardware (*things*). The peculiar genius of "American know-how" lies in the ability to examine how some dedicated pioneer has groped, suffered, and struggled to produce an outcome he deemed worthy of his time and life; after which engineers then work out a program of interlocking steps such that *anyone* can produce the same outcome without the struggle, and for that matter without the same level of commitment. The emphasis is always upon the *product*. We can mass-produce cars, after some creative person designs and hand-makes the first model. We can get everyone to paint the Mona Lisa simply by following the steps outlined in a do-it-yourself kit. Da Vinci had no such kit available to him. Now, behavioral engineers are looking at educated men, who live a life of learning, to see if they can "program" the steps they went through so everyone can look like an educated man. The engineers study one facet of how they behave now —the kind of answers they give to stock questions. And by small incremental steps, they strive to shape millions of people such that they will bear a superficial resemblance to authentically educated bachelors of the arts and sciences. But such "programmed bachelors" will not have been permitted to grope and struggle for meanings, goals, and achievement. All is to be effortless, and boring. Even their bodies would be denied the opportunity to cope with temperature extremes, periods of malnutrition, episodes of physical strain, so that the homeostatic mechanisms can be exercised. The result would have to be a nation of flabby, homogenized, replicas of one another, who had all but lost the capacity to cope with the unexpected. Man grows and fulfills his peculiar possibilities—physical, mental, and spiritual—*only through struggle,* and, moreover, struggle to find his own way. To eliminate it is virtually to annihilate all possibilities save the one actualized, the possibility of being like somebody else. Behavioral engineers are correct when they discuss the undisputable value of programmed instruction, say, of the content of textbooks. It removes "needless struggle" from the teachers' effort to impart "knowledge." They argue that elimination of struggle saves time, and frees teacher and pupil alike for free dialogue, discussion, and other unprogrammable encounters. What is overlooked is that there is something monstrous, at least to me, of having one thousand pupils reading the same book *in the same way*—which is what a "programmed text" requires the reader to do. The fact is, there are *many ways* for people to master skills or subject matter, and many ways to read a book. It has by no means been proven that programmed materials are better, than, say, lectures, demonstrations, and the struggle on a student's part to learn efficient ways to tackle subject-matter. We may have been sold a bill of goods. We may be so enamored of the scientific aura exuded by "learning packages," that we have become blind to shortcomings. But since there *may* be something of value in programmed instruction for schools and universities, "P.I." should be optional, not compulsory. One high school student I know is obliged to study English grammar from a programmed text, and it is driving him silly. I advised him to get hold of an old fashioned book and read it *sub rosa.*

"Programmers" can program men who conform to Hitler's or Himmler's image of the ideal, useful (to the state) man. They can program men who conform to the image of "men who have it made" in the U.S.A. The only thing they cannot so far program is commitment itself. Perhaps soon they will, and scientific knowledge will thereby be advanced. That is good. But each man must, by himself and for himself, select goals worth his struggle to achieve them. It is the meaningful struggle itself—not the product, the success or failure —that makes *men.* Guaranteed success without full engagement produces suave but moronic "nebbishes."

We may yet have to develop a new kind of specialist, as automation and programming of behavior eliminate struggle and risk from more realms of existence. The new specialist might be called a *struggle-ologist,* or a "de-programmer" (in fact, this is what the guru and therapist are). It will be his task to treat with "programmed man" who has enough soul left to realize he is bored to death. Perhaps he too can develop a program, whereby, in small incremental steps, he will reintroduce his client to tolerate increasing degrees of uncertainty, increasing degrees of challenge. He will be a coach of spiritual weight-lifting. His will be an "antiprogram" program.

As I see them, programmers are invaluable in settings where men want or need to function like interchangeable parts in a social system, where "training" is the objective. Some kind of learning-programs is necessary to train soldiers, or to indoctrinate people in traffic rules, or the rules in the Emily Post etiquette book. Perhaps programmed instruction is best seen as the swiftest way for a society to impart some of its past—its culture, knowledge, and skills—to the oncoming generations. But for *education,* which entails inventing and actualizing the future, I do not believe packaged teaching programs are relevant.

Imagine the fully programmed man sitting, waiting for the next frame in his teaching machine to appear—and the electricity breaks down. He no longer knows how to search for facts, though he may be surrounded by them. He is like the city boy who starves to death in the jungle, surrounded by enough protein and carbohydrates to feed a million men—but not in the form of bread, steak, salad, apple pie, and coffee. Survival training in the army and outwardbound training in the Peace Corps are embodiments of antiprogramming. But as fast as these antiprogram programs are evolved, new programs spring up. I think that like antibiotics, programming is a mixed curse-blessing. A sterile gut produced by massive doses of penicillin and aureomycin cannot cope with minor infection. A sterile soul, produced by massive doses of programming, cannot cope with the unprogrammed disclosure of the world.

A master of some art, such as surgery, painting, sculpture, or the dance, performs in ways that dazzle, mystify, and inspire someone, who then becomes his pupil. In the course of time, as the master deems his apprentice ready, he discloses to him the exercises, the techniques, the tricks out of which he has perfected *his* embodiment of the art. The pupil then imitates his master, relives his master's life, as it were, albeit in telescoped form. He ultimately arrives at the point where his master is, and then, hopefully, he surpasses his master in mastery, finally transmitting this to *his* pupil. In a sense, the master is programming his pupil, but in a slow painstaking way. The pupil must adapt himself to the master's eccentricities, thus transcending his own, prior programming. He imitates the being of his teacher.

The sophisticated teaching program is like a condensed-learning autobiography, alienated, separated from the whole being of the man who learned the ultimate performance, and reduced to some lowest common denominator—it is arranged so even people of little intelligence can master skills and verbal knowledge. There is didactic value in studying and rehearsing games of chess or bridge by which a championship was won, but the student does not thereby become a master. He only learns how someone who was dedicated and committed to excellence groped his way, and "did it." Similarly, the student of science who recapitulates great experiments experiences part—an alienated part—of how a dedicated master did it. The pupils of Carl Rogers[84] in the late '40s and early '50s learned how to help people grow as Rogers did—by reflecting and restating the patients' disclosures. But they do not thereby become that committed, groping man, Carl Rogers. They must surpass his "technique" in quest of their own ways to help people grow. Rogers gets them started, and they must then struggle on their own when they arrive at the impasses to which his technique will inevitably lead them.

One could program the project, "behaving verbally like Carl Rogers," in about an hour, given a reasonably alert moron as a pupil. But to become one's possible self, to discover one's own way of achieving goals, is not a programmable project.

The student of painting naturally reads the lives of the great artists and tries to duplicate their masterpieces; he might even re-experience the blind alleys and false starts, to get the feel of a committed man groping to actualize an image of possibility. But then he must produce his own images, and strain for their realization.

Now let us look afresh at programmed instruction, and its possibility for helping educate (not train) men. Each program, whether for mastering wiring diagrams, or the rules of French grammar, can be viewed as a highly condensed autobiography of someone who already groped to fulfill these aims, but with the bungles and blind alleys, the blood, sacrifice, sweat, and tears, left out. It is reduced to banality. If the aim of a society is to preserve a status quo, to shape someone to a criterion, to transmit past "successes" that produced the status quo, programmed teaching is relevant, and very valuable. If the aim is to inspire men to pursue even higher, more difficult goals, even here teaching-programs are useful—they can be used like encapsulated, inspirational parables, autobiographies to be studied, even rehearsed like a game of chess, and then abandoned or surpassed as one struggles to actualize higher possibilities. The true value of Pressey's and Skinner's work is twofold: programmed instruction and teaching machines serve the social system by providing a swift and sure technique for shaping people into replicas of one another, so that society's maintenance work can be done, so people can replace one another in occupational roles. The other, *educational* value of programmed instruction is that it could afford a straight and negotiable ladder for a pupil quickly to climb upon the shoulders of a master he chooses. Once he is on those giant shoulders, if he is to grow, he must leap, grope, and struggle to fulfill new possibilities. This quest cannot be simplified, and it takes courage in the face of repeated failure to make actual what was an invented possibility.

As the work of society becomes increasingly automated (see Chapter 15) men will be released from much occupational labor, and fewer men will be able to find growth-yielding struggle in the realm of work. Scientific programming may be the way in which human skills are quickly attained for this new Utopia we face. But if man is not to go mad, or become wholly robot-like himself in this impending world, then Education—with a capital E—must be reorganized, so as to awaken imagination and courage to struggle in millions. Imagination is called for so people can invent *new* values, beyond comfort, ease, and sensual enjoyment, worth pursuing (these latter will be produced automatically, by machines). And courage will be called for, so that meaningful struggle, that vital ingredient, will remain in the world.

Then, the new world will be populated by *men,* not humanoids. And these men will have the inner resources to keep inventing and producing new worlds, whenever their present world becomes static and not fit for whole men to live in.

The implication for education is clear: where training is called for, let it be done quickly and efficiently with all the technical help available. But let the schools and universities have on their staffs those whose expertise is, not training, but rather the talents of the guru. These men will aim at helping learners to transcend their own programming, to invent new goals, and to address them with vigor and courage.

12

An Exploratory Study of Body-Contact*†‡

Fourteen years ago, Paul Secord [92] and I published the first of a series of papers presenting some findings in the study of "body-cathexis"—feelings of like-dislike which people experience toward their own body. Since that time, with the exception of books by Szasz [99] and Fisher and Cleveland [18], little work has been done in psychology on aspects of bodily experience. Yet we have much reason to suspect that the way people experience their bodies, how they think, feel and fantasy about their bodies, profoundly affects their behavior and their well-being. The touch is an action which bridges the gulf many people develop between themselves and others, and between their "self" and their body. When I touch someone, I experience his body and my own simultaneously. To be touched is an almost infallible way of having one's attention seized and diverted from anything it was occupied with. As I noted earlier (Chaper 7, pp. 65–67), body-contact has important implications for psychotherapy, and for healing in general, not to mention its role in maternal care and in the sexual aspects of love. Touching another person is the last stage in reducing distance between people. Each person lives as if with an invisible fence around his body, a fence that keeps others at that distance which one feels most safe and

* Adapted from a paper read at the convention of the Florida Psychological Association in Tampa, Florida, May 1, 1964. The present version was written during my tenure as a Special Fellow of the United States Public Health Service under Grant 1-F3-MH-3374-01.

† I would like to express my appreciation to Dr. Jefferson Sulzer, now of Tulane University, for help in preparing the questionnaire used herein; to Carol Raff, Mohammed Inayat-Ullah and Zalmon Neumark for assistance with the statistical work; and to the Director of the Computing Center, University of Florida, for a grant which underwrote the cost of some of the data analysis.

‡ This paper is reprinted from the *British Journal of Social and Clinical Psychology* (1966, vol. 5, pp. 221–231) with permission.

comfortable. Let another person approach nearer than the boundary, and the one approached will step back, to keep the distance optimum —even if it means successively stepping back until considerable distance has been covered, with one approaching, the other retreating. To actually touch a person who is thus walled behind an invisible fence is often to invite violence or panic. Out of such considerations, I commenced the investigation which is reported here. The study can be viewed as an effort to bridge the gap between the methods of phenomenological analysis and psychological research in an area we are all close to—our bodies.

We know that touching another person is a significant act. Touches can convey love, goodwill, hate, and myriad other meanings (Frank[20]). Lovers arouse their paramours, mothers soothe their infants, and healers relieve their patients, all with a touch. We also know that there is much variation between groups and individuals, and between settings in the amount and style of permissible body-contact.

As investigators, we have encroached upon many realms deemed sacrosanct. We have inquired into people's sex lives, probed their religious sentiments, peeped into their unconscious fantasies, we have even eavesdropped on the psychotherapeutic interview. But for all this, we know little about the conditions under which a person will permit another to touch him, the meanings people attach to touching and being touched, the loci of acceptable touch, and little of the consequences of body-contact. It is as if the touch-taboo most of us learned in childhood has produced a scotoma of our professional vision, making us describe man in our textbooks as if he did not come closer to his fellows than a foot or so. Illustration of such differences is provided by some observations I made during pilot stages of the present investigation. I watched pairs of people engaged in conversation in coffee shops in San Juan (Puerto Rico), London, Paris, and Gainesville (Florida), counting the number of times that one person touched another at one table during a one-hour sitting. The "scores" were, for San Juan, 180; for Paris, 110; for London, 0; and for Gainesville, 2. On another occasion, I spent two hours walking around the Teaching Hospital at the University of Florida, seeking episodes of body-contact. I watched nurses and physicians tending to patients, I observed relatives in conversation with patients, and I patrolled corridors, watching interchanges between nurses and nurses, physicians and nurses, and physicians with each other. During this time, two nurses' hands touched those of the patients to whom they were giving pills; one physician held a patient's wrist as he was taking a pulse; and one intern placed his arm around the waist of a student nurse to whom he was engaged. Clearly, not much physical contact was in evidence. By contrast, I have seen happily married spouses touch one another dozens of times before others—a kiss, a handclasp, a hug. And miserably married persons whom I have seen in psychotherapy have often complained of too little, or too much physical contact. Finally, I have encountered individuals who become furious, and jump as if stung if they are brushed against, or touched on the shoulder or chest during a conversation.

It is time for systematic study of the parameters of touching. I suspect that many people suffer from deprivation of physical contact during their adult lives, but there is no way to prove this without knowledge of normative and desired touching patterns, and their sources of variation. The present study was undertaken as a first step in this direction.

Method

Materials and Procedure

The term *body-accessibility* was proposed as a general term to describe the readiness of a person to permit others to contact his body. We can make our bodies accessible to others via several sense modalities, viz.: touch, sight, smell, and even taste. In the present study, I confined myself to the tactual and visual modes. I constructed a questionnaire that would inquire into the site of visual and tactual contact with their bodies which Ss permitted certain "target-persons", and the extent to which the Ss had seen and touched the bodies of those others. No inquiry was made into the frequency with which the contact occurred. The questionnaire was developed as follows:

A drawing of the body was prepared (see Fig. 1), with 24 regions demarcated. The idea for such a diagram was suggested by beef-charts on which butchers delineate the various steaks and chops. This diagram was to serve as a guide to Ss for indicating which regions of their bodies had been seen and touched by the mother, father, closest friend of the same sex, and closest friend of the opposite sex, and which regions of these target-persons' bodies they had seen and touched. A booklet was assembled, with face-sheets for biographical and demographic data, and pages inscribed with a diagram referring to each of the target-persons. Four columns and 24 rows were drawn below the diagram. The Ss were requested to indicate with a check-mark in the appropriate column, (a) which regions of their own body had been seen, unclad, by the target-person in question, (b) which regions of the target-person's body they (the Ss) had seen unclad, (c) which regions of their own body, clad or unclad, had been touched by the target-person, and.(d) which regions of the target-person's body they had had physical contact with.

Entries were to be made only if visual or tactual contact had occurred within the past 12 months. No inquiry was made into the frequency, circumstances, or meaning of the contact; a man could make an entry if he had wrestled once with his male friend, or if he had repeatedly kissed his mother or girl-friend. We were seeking to measure sheer occurrence and locus of body-contact, visual and tactual, under any and all circumstances in the past 12 months.

The questionnaire booklets were administered by the writer or his assistant to a total of 380 college students who were tested in groups. The Ss responded anonymously. Their co-operation was enlisted by explaining the purpose of the study, and the need for honesty in responding. There was considerable laughter, and some embarrassment expressed by the Ss over the nature of the task, but they complied with a great deal of interest. Only the returns from unmarried Ss between the ages of 18 and 22 years were analyzed—a total N of 168 males, and 140 females.

Each S's entries, classified by *mode* (visual *versus* tactual), *direction* (being seen or touched *versus* seeing or touching), and *target* of contact were summed for statistical analysis. The percentage of Ss reporting that they had touched each target-person, and had been touched by them was also computed separately for each of the 24 body regions.

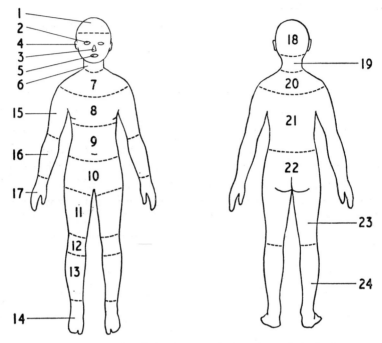

Fig. 1. Diagram of the front and rear view of the body
as demarcated for the Body-Accessibility Questionnaire.

Results

Reliability of the Questionnaire

Odd-even reliability coefficients were calculated for the visual and tactual contact scores of 50 male and 50 female Ss selected at random from the total sample. The r's (corrected for attenuation) ranged from a high of ·98 for tactual interchange between the male Ss and their fathers and same-sexed friends, to a low of ·27 for the scores depicting the visual accessibility of the female Ss to their fathers. All the tactual contact scores showed reliability coefficients above ·85. Examination of the visual contact scores showed that the lower r's resulted from restricted variance in the pairs of subtotal scores.

It was concluded that the questionnaire measures had adequate consistency for a survey-type study.

Analysis of Contact Scores

Means, *SD*'s, and "critical difference" values for the several contact scores of 25 males and 25 females, selected at random are listed in Table 1.

Table 1. *Means, SD's and critical difference values* for the various body-contact scores*

Target		Ss See		Ss seen by		Ss Touch		Ss Touched by	
		Mean	SD	Mean	SD	Mean	SD	Mean	SD
Mother	Males	19·64	2·54	21·60	3·92	6·88	4·88	9·56	7·84
	Females	21·76	2·48	22·12	2·28	9·44	5·48	10·60	5·16
Father	Males	22·96	1·52	23·00	1·52	6·08	5·84	6·80	6·04
	Females	21·60	2·76	19·88	2·60	9·24	6·12	9·44	5·60
Same-sex friend	Males	23·20	2·20	23·24	2·20	9·76	7·92	10·04	7·80
	Females	21·84	3·08	21·68	3·20	9·88	7·00	10·12	6·80
Opposite-sex friend	Males	19·96	5·80	19·76	6·20	19·72	6·88	18·72	7·44
	Females	20·72	4·16	21·08	2·92	19·04	6·62	19·88	5·84

* Critical differences for P < ·05 = 1·61; P < ·02 = 1·91; P < ·01 = 2·12; N = 25 males, 25 females.

Analysis of variance showed significant ($P < ·001$) differences in overall scores between modes of contact ($F = 293·27$) and target-persons ($F = 25·36$). The interactions for mode-by-target ($F = 72·54$) and sex-by-mode-by-target ($F = 4·07$) were also significant beyond the ·001 level of confidence. The *F*-ratios for the comparison between sexes, and for sex-by-mode and sex-by-target interactions were not statistically significant.

Visual accessibility. The means listed in the first two columns of Table 1 show that the bodies of the *S*s and the target-persons were reportedly more accessible to visual contact than to touching, an exception being in the *S*s' relationship with their opposite-sexed friend. There the visual and tactual contact scores were more nearly similar. From 20 to 23 body regions were mutually accessible between the *S*s and each of the target-persons, likely attributable to the fact that the study was conducted in Florida, where people spend considerable time throughout the year clad in bathing costumes.

Tactual accessibility. The means in the two right-hand columns of Table 1 show that compared to visual contact, relatively few body regions were touched in the relationship of the *S*s with their parents and friends of the same sex. This is graphic illustration of a touch-taboo, at least in those relationships. Substantial means for touching were found for the relationship with the opposite-sex friend, happily enough, indicating that the touch-taboo is not wholly generalized. These findings suggest that most regions of a young adult's body remain untouched unless he has a close friend of the opposite sex.

The scores for exchange of physical contact with parents showed an interesting pattern. The males were reportedly touched by their mothers on as many regions as the females were, but they did not touch their mothers' bodies in as many places as their mothers touched them, nor on as many as the females touched their mothers. Moreover, the females touched their fathers on more regions than the males did, and they were touched on more body areas by their fathers than were the males. When it comes to physical contact within the family, it is the daughters who are the favored ones.

Inter-modal correlations. The questions were raised, "Is there a correlation between modes and directions of body-contact? That is, are seeing and being seen, touching and being touched mutual transactions? And is there any relationship between visual and tactual accessibility?" To answer these questions, *r*'s were computed for the 25 males and females (whose scores were recorded in Table 1) between (*a*) their summed scores for seeing the bodies of the 4 target-persons, and the summed scores for being seen by them, (*b*) scores for touching and being touched, (*c*) seeing and touching, (*d*) being seen and being touched, (*e*) being seen by the others, and touching them, and (*f*) seeing others, and being touched by them. The *r*'s are shown in Table 2.

The highest *r*'s were between directions of contact within modes, suggesting a strong "dyadic effect" in disclosure of the body to the

Table 2. *Intercorrelations among scores for various modes and directions of body-contact**

		See others	Seen by others	Touch others	Touched by others
See others	Males		·91	·59	·61
	Females		·95	·58	·60
Seen by others	Males			·66	·74
	Females			·59	·64
Touch others	Males				·96
	Females				·97

*N = 25 males, 25 females.

other's sight and touch, similar to that noted in the study of self-disclosure (cf. Jourard[37]; Jourard & Landsman[42]). The r's between modes of contact were lower, indicating that visual and tactual accessibility were somewhat more independent of one another, though they were still significantly correlated.

Tactual Accessibility of Regions of the Body

Table 3 shows the percentage of the 168 males and 140 females who reported touching, and being touched by, each of the 4 target-persons on the 24 regions of the body distinguished in Figure 1. Considerable variation between bodily regions may be noted, ranging from a high of 94 per cent (for females reporting being touched by their opposite-sexed friend on the back of the head and neck) to a low of zero, with regard to tactual interchange between the females and their fathers in area 10, the genital region. A target-by-region interaction is attested by

Table 3. *Percentage* of Ss who report touching, and being touched by, various target-persons, on twenty-four regions of the body*

Body region No.†	Touch		Touched by		Touch		Touched by		Touch		Touched by		Touch		Touched by	
	Mother				Father				Same-sex friend				Opp.-sex friend			
	M	F	M	F	M	F	M	F	M	F	M	F	M	F	M	F
1.	63	77	74	78	35	65	47	69	50	68	49	65	89	92	86	89
2.	31	39	44	44	18	35	7	34	23	28	23	31	81	78	79	82
3.	41	51	53	52	22	48	22	46	30	28	28	29	88	85	85	84
4.	41	46	53	42	22	42	23	43	33	28	34	29	87	89	84	86
5.	54	49	59	52	18	50	16	52	22	31	20	31	93	93	90	89
6.	52	57	58	56	31	51	36	59	44	42	44	42	89	90	86	88
7.	35	54	54	55	43	52	45	48	53	49	55	50	88	83	84	82
8.	8	6	29	9	23	22	24	6	39	6	41	6	73	70	76	52
9.	15	24	27	21	20	27	21	21	39	20	41	21	81	72	78	72
10.	1	2	2	2	1	0	2	0	10	1	9	1	53	42	50	44
11.	10	15	21	16	16	15	14	16	31	18	31	18	78	62	72	67
12.	15	18	24	30	19	20	19	22	36	25	35	25	79	70	73	79
13.	18	21	26	29	19	18	19	20	36	23	34	23	77	68	70	72
14.	21	24	30	31	21	25	20	25	34	28	33	27	73	65	67	67
15.	70	72	71	75	59	72	59	70	71	75	70	75	88	89	86	89
16.	74	73	73	76	61	75	61	74	71	79	71	80	89	90	89	88
17.	83	78	82	82	86	82	86	77	88	81	87	82	93	90	92	89
18.	49	66	64	71	36	56	43	62	48	67	47	71	88	89	86	94
19.	54	59	60	60	40	56	46	58	48	54	46	60	89	91	88	94
20.	61	71	67	76	57	72	57	67	57	67	58	74	89	88	85	92
21.	34	50	50	59	39	52	34	51	43	52	45	55	88	82	83	83
22.	6	14	13	17	8	5	11	13	21	12	22	14	61	48	54	58
23.	12	15	21	19	14	15	16	16	29	19	30	22	73	61	68	69
24.	18	20	26	29	18	18	19	21	33	23	34	24	71	65	71	72

* Based on N = 168 males, 140 females.
† The numbers refer to regions shown in Fig. 1.

the relative deluge of tactual contact reported by both sexes in relation to opposite-sexed friend in contrast to the contact reported with the other three target-persons.

Similarity between the sexes in their reported receptivity to the touch of others on each of the 24 regions of the body was shown by r's of ·97, ·85, ·85 and ·88 between the percentages of males and females indicating being touched on each region by their mothers, fathers, same-sexed friends, and opposite-sexed friends respectively (with $N = 24$ body regions). These r's likely signify that males and females share norms governing which body-regions they will make accessible to others' touch, and which they will withhold from the touch of others.

Tactual Accessibility as a Personality Trait

If body-accessibility is a personality trait we should expect to find correlations in our present data between the number of body regions exposed to the touch of one target-person, and the number exposed to the touch of others. Table 4 shows intercorrelations for the total "being touched" scores reported by 50 male and 50 female Protestant Ss for their relationships with each of the 4 target-persons. In general, the

Table 4. *Intercorrelations* among scores for extent to which Ss† were touched by each of four-target-persons*

	Mother	Father	Same-sex friend	Opposite-sex friend
Mother		·64 (·87)	·46 (·80)	·35 (·39)
Father			·45 (·72)	·30 (·38)
Same-Sex Friend				·36 (·38)

*$N = 50$ males, 50 females, all Protestants.
† The r inside parentheses is for the females Ss, while that outside parentheses is for the males.

females show higher r's than the males, suggesting more consistency in attitude and behavior regarding body contact, or perhaps less discrimination than the males in accepting or spurning the extended hand of others. Also to be noted in this table is the consistently smaller size of the r's in the column for the friend of the oposite sex; evidently one cannot as well predict the amount of body exposed to touch in the heterosexual dyad from that exposed in the relationship between an S and his parents or his same-sexed friend.

Some Further Group Comparisons

Several exploratory analyses were made of differences in mean "being touched" scores when the total sample was classified by age, religious denomination, and level of self-rated attractiveness.

No significant differences were found to be associated with age, but this was hardly surprising, in view of the limited age range under considerations, viz.: from 18 to 22 years. For the interdenominational comparison, one significant ($P < \cdot 05$) difference was found: Protestant ($N = 89$) and Catholic ($N = 18$) girls reported being touched by their male friends on an average of 20 body regions, as compared to a mean of 16 regions for the Jewish girls ($N = 28$). The reasons for this difference are not clear, but the presence of a difference of this sort points to the value of future comparisons among various sociological groupings of their practices with respect to body-contact.

All of the Ss had been requested, on the face-sheets of the questionnaire booklet, to rate their attitude toward their bodily appearance by checking one of 4 adjectives, viz.: very attractive, attractive, plain, or average. The Ss who checked either of the first two terms ($N = 60$ males, 78 females, designated the *Attractive* group) showed higher "being touched" scores than those checking the latter terms ($N = 89$ males, 60 females, designated *Plain*) *vis-à-vis* all target-persons. The single exception was in the case of the *Plain* females, who reported receiving contact on more body areas from the girl-friends than did the *Attractive* girls. The only significant ($P < \cdot 02$) critical ratio that was found in these comparisons was for the males, with respect to the range of contact received from their girl-friends. Of course, it was the *Attractive* males who reported the higher means. One does not know whether the *Attractive* Ss regarded themselves as such because they had been touched on more body regions, or whether others touched more of their body surface because their bodies appeared more inviting and attractive.

Discussion

The most important finding in the present study is that body-accessibility can be reliably measured. Provided that Ss will respond to a questionnaire with honesty, a way is opened for investigation of diverse questions, from those relating to group differences to the study of personality correlates of body-accessibility.

I am going to confine the remainder of this discussion to touching, not because visual accessibility is less important—indeed, there are probably marked differences between cultures, and between individuals in readiness to reveal the body to others. Rather, it is because there was less variance in visual accessibility scores, and because I included this dimension in the study primarily for purposes of comparison with touching.

The touch data prompt a number of questions. Why is less of the body exposed to touching in the Ss' relationships with parents and same-sexed friends? Why does the most extensive body-contact occur in relation to the friend of the opposite sex? Is it that the "touch vocabulary" in America is limited only to sexual meanings? What about age trends? My sample was confined to young unmarried adults. Would we find patterns of contact similar to those noted in the study of self-disclosure, where increasing age brought about a decrease in confiding between a person and his parents and same-sexed friend, and increased disclosure to the opposite-sexed partner (Jourard[38])?

Why do sons exchange physical contact of fewer body regions with their parents than daughters do? Is there some taboo which restricts the number of points for physical contact between fathers and sons? Several of the males reported that they could recall *no* physical contact with their fathers! And why do we find the mother-son touching asymmetry? Why can mothers touch their sons on more areas than the sons can touch them? Is it because mothers can contact more body-surface without sexual significance than the sons can?

Why did the Jewish females report fewer regions of their body were touched by their boy-friends than the Protestant or Catholic girls? Is it that the bodies of Jewish girls are less accessible? Or is it a function of the fact, noted by a colleague, that at the University of Florida, the Protestant and Catholic girls are outnumbered by Protestant and Catholic men, whereas the Jewish men and women students are about equal in number—the implication is that the Jewish girls, if they date within their faith, have fewer men to whom they can grant access to their bodies. Or it may mean that the men are more reluctant to touch many areas of a Jewish girl's body.

In an earlier paper (Jourard & Secord[44]), we reported that Ss' attitudes of like and dislike toward the appearance of their bodies were related to their parents' attitudes to their (the Ss) bodies. That is, the Ss tended to like their bodily appearance if they believed their parents did. This finding may be linked with the present data, which showed that Ss who rated themselves as "attractive" in appearance reported receiving more physical contact than those who saw themselves as less attractive. The hypothesis may be proposed that parents convey their acceptance of their children's bodies through physical contact, and the children come to experience themselves as acceptable in appearance in this way. More specifically, the children may come to like or accept only those areas of their bodies which the parents have touched or caressed in a positive way. Presumably, a person who likes and accepts his body will invite and accept more physical contact than one who experiences his body as unattractive or bad.

The presence of significant correlations among the various scores depicting touch received from others is especially interesting. It implies that readiness to enter into broad-range touching relationships with others is a dimension of personality which cuts across role-relationships. Presumably there are people who freely exchange touches with others, and another population which sharply restricts the points of physical contact. Through the use of questionnaires, it should be possible to locate the "mustn't touch" people, and study other dimensions of their personalities. The large SD's found for the measures of touching offer additional warrant for studying personality correlates of tactual accessibility.

Body regions were found to be highly variable in touchability. The hands, arms, shoulders, and top of the head received the most contact, while the areas most obviously linked with sexuality were touched less. A more detailed study of touching in the marriage relationship seems especially warranted, in view of the close association between touching and sex. Perhaps we would find a correlation between expressions of marital satisfaction and the number of body regions that are included in the loving caresses of spouses.

I think that body-contact has the function of confirming one's bodily being. We live in an age of "unembodiment" (Laing[54]), or disembodiment, and I believe that the experience of being touched enlivens our bodies, and brings us back into them. This is one implication of references in novels to the loved one who "came to life", or was "turned on", or "realized I had a body" in response to the lover's touch or caress. The

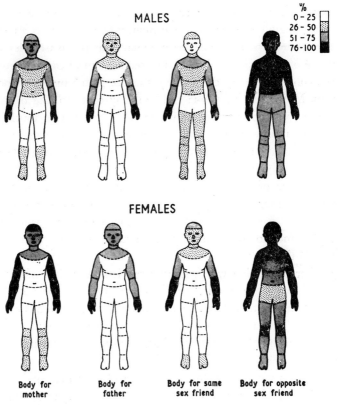

Fig. 2. The Ss' "Body-for-Others", as experienced through amount of touching received from others. Percentages are based on $N = 168$ males and 140 females. The darkest portions signify that from 76–100 per cent of the Ss reported being touched by the target-person in question on the body-region indicated.

data reported in Table 3 permit us to depict a dimension of body-image in addition to the "boundaries" mentioned by Fisher and Cleveland,[18] and cathexis (Jourard & Secord [44]): viz., our Ss' *experienced* "body-for-mother", "body-for-father", "body-for-same-sex-friend" and "body-for-opposite-sex-friend". Figure 2 shows a front view of an hypothetical S in this study, with the regions that have been touched most by a target-person shaded in most heavily, and the lesser-touched regions shaded more lightly. The diagrams suggest, for example, that a male's *experienced* body-for-father is composed primarily of hands, head, shoulders and arms, whereas for his girl-friend, much more of his body is experienced, and is included in the relationship. We might propose on the basis of these findings that only those persons who have a relationship with others that includes touching and caresses will have a fully experienced body and a fully embodied self (Laing,[54] pp. 67–81). Sartre's[86] superb discussion of the way in which a caress incarnates the flesh of the one caressed as well as the one caressing certainly suggests this (cf., pp. 389–397).

Kessen & Mandler[50] have stated that physical contact between a mother and her child is a "specific inhibitor" of the unlearned, periodic "fundamental distress" to which children are subject, and which is the *anlage* of anxiety in the adult. Indeed, Harlow's[28] monkeys ran to the surrogate "mothers" of terry cloth, and even of wire, presumably for the comfort they derived from contact when they were frightened or stressed. The animal data suggest that contact is the primitive language of love. If this is true, then extensive physical contact may indeed be the natural or primordial sedative and tranquilizer, one without the dangerous side-effects of pharmaceutical compounds. Perhaps people rely on drugs because they do not receive enough contact, caressing, or body-massage in their everyday life. But touching must also be a disturber, especially for defensive people, or for those engaged in tasks involving concentration. It would be interesting to study what happens to an Ss' pulse, his reading efficiency, his learning ability, or his willingness to disclose personal information in an interview when he is being touched by the experimenter or by some other person, e.g., his mother, or a friend of either sex.

In the introductory section of this paper, I noted the rarity of body-contact that occurred in a general hospital setting. I have made similar observations in mental hospitals in the United States, where physical contact of any kind between professional staff and patients, and among patients is discouraged as a matter of policy. By contrast, at a French mental hospital which I visited (in 1964), physical contact is deliberately encouraged, and is seen as an important aspect of the total rehabilitative plan. Patients receive massage, and they engage in all manner of group activities, such as games, in which touching takes place (cf. Sivadon & Gantheret[95]).

We may conclude from this exploratory study that body-accessibility is a promising field for further study. In future investigations by the questionnaire method, I would recommend modifying the way in which body regions are demarcated. Our division of the body was somewhat arbitrary, and did not assign distinct status to such important body zones as the cheeks, or the ear-lobes. It would be valuable, too, to construct a verbal questionnaire, to inquire especially into the meaning and the frequency of contact, e.g., "On what regions of your body have you been kissed"? "Do you receive a hug or embrace from parents"? "How much contact would you like, and how much do you get from a given person"? It would be possible in this way to obtain a better picture of the role of body-contact in an individual's interpersonal life.

Summary

A body-accessibility questionnaire was submitted to 168 male and 140 female unmarried college students. The aim was to determine the extent to which college students permit their parents and closest friends of each sex to see and touch their bodies, and the extent to which they have seen and touched the bodies of these "target-persons". The bodies of the Ss and of the target-persons were reportedly more visually than tactually accessible. The greatest range of tactual interchange occurred between the Ss and their closest friends of the opposite sex. Significant relationships were found between the measures of seeing another's body and being seen by that person, and between touching the other's body, and being touched by him. The male Ss touched fewer regions of their mothers' bodies than were touched by their mothers, and they were not touched by their mothers on as many regions as the females were. The females exchanged physical contact on more areas of the body with their fathers than did the males. There was also significant correlation among the measures of contact with each of the target-persons under consideration, suggesting that body-accessibility is a personality trait. Protestant and Catholic females reported being touched by their boy friends on more body regions than did Jewish females. Ss who rated themselves as plain or unattractive reported being touched on less of their body surface than did Ss who rated themselves as average or attractive in appearance. There was much variability in body-accessibility associated with region of the body, and both sexes showed similarity in the regions which were most, and which were least accessible to the touch of others.

13

Growing Experience and the Experience of Growth

Growth has always fascinated man, but he has studied it only from its "outside." None of the scientific accounts of growth and development are informed by the experience of the one growing. Instead, we have accounts of physical and behavioral development, as these appear to the scientist's eyes, or as they leave traces on his recording apparatus, to show up as "growth curves" in a scientific treatise. The other side of growth needs to be shown, if for no other reason than to round out the story. The present chapter offers an essay toward a "phenomenology of personal growth."

Everything looks different when I visit the neighborhood where I grew up. The stores and houses look smaller, decayed, less imposing than I remember them to have been. My old school chums are balder, fatter; some look defeated and resigned, and others are smug, more self-satisfied than they were when I knew them years ago. Their change appears to me as a kind of fall, a failure to realize many of the dreams which I knew animated them in their younger days. My own change (which I become acutely conscious of at times like these) feels to me like growth. I feel that I have grown, while they have just grown older.

What is growth? What is my growth? How does it appear from the outside, from the point of view of another? Do I experience my growing? Or do I only see a difference, say, between old and more recent pictures of myself and conclude that I have changed. Indeed, I have heard tape recordings of my speech and seen moving pictures of myself taken several years ago; and seeing how I looked and sounded makes me almost nauseous. I don't recognize myself as the source of those impressions. I experience myself from the outside, and can't recapture the "feel" of the person I was. Yet at times I have undergone some engrossing experience and, in a flash, realize that I am changed. I experience myself and the world in new dimensions, as if a veil has been suddenly lifted.

What is the essence of this change? Is it growth? What brings it about? Can I help it along, or hinder its occurrence? Can another person bring it on? Prevent it? In this chapter, I am going to speak of growth from an "inside" point of view, of the growth of experience and the changed experiencing that is growth. There are many accounts available about growth as it appears on the outside, as recorded by instruments or by scientific observers, but few about growing awareness. Since I *am* my awareness, an account of growing, changing awareness must at the same time be an account of my growth.

Growth is the disintegration of one way of experiencing the world, followed by a reorganization of this experience, a reorganization that includes the new disclosure of the world. The disorganization, or even shattering of one way to experience the world, is brought on by new disclosures from the changing being of the world—disclosures that were always being transmitted, but which were usually ignored.

Being Is Change

Change is in the world. The being of the world is always changing. My body is in the world, and it changes from instant to instant. Things and other people are in the world; and they metamorphose, swiftly or ever so slowly. I may not be aware of the change that *is* the world. The world-for-me may not appear to change; but rather it may seem congealed, constant, fixed. I may also experience my own being as unchanging.

In fact, people *strive to construct* a stable world, a world they can control and get their bearings in. A view of the world exclusively as constant is an achievement—a *praxis,* not a "given." A naïve view of the world sees it as *both* a "buzzing, blooming confusion" and as stable and "structured." We simply cannot navigate in a world that changes swiftly. And so we "freeze" it by pledging not to notice change until it has reached some critical degree, until it has gone so far it can no longer be ignored. Then, we might acknowledge it. If everything changed during the night, and you awakened to a new experience of yourself and the world, you might be terrified. But if suddenly, the world froze, so that as everything now is, it would remain for eternity, you would be horrified. It would be hell—a hell of perfect predictability and boredom.

The disclosure of change is going on all the time. Change is *experienced,* however, only at moments. The awareness of change is frequently the experience of *surprise:* the "unexpected" has just been presented to us.* The world, or my own bodily being, is not as I had believed it to be. My expectations about being, my concepts and beliefs about the world, have just been disconfirmed. The awareness that things are different is not growth, though it is a necessary condition of growth. A growth *cycle* calls for (a) an acknowledgment that the world has changed, (b) a shattering of the present experienced "world-structure," and (c) a restructuring, retotalization, of the world-structure which encompasses the new disclosure of changed reality.

The retotalization of experience which consummates a growth cycle happens when a person sets goals and projects for himself, when he envisions a possibility and sets about trying to bring it to fruition. In fact, the growth cycle is often tripped off by a *failure* in goal-seeking. As one sets about trying to make or do something, he finds that his initial concepts and beliefs about what and how things *are,* are false. They do not ground accurate predictions about the world and oneself.[48,94] Faced with failure, he must then suspend his present beliefs and let the world disclose itself to him as it *now* is. If he does this, he can revise his concepts and get on with his project.

* Psychologists will note the relation of the present phenomenological theory of growth to Festinger's (1957) considerations of "cognitive dissonance." "Balance" theories, as well, as in Heider (1958) or Secord and Backman (1965), also bear upon this question. Shaw's (1966) concept of "upended expectations" is a cognate term, and Kelly's (1955) dialectic of "construing" and reconstruing of experience is likewise related. Murphy's (1947) and Werner's (1948) formulations of the stages in perception, from the global and undifferentiated, through the differentiated, to the integrated or unified stage, is a relevant theoretical formulation of growth, taken over from biological views of physical growth. Finally, the dialectic as formulated by Hegel and Marx, and reformulated by Sartre in phenomenological terms (1960, 1963), and expounded by Laing and Cooper (1964), provides a framework within which the present chapter may be viewed.

A growth cycle can also be triggered when goals and projects turn stale; when money can no longer buy anything that the person wants; when the fame that was once the person's glory has turned to ashes; and when the love of that woman, long-pursued, is now experienced as cloying, suffocating possessiveness. The lack of fulfillment when long-enjoyed goals are achieved signifies, however indirectly, that *our personal being* has changed, unnoticed by us. Our *concept of ourselves,* as the person who would be fulfilled by this pleasure or be made happier by that "success," *has gotten out of touch with the reality of our being.* We are in for some surprises. The boredom signifies the imminence of growth. The time is ripe for the experience of new goals, and new unfoldings of our being. It is time to let the world and ourselves disclose their being to our experience. We may undergo this new experience (if we let it happen) in delight, or in the terrifying realization that we are going out of our minds.

The world is full of Being, of many beings—some human, some animal, some inanimate. Being has many forms. Every being in the world can be likened to a kind of broadcasting station, transmitting signals of its being to other beings in the world. This transmission is ceaseless. As people and things and animals exist, they change; and they broadcast the fact of this change into the world. You and I are both beings, but beings of a special kind. We have (or are) awareness. We are embodied consciousnesses. We experience the transmissions that originate in our bodies; and through our bodies, we experience some of the transmissions of being that originate elsewhere.

As human beings, we originate transmissions of our being, and we receive transmissions from other beings. My being discloses itself to me—I experience my own being—and it is disclosed to you through my appearance and behavior. *My* experience of *my* being is different from *your* experience of *my* being. And my experience of the being you disclose to me differs from your experience of your own being.

Our Concepts "Freeze" the World and Blind Us

Man is a *concept-maker.* He forms *concepts* of the being of the world, and of his own self-being. A concept is an abstraction from what *is.* From a phenomenological and existential perspective, *a concept is a commitment to stop noticing the changing disclosures (dis-*

closures of change) *incessantly being transmitted by the beings in the world.** When I identify something as a cow, I rubricize it. I let it disclose enough of its being for me to classify it into the category *cow*. Then, I stop receiving, though the cow hasn't stopped sending. It is a cow. It is this very cow, Bossie. Bossie is that cow which presents itself to me as black and white, of the kind "Holstein," with a big chip flaked off her left front hoof. I "know" Bossie. I can anticipate what she will do, on the basis of her past disclosures to me and my awareness of these disclosures. I can get milk from Bossie. She will kick me if I approach her from the right side. And so on. But Bossie is continually changing, and these changes are continually revealed to the world. So long as I think of Bossie as I always have, I ignore these disclosures. I address Bossie as if she has not changed. Indeed, for the purposes I pursue in my transactions with Bossie, these changes may not make any difference, until enough change has occurred that my predictions about Bossie are not borne out, and my purposes are thwarted. I start milking Bossie, and no milk comes. I say, "Something's wrong. Bossie is different. She has changed. She is not the Bossie I knew." Of course she isn't. She never was. No sooner did I form a *concept* of Bossie (stop perceiving her disclosures) than it was out of date. When I say, "Bossie has changed," all I am doing is belatedly acknowledging a change that has been inexorable and continuous. For my purposes (getting milk out of her), she did not change. When my purposes were thwarted, I was forced to expand my awareness of Bossie, to suspend my concept of her being, and to let her being address me. My concept of Bossie (which terminated my perception of the multiple disclosures of her changing being) enabled me to fulfill my milking project. When the project was stymied, my concept became perceptibly incongruent, out of date with the actuality of Bossie's being. In fact, if I propose some new projects that involve Bossie, I may find that my concept of her being requires revision. I may wish to enter her in a race. I believe she is a fast runner and can win me a prize. I test her—I put her in a situation where she can

---

* Gendlin's [24,25] formulations have strongly influenced the present exposition. His analysis of personality change is of the most far-reaching theoretical and practical significance, in my opinion.

disclose her running ability. I find her slow. My concept of Bossie's being must now include the assertion that "she is slow."

Growing, Suspended Concepts, and the World's Disclosure-to-Me

Enough of cows, and enough of Bossie. I am going to contend that when my concepts—of myself, of you, of cars, of cows, of trees, and of refrigerators—are shattered, and I again face the world with a questioning attitude; when I face the being in question and *let it disclose itself to me* (it always was disclosing, but I paid it no attention after I conceptualized it); and when I re-form my concept on the basis of this newly received disclosure—then, *I have grown.* I will suspend my concepts when my projects in life (which depend on accurate concepts of reality for their fulfillment) are thwarted, when my predictions about how things will act or react prove wrong. Then, if I adopt the attitude of "let the world disclose itself to me," I will receive this disclosure and change my concepts; and I will have grown.

My concepts of being can change under more pleasant circumstances than failure. In those rare moments when I have gratified all of my urgent needs—I have done my work, I feel good and fulfilled, and I want nothing out of the world just now—then the world will disclose all kinds of new faces to me. I am letting the world "be itself, for itself." I may then notice all kinds of things about my friends, trees, the sky, animals, whatever is there; things that call upon me to enlarge my previous concepts of those same beings. Thus, success and gratification can be psychedelic (consciousness-expanding). They can open up my world for me and let me experience it in new dimensions.

You may notice that I appear different from the last time you saw me. My behavior and my verbal disclosures will show a change to you. You will say of me, "He has changed, he has grown." You will have to modify your concept of me at that time. *If you do, then you will have grown.* Your action toward me will reflect your changed concept of me, your changed experience of me. And I shall then say to you, "You have changed; you have grown." You will feel confirmed in your being. You will feel understood; you will feel that the disclosure of your changed being—in words and actions—has been received and acknowledged by me.

I have a certain concept of my being, of myself. This is my *self-concept*. It is my belief about my own being. My being discloses itself to me in the form of my intentional experience of myself. I experience the feel of my body's existence. I experience my own action from the inside. I form a concept of myself—what I am like, how I react, what I am capable of and what I cannot do—on the basis of this self-experience. You may also tell me what and who you think I am, on the basis of your experience of the outside of my being; and I take your belief into account. We may agree that I am thus and such a kind of person—a man, a psychologist, kind, strong, able to play a fair game of handball, unable to sing in key, etc. Once I have formed this concept of who and what I am, I proceed to behave in the world as if that is all and everything I am or can be. My behavior, my self-disclosure, endlessly confirms my self-concept. It is as if I have taken a pledge to present this and only this as my being.[26]

In fact, my being, like all Being, *is change*. This change discloses itself to me through my experience and to others through my behavior. But if you and I have formed a concept of my being, neither of us pays attention to the ceaseless transmission of my changing being. It is transmitted, but no receiver is tuned in to acknowledge the change. Things can get more complicated. I may notice the changes, and change my concept of myself accordingly. You may not notice the changes. You treat me as if I were the same person. I do not recognize myself as the one you believe I am. I feel you are talking to somebody else, not me.

Or, you may notice the changes before I do, and change your concept of me accordingly. Again, I may not recognize the "me" that you seem to be addressing. Your concept of me is disjunctive from my self-concept.

Or, I may display and disclose the newly experienced facets of my being to you. You may say, "I don't recognize you. You are not yourself today. I don't like the person you seem to be. I'll come see you when you have gotten back into your 'right mind.'" If you thus disconfirm my newly experienced and tentatively disclosed being, and if I am unsure of myself, I may try to suppress and repress my newly emerged being and seek to appear to you and to me as the person I *was.* If I do this chronically, and successfully, I enter an untenable situation; and I may become mad.[54]

Growing and the Modes of Experiencing

There is also another way in which I might grow through a relationship with you. I may have a fixed concept of you and hence behave toward you in an habitual, stereotyped way. My action toward you is predictable. I always become aggressive in your presence. I experience you as a source of harm to me; and I attack first, to protect myself. My concept of you is that you are menacing, that you harbor ill will toward me. *When I experience you, I may not be undergoing a perceptual experience, but rather an imaginative experience of your being.* I tune out your disclosed being, and I replace it by an imaginative experience.[88] Or a fantasy[54] experience. Imagination veils perception. In fact, much of our experience of the people in our lives, even when they are face-to-face with us, is *not* perceptual, but *imaginative,* or fantastical.*

The perceptual mode of experiencing entails the readiness to receive inputs of disclosure from the other, such that one's awareness of the other is a changing awareness. But the imaginative and fantasy modes of experiencing "tune out" fresh disclosures. My image of you remains fixed, unchanged by your disclosures, because I do not pay them any attention. Now, if you can break through my imaginative experience, or my fantasy image, of you; if you can catch my attention, by a shout, a blow, a scream of pain or joy—I may, as it were, "wake up" from my daydream-like experience of your being and undergo a fresh perceptual experience of you. You will surprise me. If you do this, if you get me "un-hung" from fixation on these modes of experiencing you—the imaginative and the fantasy modes—so that I can now perceive you, I shall have grown. My consciousness of you will have expanded. My awareness will have grown; and where I had previously been aware of you only as an image or a concept (though I wasn't *reflectively* aware that this was an image), now I

---

* Laing's (1961) analysis of fantasy as a mode of experience is a contribution to phenomenology of high importance. He shows what Freud's "unconscious" is like as it is embodied in our conscious experience of the world.

can experience you perceptually. If my consciousness expands so that I can experience you or the world in many more modes than I could hitherto—imaginatively, perceptually, recollectively, in the mode of fantasy—then I have grown. I *am* my awareness; and if my awareness expands, *I* have grown.

My world of awareness may not only be fixed in one *mode* of experiencing, e.g., the abstracting, conceptual mode or the imaginative mode; my world may also be confined to some one or two sensory "channels" of awareness. For example, I may limit my clear awareness only to visual and auditory impressions and exclude the worlds of smelling, tasting, or the feel of my own body. If you can turn me on to my feelings, to smells, to tastes; if you can wake up my imagination; if you can get me to experience the feel of my body—you will have expanded my awareness and helped me to grow. You could caress me (cf. Sartre,[86] pp. 389–391) out of my "mind" and into my experience of my body (see also Chapter 12).

Growth Through Suspension of Self-Concept and Self-Consciousness

If I, from time to time, suspend my concept of myself and "tune in" on my being, if I meditate or reflect on my experience, then I must re-form my self-concept. I shall believe myself to be different. I shall act differently. I *am* different. Moments of meditation are the times (rare in our culture) when we try to let the changing flux of our being disclose itself to us.[51,63] If we learn how to do it or let it happen, meditation can give us the *experience* of transition in our being and can yield transitional experiences.[94] In meditation, too, we let the world disclose more of its changing being to us; and we may find ourselves experiencing more of the variety in the world.

But meditation is not the only occasion when our self-concepts are put into question and temporarily suspended. Whenever we are unselfconscious, whenever our attention is fully focused upon some task or some project, our being changes; and our changing experience of our changed being goes on spontaneously. We let our personal being *happen*. We do not try to monitor and control it so that it conforms to a concept, yours or mine, of my being. Fascinated engagement at *anything* can let change happen and be experienced such that the next time I reflect upon myself, I find my experience of myself different from how I remember it the last time I reflected. And my concept of myself will have to change to encompass the new experiencing I have undergone. Challenge, fascination, total involvement in some task or project such that self-consciousness and self-conceptualizing is *not* the mode of experience, will permit the changed self-being to be experienced.

Growth Through Dialogue

If I engage in conversation with you, in dialogue; and if you disclose your experience of yourself and of me to me in truth; and if I receive your continuing disclosure; and if I disclose my experience of myself and of your disclosures to you in truth—*then I must be letting change happen* and be disclosed to us both. If I reflect upon my experience of the dialogue, I must notice that I am different from the way I was when we began the dialogue. But if I have (as it were) pledged myself to appear before you and to myself as *this* kind of man and no other, then my intentional disclosures to you will be very selective. Perhaps I will lie to you, to preserve your present concept of me, or at least *my* concept of *your* concept of me. Indeed, if my pledge of sameness is made to myself, then every time my *actually* changed being discloses itself to me, I will become threatened and repress it. I will pretend to myself I did not have the experience of hatred, or of anxiety, or of lust. And I will believe my own pretense to myself. Then, I shall not grow. My concept of myself will become increasingly estranged from the ongoing change of my being. If my self-concept is too discrepant from actuality, the disclosure to me of my changed being will become more insistent. I will then have to pretend and repress much harder. If the change is too great, the experience of change will no longer be repressible. It will declare itself in my experience and perhaps in my behavior; I may become terrified and feel I have "gone out of my mind." Actually, I have, if by "mind" we mean "self-concept." If still I insist on trying to appear to you as the same person I was, I may develop neurotic symptoms. Or if I am terrified enough, I may become psychotic.

Growth and Your Experience of Me

You can help me grow, or you can obstruct my growth. If you have a *fixed* idea of who I am and what my traits are, and what my possibilities of change are, then anything that comes out of me beyond your concept, you will disconfirm. In fact, you may be terrified of any surprises, any changes in my behavior, because these changes may threaten your concept of me; my changes may, if disclosed to you, shatter your concept of me and challenge you to grow. You may be afraid to. In your fear, you may do everything in your power to get me to un-change and to reappear to you as the person you once knew.

But if you suspend any preconceptions you may have of me and my being, and invite me simply to be and to disclose this being to you, you create an ambience, an area of "low pressure" where I can let my being happen and be disclosed, to you and to me simultaneously —to me from the inside, and to you who receive the outside layer of my being.

If your concept of my being is one that encompasses more possibilities in my behavior than I have myself acknowledged; if your concept of my being is more inclusive and indeed more accurate than my concept of my being, and if you let me know how you think of me; if you let me know from moment to moment how you experience me; if you say, "Now I like you. Now I think you are being ingratiating. Now I think you can succeed at this, if you try"; if you tell me *truly* how you experience me, I can compare this with my experience of myself, and with my own self-concept. You may thus insert the thin edge of doubt into the crust of my self-concept, helping to bring about its collapse, so that I might re-form it. In fact, this is what a loving friend, or a good psychotherapist, does.

There is another way you can help me grow and that is through challenging me and encouraging me to attempt new projects. We actually construe and conceptualize the world and ourselves in the light of the projects we live for. It is our commitment to these which structures our worlds. The beings in the world, including our own being, reveal different faces of themselves to us, depending upon the projects we are pursuing at the moment. The trees in the forest reveal their timber footage to the lumber merchant, the bugs in their trunks to the insect-collector, and their colors to the painter. My muscular strength or weakness reveals itself to me as I try to chop the forest down, and I form a concept of my muscular strength. I may never come to question or doubt this estimate I made. My self-concept gets frozen if my projects are frozen, and if I become too adept and skilled at fulfilling them.

Suppose, when I find my existence dull and boring, I decide to try some new project—to write a book, climb a mountain, change jobs. I tell you of this, at first, faint resolve. I am afraid to try, because, as I presently think of myself, I don't believe I have the capacity to succeed. If you encourage me to try and encourage me and support me when the going gets rough, so that I stick with the project with more and more singlemindedness, I discover in myself transcendent powers I never experienced before and never imagined I had. I do not and cannot transcend my *possibilities;* I don't know what these are and won't know until I stop living. I only transcend my *concept* of what my possibilities might be. You can help me transcend my self-concept by challenging and supporting me in new projects that I undertake.

Even the decision to *attempt* something new results in a new experience of myself and the world, *before* I actually get going. If I decide to start a new book, I begin to experience friends as interferences in this project; movies and television, formerly very inviting, become dull and boring. The whole world and my experience of myself change with the change in projects. If you help me give up old projects that are no longer satisfying, delightful, or fulfilling and encourage me to dare new ones, you are helping me to grow.

Contemplation, Meditation and Growth

You can help yourself grow if you will engage in aimless contemplation and meditation. To contemplate the world before you, in its visual, auditory, olfactory, and tactual dimensions means simply to let the world present itself to you. You are not searching for anything when you contemplate. Rather, you are letting the world disclose itself to you as it is *in itself.* You can do this only when you suspend your work, your striving, your goals and projects. When you suspend your projects in this way, you open the "doors of perception," and let birds, trees, other people, in fact everything disclose itself to you. All these beings always were, but you didn't notice so long as you were involved in some task or mission. Such contemplation yields a different experience of the world, which must change your concepts of the world, and it thus fosters growth. Maslow (pp. 109–118)[62] has described such contemplation as "B-cognition," and has pointed out that it has dangers as well as delights. The dangers, of course, are that one might simply revel in the sheer beauty of evil rather than do something about it. But it cannot be gainsaid that contemplation of the world in this aimless way enriches experience.

Instead of gazing upon the world and letting it disclose itself to you through your eyes, ears, nose, and hands, you can meditate upon your own experience of your bodily being. Perhaps close your eyes, or seek a tranquil setting with no sudden distractions. Let your experience happen without direction. Engage in free reverie. You may find yourself now recalling something of the past, now vividly imagining—in playful ways—all kinds of possibilities. You may find yourself experiencing anger for somebody, love for somebody else, you may find you have aches and pains you hadn't noticed before. Some of your self-experiencing may be frightening. It may help you to meditate if, instead of closing your eyes, you gaze with or without fixed focus at a mandala, or a flower. If you gaze long enough, your experiencing may turn on fully and freely. Instead of being frozen into some one mode of experiencing—say, perceiving, or imagining, or remembering—which may be customary for you, you may find that you become "unglued" and then integrated. You experience perceptions fused with memories fused with imagination fused with conceptualizing fused with fantasy fused with emotion. This richness may truly shatter your self-concept, so that when you "pull yourself together," you are truly a different person from the person you thought you were.

As I said before, your being and mine are always in process of change, in consequence of the way we live, the passage of time, and sheer past experience. But living as we do mostly at a conceptual level and for definite projects—dealing, not with concrete things, but with *concepts* of things and people and of ourselves—we reflect quietly upon our awareness of ourselves, we suspend the concepts, and we let our being disclose itself to us. And thus we grow.

Growing Out of Our Minds

Growing entails going out of our minds and into our raw experience. Our experience is always of the disclosure of the world and of our own embodied being. When we function smoothly, habitually, and effectively in the world, our concepts are confirmed; and we do not receive new disclosure. When we meet impasses and failure in the pursuit of our projects, then our habits, concepts (a habit can be seen as the "outside" of a concept), and expectations are challenged, or upended.[94] Failure of our projects gives us a whiff of the stink of chaos, and this can be terrifying. Our concepts get cracks in them when we fail. Through these cracks, the encapsulated experience "contained" by the concept might leak or explode; or through the crack there may occur an implosion of more being. When there are no concepts, there is nothing—no-thing we can grapple with, get leverage on, in order to get on with the projects of living. There is the threat of pure chaos and situationlessness. If we experience the pure nothingness, we become panicked, and seek quickly to shore up the collapsing world, to daub clay into the cracks in our concepts. If we do this, we don't grow. If we let the concepts explode or implode and do not re-form them veridically, we appear mad, and are mad. If we re-form them, to incorporate new experience, we grow.

Once again, we must consider projects, this time in relation to *integration,* a vital and crucial phase of growth. When our projects are obstructed, because our concepts are out of phase with being, the concepts must explode, or become fractionated, differentiated into parts. We experience chaos. Our commitment to the old projects, or recommitment to new projects, serves as the field of force which organizes the fractionated experience of being into meaningful wholes, concepts, gestalten. Growth is our experience of our concepts and percepts being detotalized and then retotalized into newly meaningful unities.

I know I am ready to grow when I experience surprise—a dissonance between my beliefs and concepts and expectations of the world and my perception of the world.[16] I am also ready to grow when I experience boredom, despair, depression, anxiety, or guilt. These emotions inform me that my goals and projects have lost meaning for me; that my being has gotten too big, too out of phase with my concepts of my being. I have a choice at these moments, if indeed I can experience them. I may have become so unaccustomed to and maladept at reflection and meditation that I simply don't notice these all-is-not-well signals. And I continue to pursue my projects and to believe my beliefs as if experience were confirming them.

But if I do acknowledge the signals, my choice is either to meditate, suspend my concept and preconception of self, and let my changed being disclose itself to me, even when it hurts (it frequently does); or to decide to affirm the project of being the same (an impossible project, but one that many people try to live). If I decide to try to be the same, then I will repress my experience of change, of all-is-not-well signals. I have resolved, really, to stop perceiving myself.

The invitation to suspend preconceptions and concepts, to let being disclose itself, is actually an invitation to go out of one's mind. To be out of one's mind can be terrifying; because when projects are suspended, and experiencing is just happening, myself and the world are experienced as infinite possibility: anything might be possible. Since nothing *definite* is possible, purposeful action is *im*possible. Yet, if a person can endure this voyage within his own experience—his Odyssey within—he can emerge from it with a new concept of his being and with new projects; the new concept of being will include more of his being in it. But this new integration will last only so long, and then the entire process must be repeated again. A sentient life is an endless series of getting out of one's mind and concepts, only to re-enter and to depart again.

Surprise and Growing

The experience of surprise is a sign of one's readiness to grow. Amazement and wonder signify that one's concepts of self and of the world and of other people are "loose," ready to be re-formed. The "know-it-all," the "cool" one, has pledged himself never to be surprised. Everything that the world discloses is no more than an unfolding of what he has expected and predicted, or so he tries to convey to others. But when a man can be dumbfounded and surprised at what comes out of him or at what his friend or spouse is capable of doing and disclosing, he is a growing person.

In fact, if I intentionally adopt the "set" that all of my concepts are tentative and provisional, I invite others, myself, and the world to reveal surprisingly new facets of their being to me, so that even my daily life can be an unfolding of newness, where simply perceiving the world or the self is a source of endless variety and surprise.

If I am with you, and I have willfully adopted the set that I do not know and cannot ever fully know all your possibilities, my very presence embodies an invitation to you to surprise me, to show off, to transcend your (and my) previous concepts of your being. I can tell when I am in the presence of a person with a closed mind. I feel constrained to shut off most of my possibilities. But in the presence of a wonder-er, I feel an absence of prejudgment, a permissive acceptance; and my terror and self-consciousness about revealing surprises is diminished.

In short, if you and I retain our capacity for surprise, we aid and confirm one another's growth.

Psychedelic Drugs and Personal Growth

There are many ways to "turn experiencing on," whether we are speaking of perceptual awareness in any of the sense modalities; imagination; remembering; or fantasy. I've mentioned the opportunities for this to happen in dialogue, in failure at projects, in boredom, and in fascination. The psychedelic drugs have this power to turn a person on, probably by (somehow) disengaging him from any and all attachments and projects in the "outer" world. This drug-induced liberation from attachments destructures the world of experience and permits all kinds of experiential changes to happen. The world gets unglued and destructured from its usual forms. I shall describe one such experience now, in illustration of some of the points I made earlier.

On the occasion of which I write, I was in the company of a physician who had himself, many times, taken the psychedelic trip. He was my guide and teacher. I took the dose of the drug in a shot glass of water and sat chatting with the others, fellow travelers. Before long, I began laughing—it was a gigantic joke, a hoax, but the laugh was on me. Everything I could see or hear or think seemed so arbitrary and unnecessary and it could have so easily been diffierent. I could have been somebody else. There seemed no necessary reason why things fell when they were dropped; why not float, or scoot off sideways? Then, I noticed the wire of the telephone receiver, close to my hand. A dim beam of light fell upon it, and it had an exquisite and fascinating iridescence. It seemed to give off a ruby glow. (Ordinarily, I am rather color-blind, or insensitive to subtle variations in hues.) I spent what seemed eons of time holding the cord, dangling and twisting it, fascinated with each new configuration that was produced. I felt as if veils had been lifted from my eyes, ears, nose, skin, and my sense of my own body. Sounds from the street would catch my attention, and it was as if I was truly hearing for the first time, as if wax stoppers had been removed from my ears. Everything was as important as everything else. I would note the feel of the chair against my backside, or the texture of a desk-top, and nothing else existed. Odors, tastes, the sight of the flames in the gas fire—each of these presented itself to me, and I would note them, become them: my consciousness *was* these things and was *of* these things.

Perhaps an hour might have passed, by earthly time. I found myself flipping from the perceptual mode of experiencing to the imaginary mode. I could imagine something, and my image was as real as any perception. At a whim, I could transform my image of a person into a dog, cat, or locomotive; and each was as real as any perception.

Then I was truly swept away on a journey back through time. I experienced the sound of the song, "Ramona, I see you by a waterfall." Peculiar faces I couldn't then recognize, of very demure dandies, with fedora hat, bow tie, and devilish looks in their eyes, appeared and then disappeared. A phrase was uttered by somebody, some baby-talk gibberish I couldn't decipher. I experienced a period of my childhood, perhaps when I was two—a precocious peanut of a child, sentient, but regarded as a doll, like the midget in Gunter Grass' novel, *The Tin*

Drum. The dandies were the teen-agers of the late 1920s—my older brother and his friends and an older cousin, who, when praised for their neat garb, would make a certain coy gesture. The song, "Ramona": my mother would put me on the counter of our store and ask me to sing that song, "Ramona, I preshoo kanishiks"—and that was the babytalk. The elephants' legs: fat women in the store, me reaching to their knees, they in short dresses, stocking-tops turned down.

But I didn't stop there—I meaning my experience. From time to time, I would experience what I thought was the universe—a spiral wave of nothingness that would move in a spiral path, cast itself into a configuration that I felt was the being of a whole millennium; then it would fold back on itself, only to flow again to cast out another, higher way for the world, the people, to be. I heard a ghostly laughter, howling about what a joke it was to end one configuration—that everyone in it thought was God's plan—only to have it washed out of existence to be replaced by another.

In one of these moments of the universe's movement, I became a lion. I felt my claws tense—front paws and back; my mouth curled involuntarily into a snarl, that became a strangled gargle, finally to be released as a full-throated roar. The release of the roar was one of the most satisfying, and I think integrating, experiences of my life. I felt myself extending from my center right out to the edges of my body, perhaps filling it and living it for the first time. It is, I can assure you, a magnificent experience to feel your toes as your own, like talons, and as an integral part of yourself, rather than those little nubs experienced as "way down there."

From time to time, I would flip back into the mode of perception, and experience the world outside my own skin. It was constantly changing appearance, as if the edges of things—which ordinarily confined and contained their being—became waxy or actually ruptured, so that the insides were disclosed.

Several hours later, I and my fellow voyagers began to surface. It was like an experience of being reborn or reincarnated. At midnight, we went to a nearby Cypriot restaurant—a psychiatrist, a social worker, a writer, a young physician, and myself. We ate as if for the first time. The feel of jaws and teeth rending meat and bread was exquisite.

Psychedelic Drugs: "Not for Everybody"

The various consciousness-expanding drugs are the subject of keen interest to laymen and to scientists at the present time.[7,58] College students, artists and writers perk up when they hear of personal narratives of a psychedelic trip. Psychiatrists, psychologists, and pharmacologists conduct experiments with LSD-25, mescaline, psylocybin, morning-glory seeds, marijuana, peyote buttons, and anything else that reportedly turns one on. Some psychiatrists include psychedelic drugs as part of their psychotherapeutic armamentorium, using it and sometimes abusing it as a cure-all. I would like to consider here some implications of psychedelic drugs for personal growth and for personal disintegration.

I have said above that a person's consciousness expands whenever he lets more of the possible disclosure of the world reach his perceptual "field," and when he allows his capacities for remembering, imagining, fantasy, thinking, and bodily-experiencing to be activated and admitted to consciousness. Many events and factors can produce such a turn-on of consciousness, as sages and mystics have long known. Thus, the disciplines undertaken by the yogis, the exercises and rituals of the Sufis and of the Jewish mystics, the meditations of the Zen master, all are means that have been adopted in the past to lift consciousness out of its usual rubrics and limits. The Indians who ingest peyote and those who attain ecstatic levels of consciousness through wine or other alcoholic beverages attest the fact that man has always sought to transcend his usual consciousness, and that he has had recourse to pharmacological means. Drug users, both of the opiates and of the nonnarcotic varieties, such as hemp, give reports of the alteration of their experience that the drugs induce.[102] The more powerful psychedelic drugs now available simply reveal technological progress in a quest for new experience that is ages old.

The question I would like to address here is, "What are the values and what are the risks that are entailed in attempting to abet growth through the use of drugs?"

The general answer I would offer is that everything depends upon who is doing the drug-taking, what he is taking the drug for, what is his preparation for the experience, and with whom is he involved when he takes the drug. I believe that taking such drugs as LSD or hashish for "kicks" is no more or less harmful than taking a ride on a roller coaster or getting drunk. Taken too often, as an escape from a reality that might be changed with a bit of courage or ingenuity, the drugs can be harmful. I have seen patients who sought help because, after 1, 20 or 50 LSD trips, taken without guidance, they found they were so un-hung from usual values and goals that they couldn't find anything worth doing in this world except contemplate the "suchness" of the world. Such "nonattachment" is seemly for a wise old man preparing for his forthcoming death, but appears premature and unearned in young men—especially when there is much to be done in this world and much to be enjoyed. But I have also seen people in their twenties, or forties, who have enlarged their perspectives and liberated long-dormant capacities of feeling, striving, enjoying, and doing, after an experience produced by a drug. The drugs simply yield an enrichment of, and liberation from, one's usual intentional experience. So does a visit to another country, or a dialogue with a teacher or a psychotherapist. Whether or not this experience is worked through and integrated with the total being of the person seems to depend upon whether the person is prepared to grow. And it also depends upon whether or not the person is involved in a *continuing* relationship with some other person who can function as a teacher or guru, or as a spiritual adviser.

In short, I do not see the psychedelic drugs as an unmitigated blessing or menace. I think it a mistake to assign exclusive regulation of their use to physicians. There is no guarantee that physicians are any wiser in the prescription of these consciousness-releasing agents than, say, a minister would be. In fact, if more ministers were educated men of the world and capable of midwifing a man's growth, I could see sense in having marijuana or LSD available in churches, which could then serve as retreats where a person could go to seek healing and growth. But prayer, meditation, and church ritual can also be psychedelic experiences, as can an inspiring sermon, or a dialogue with a clergyman. Since the drugs yield a powerful experience, and since the young and the ignorant are to be guided and protected by the old and the wise, regulation and "dosing" of experience should be in older, wiser hands. But whose hands? Who are the wise ones, the teachers?

The authenticated reports of serious breakdown and deterioration, and of chromosome damage following the ingestion of LSD or mescaline must be taken into account. Instances with which I am personally acquainted have led me to the tentative conclusion that the people so afflicted were brittle, defensive people, incapable of facing *any* intense experience of change. Hence they were ill-advised to take drugs, just as they might have been ill-advised, say, to live in another culture. They were not prepared: they were not involved in a guiding relationship with a therapist or teacher, or the therapists with whom they were involved were not qualified to help the person through the period when ego-disintegration was taking place.*

* In Chapter 15, I discuss psychedelic drugs further.

14

Experience and Artistic Self-Disclosure

*This chapter could well be subtitled "A phenomenological analysis
of human possibility." It has seemed to me that artists in society embody and disclose possibilities of experiencing that are available to
everyone, but are generally stifled. If every madman is an ineffective
revolutionary, and every sick person is an anarchist who failed, then
each artist who produces art successfully points the way toward new
modes of experience and action. The true revolutionary, who changes
men's minds and spirits, is not the political fanatic or the religious
zealot, but the man who wields the painter's brush or the poet's pencil,
or he who composes and produces sounds no man has heard before.
I presented the remarks in this chapter at a meeting of a seminar called
"Art and Civilization," attended by an invited group of artists, with
a smattering of people from other disciplines.*

The world—Being—discloses itself without surcease. The world discloses itself in forms and patterns and as change. The being of the
world is revealed in splendiferous variety, depending upon the nature
of the "surface" from which it is refracted.*

The world-for-man is a world refracted in human intentional consciousness.[34],[64] This magnificent and mysterious entity, consciousness,
is but little understood. Indeed, it can only be understood by a being

---

* This analysis, like those in the previous chapters of this section, draws
heavily upon the work of Laing and his associates. Laing[57] writes "The
human race is a myriad of refractive surfaces staining the white radiance of
eternity. Each surface refracts the refraction of refractions of refractions. Each
self refracts the refractions of others' refractions of self's refractions of others'
refractions. . . .

"Here is glory and wonder and mystery, yet too often we simply wish to
ignore or destroy those points of view that refract the light differently from
ourselves."

such as itself or by another consciousness; for understanding is given only to human consciousness. Being can be refracted by animals, and by man-made instruments; but understanding of the being revealed to an animal or a machine is possible only if the animal or machine somehow transmits its refraction of the being of the world to a human consciousness. And a consciousness can attain some measure of self-understanding by transmuting itself into a reflective consciousness.

The study of consciousness, at least from a disciplined, scientific standpoint, is still in its infancy. We are still in the descriptive and taxonomic stages, with a crude beginning at experimental analysis of experiential change. I shall draw on the little we now know and suspect about that marvelous being—my consciousness and yours—to discuss art, and its relation to human possibility.

Some Characteristics of Consciousness

Reflection shows that any consciousness of the world is subject to transmutations, which are as miraculous as the alchemical transubstantiation of base metal to gold. The differing modes for anything to appear to someone's consciousness include: the *perceptual* mode—seeing, hearing, tasting, smelling, and touching something. The *recollective* mode refers to man's capacity to re-experience past consciousnesses; we call it remembering. The *conceptual* mode is the name for a "thinking" and abstracting consciousness, the awareness of the acts of thinking about something as one of a kind, and reasoning about it. The *imaginative* mode is the name which refers to an experience of possibility. The *fantasy* mode is a paradoxical form of consciousness, because it is not conscious at the time of its occurrence, except under rare and special circumstances. Yet it is always present as a kind of shadowy background to any and all consciousness-modes.[54] We know of our fantasy consciousness after it has just gone through a detectable change, as when we experience ourselves as empty, sucked dry, following an encounter with a very dependent bore.

Another mode of being-conscious-of-something is the *anticipatory* consciousness: the experience or expectation that something is going to appear in perception, or memory. Probably this is a subclass of imagination.

Construing, or giving-meaning can perhaps be regarded as a mode of experiencing the world, though it seems to be dependent upon the act of reflecting upon one's perception, or other modes for experiencing.

And it is perhaps meaningful to regard the experience of *willing* (trying to make something appear) as a mode of consciousness.

Feeling and emotion may be designated as *qualities* of intentional experience. In a person with a unified consciousness, feelings are fused with every perception, memory, or imaginative act. The person feels alive because he feels. But feelings and emotions arise only when an individual is committed to goals and projects in the world, when events and actions help or hinder his successes. And feelings will be felt only if a person has not excluded them from his consciousness by acts of repression.

Every mode of consciousness is dependent upon the basic, perceptual consciousness. Without inputs of intentional perception, the other modes of experiencing become static and irrelevant as guides to effective mastery of the world and successful adaptation of the self in the world. All modes of experiencing are fed by inputs of the world's disclosure, refracted and detected by the several sensory channels— the eyes, ears, nose, mouth, and skin.

Consciousness of the world's disclosure is always patterned and structured. The pattern and structure of your experienced world is a function of your projects, goals, needs, and values. This means that you and I, chronically pursuing security, wealth, fame, love, or whatnot, are cognizant only of those aspects of the world relevant to the attainment of these ends. To all else, we are effectively blind. It is not strictly true to say we are blind to aspects of the world not relevant to our projects. Rather, the unattended aspects of experience blur into the background of our consciousness. We have a subsidiary consciousness of them rather than a focal awareness (to use Polanyi's[72] apt terms). They are *ground* rather than *figure,* in the language of Gestalt psychology. Thus, the structure of a given mode of consciousness, say, the perceptual or imaginative mode, can be analyzed into its components of the focal awareness—that which is explicitly attended to—and the subsidiary awareness of the background experience.

The possibility of our consciousness functioning in a unified, fully turned-on way is limited by our projects. If attainment of goals is impeded by attention to inputs from some sensory channels, we blot that face of the world out of being. Thus, most of us functionally amputate our noses, our taste buds, and our capacity to feel something when we touch it, because these experiences may divert us from attaining our goals in the world. If our imagination diverts from restless or anxious scanning of the world, as we seek the main chance or the chief danger, then we blot this possibility out of being. And if feelings, or a body-consciousness, diverts from our serious business, then we blot that out. The upshot is that a typical man's consciousness is a distorted, fragmented, disunified being, only half-functional. The fragmentation, compartmentalization, and mutilation of experience is undertaken by a man himself. He effects various praxes upon his experience, such as I've alluded to. For example, he blots some of his consciousness from existence. He separates his experience of his "mind" from his experience of his body, and produces the pernicious and perennial dualism that impedes our attainment of harmony with our world. And by conceptualizing the world, man freezes it. He must attend to constancies, and give them names, else he could not navigate or transact effectively. And many of us repress our feelings, such that perception, recall, or imagination are "cold" and lifeless. Every concept is an abstraction from a more global experiencing of the world; and this means that so soon as something is named, the person stops perceiving it: he closes off his reception of the being's transmission of its essence.

Thus, most of us live in a conceptual world, unrefreshed by new perceptual experiences of the beings we have named. This can get to be a stagnant world, one that sensitive men feel to be suffocating and boring. And because the social world in which we live resists change—for reasons Marx made abundantly clear—we are shaped and socialized, such that our imaginative consciousness becomes crippled. Our feeling-consciousness becomes reduced in intensity and variety. Our willing-consciousness virtually vanishes; and we experience ourselves, not as creatures who live and decide, but as beings lived by social pressures, or glandular explosions. We construct barriers that separate our various modes one from the other, and allow ourselves to experience them serially, never in a unified, simultaneously active way. One minute we perceive; the next minute we imagine; the next we remember; the next we think. There is no reason for us to believe that serialized consciousness is natural, more God-given than unified experience, such as happens to average people in rare moments of ecstasy, in "peak experiences" [62] and in certain drug-induced states, and in so-called mystical or transcendental experiences. Indeed, there is some reason for suspecting that in young children, before they are socialized, a unified consciousness, fully turned-on, is the mode. And in certain madmen and outsiders[112]—those who have "checked out" of the usual social games, or who have somehow escaped complete engulfment by their culture— we can suspect that their consciousness has eluded the fate that the average person is subject to, or has willingly submitted to. The capacity for a specialized consciousness, one usually atrophied in the average man—as in seeing, or imagining, or thinking and reasoning, or feeling—enters into the evolution of that man we call an artist.

The Consciousness of the Artist

The genius in the arts is probably a specialized "experiencer," who from time to time attains to a unified and turned-on consciousness. This is part of the story of what an artist is—a person with an unreduced consciousness, capable of functioning fully in modes unavailable to the average man, and capable of moments, days, or a lifetime in a unified state of consciousness. A producing artist must also be an honest portrayer of his experience—whether it be visual, auditory, kinesthetic, or other kind of experience. One can have an artistic consciousness and be a poor craftsman, unable to transmute a memory, imagination, fantasy, or thought into the possibility of a perceptual, recollective, emotional, or imaginative experience in another person. Unless the artist produces, and produces artfully, he is only an artist in *his* consciousness, an artist-for-himself. He only becomes an artist-for-others when he externalizes his experience, embodies it in some idiom— words, paint, clay, sounds, the movements of the dance.

An artist-for-himself is one who seeks to produce for his reflective awareness a portrayal of his imaginative experience of some aspect of the world. Where others only perceive the world in its relevance to their usual concerns, the artist—detached from such concerns—perceives more and differently from the average person, receiving more of the possible disclosure of the world. And he enriches his perception by unifying it with imagination, memory, and passion. He does not perceive only those aspects one can eat, spend, or use to gratify this need or that. He experiences more of the world-for-itself.

And, since his capacity for imagining has not been socialized out of him, he can perceive in a way that is unified, fused with imagination, memory, feeling, willing, etc. He can have a tasting experience of a vision, a feeling experience of a sound; and he can experience recalled associations and imagine possible variations of what the average man only sees a little of, and calls a woman's hip.

Now, take this artist-for-himself. Let him present the objectifications of his experience in a painting, novel, poem, play, dance, or song. It now becomes part of the being of the world. It can have a being-for-others, whereas before the disclosure it had a being only for the artist himself. Since the artist is part of the world for Others, as they are Other to him, he provides the possibility for these others to experience striking change. Since man can transmit his consciousness to his fellows, and since men seem (unless it is trained out of them) responsive to their fellows as beings like themselves—the disclosure of the artists, which is always metaphor, can affect the consciousness of his audience.

Consciousness appears to be protean. It can assume an infinity of forms and structures. In principle, I can influence your consciousness of the world. I can clearly influence the way you construe[48] or name your consciousness of things and people. I can invite you into the imaginative, recollective, or conceptual modes. I may even be able to reintegrate your fragmented consciousness, and trip off a unification that you may experience with explosive force. I may be able to persuade you to suspend your projects, and simply let the being of the world disclose itself to you playfully, pointlessly, so that your perceptual consciousness is expanded, only to shrink when you once more assume your projects. An artist can affect you in these ways.

It is because an artist is not entirely socialized that he can experience in modes, channels, and intensities not easily available to his fellows. It is because in his being he embodies possible modes of being that could be attained by others, that an artist can be an agent of social change and personal growth for others. Political leaders know this and seek to annihilate or geld artists whose work is inflammatory, threatening to produce new consciousnesses in many people, consciousnesses of themselves and of new possibilities in the world that will produce changed behavior in the world. The politicians want people to behave in ways that won't rock the boat or the prevailing power-structure. Behavior is mediated by consciousness. They have a vested interest in controlling the consciousness of people, so that behavior will remain in the safe, predictable, controllable range.

If an artist, through his disclosed experience, induces a viewer to imagine new possibilities of action; if he broadens and deepens a man's understanding of some aspect of the world; if he alters a man's experience and concept of himself—he is thereby mediating growth of the other. This change in the other will mediate changed behavior—as, voting behavior, interpersonal behavior. This all produces consequences in the social order. If an artist can be invalidated, by being regarded as a madman, then his message may be kept from the world. It likely takes courage to be an artist.

In a way, artists, at least in America as Henry Miller experienced and described it, need a certain measure of protection, if they are to flourish. It's not too farfetched to say that artists experience the world vicariously for the philistine. Just as people with strangled imaginations let the comics, movies, and TV do their imagination for them, so an artist whose work is allocated to the museum and art gallery is doing imagining for others. People go for a titivating peek now and then, only to return to sameness.

If producing and surviving artists are protected, or learn to protect themselves so they can survive and get on with their work, it is also true that the public is somehow shielded from the possible impact of an artist's work on its consciousness. Public education is such as to insure that poetry, painting, drama, and innovations in the novel and dancing will not be sampled. They are the fare of oddballs, snobs, the avant-garde, who are not to be taken seriously by practical men and good fellows who stay busy, as they ought. If an artist's work does see the light of day, it most assuredly reaches the consciousness of only the few. The layman, trained and brainwashed to be suspicious of any innovations in his experience, feels comfortable only with the cliché. His patronage of the arts is limited to TV, *Playboy* pinups, movies, "pop" tunes, and the poetry page of the *Saturday Evening Post,* which is not a magazine calculated to awaken people to enlightenment about their social-economic system.

Take any art form, and ask is it designed to enlarge and stretch human consciousness, or does it function so as to keep people with their experiencing modes and habits confirmed. Look at architecture, automobiles, matchbook covers, the sounds on radio—the media for expression. The artists' consciousness is separated from all these possible sources of encounter with his fellow man, the philistine who is asleep.

An "Invisible Insurrection"

I am reminded here of an ingenious plan outlined by Alexander Trocchi,[103] a British novelist and poet. He has described "Project Sigma, a revolutionary proposal for an invisible insurrection of a million minds." He speaks, not of a political revolution, but of a cultural *coup de monde.* "The cultural revolt must seize the grids of expression and the powerhouses of the mind," as Trotsky seized the railway stations and powerhouses while the police guarded the Kremlin.

> Intelligence must become self-conscious, realize its own power and . . . dare to exercise it. . . . What is to be seized is not an arsenal nor a capital city . . . *but ourselves* (the million or so creative, artistic consciousnesses which presently are in contact with Everyman only through the mediation and monitoring of middlemen—businessmen, politicians, establishment people who insure that only those products of consciousness reach Everyman after they have first been assessed for money-earning power, and political asepsis).

Trocchi continues:

> We . . . reject the idea of a frontal attack. Mind cannot withstand brute force in open battle. It is rather a question of perceiving . . . what are the forces that are at work in the world and out of whose interaction must come to be; and by a kind of mental ju-jitsu that is ours by virtue of intelligence, modifying, correcting, polluting, deflecting, corrupting, eroding, outflank-

ing . . . inspiring what we might call the invisible insurrection. It will come on the mass of men, if it comes at all, not as something they voted for or fought for, but like the changing season.

The Scottish writer goes on to speak of the current problem of "leisure," noting how man has forgotten how to play, and is utterly dependent upon entertainment, no form of which widens his consciousness.

Contemporary man expects to be entertained; . . . art is something of which the majority seldom thinks, except derisively. This sorry state of affairs is unconsciously sanctioned (even fostered, I add) by the stubborn philistinism of our cultural institutions. Museums have approximately the same hours of business as churches, the same sanctimonious odors and silences, and a snobbish presumption in direct spiritual opposition to the vital men whose works are closeted there. What have those silent corridors to do with Rembrandt, and the no smoking signs to do with Van Gogh? . . . Art can have no existential significance for a civilization that draws a line between life and art and collects artifacts like ancestral bones for reverence. Art must inform the living; we envisage a situation in which life is continually renewed (I would say consciousness is continually renewed and expanded) by art, a situation imaginatively and passionately constructed to inspire each individual to respond creatively. . . . We envisage it . . . but it is we, now, who must create it. For it does not exist.

Trocchi points out that the political-economic structure of Western society is such that the gears of creative intelligence mesh with those of power such that creative intelligence is prohibited from initiating anything, and it acts only at the behest of vested interests that are antipathetic toward it. Trocchi suggests that the creative intelligences must have control of their means of expression, by eliminating the brokers.

How to begin?—asks Trocchi. At a chosen moment in a vacant country house not far from London, he proposes to foment a kind of cultural "jam session." Out of this will evolve the prototype of a spontaneous university. The building will be large enough for a pilot group of astronauts of inner space to situate itself, . . . the entire site to allow for spontaneous architecture and eventual town planning.

The adventure, in a capitalist society, must pay. Trocchi envisions an agency to handle all the work of individuals associated with the university. Art is fantastically profitable, but it is not the creators who reap the benefits. An agency founded by the creators and operated by highly paid professionals could harvest new talent long before professional agencies were aware it existed.

He envisions an international organization with branch universities all over the world, near every capital city, autonomous, unpolitical, economically independent. Resident professors will be creators; staff and students international. Membership in one branch entitles one to membership in others, travel being encouraged. The object of each branch is to supercharge the cultural life of each capital city as it promotes cultural exchange internationally, and functions as a nonspecialized experimental school and creative workshop. Each branch serves as the nucleus of an experimental town to which people will be attracted; and after a stay, they will derive a renewed and infectious sense of life. The economic structure would come from commissions on sales of original work; money from patents and applications; retail income from a museum restaurant, music performances, etc.; and fees and gifts and subsidies.

Trocchi concludes:

> The cultural possibilities of this movement are immense, and the time is ripe for it. The world is awfully near to the brink of disaster. Scientists, artists, teachers, creative men of good will everywhere are in suspense. Waiting. Remembering that it is our kind even now who operate, if they don't control, the grids of expression, we should have no difficulty in recognizing the spontaneous university as the possible detonator of the invisible insurrection.

Alexander Trocchi's vision and the beginnings at an action-blueprint seem to me to be prophetic, and even practical. Certainly, if my analysis of the phenomenology of being-an-artist is sound, there must be implications for the growth of persons exposed to art, and repercussions on the structure of society. I think we need to produce and live in a psychedelic world, where other people and the material surroundings have a consciousness-expanding effect upon us, awakening the artist in all of us, unifying our head with our hearts and bodies and our imaginations with our feelings and intellect, and bringing an artistic dimension into everything we do and are. The alternative is to be a turned-off, useful tool, or an impotent, ignored or martyred creator whose creations collect dust.

Part Four

*Some Conclusions and
Prospects for
Humanistic Psychology*

15

The Human Challenge of Automation

In the next moment of history, machine regulated machines will wrest our livelihoods for us. When that moment arrives, we may well not know what to do with ourselves and our time. Man is the only being for whom life poses the existential question most starkly: "What shall I do and be?" So long as he answered, "Live!," for millennia the question was settled; because securing the means for living always commanded the greater part of every man's time and energy. The biblical injunction to observe the Sabbath was epochal because it enjoined man to pause, so he might realize there are other things to do besides work to stay alive, amass power, and indulge senses. But what will happen when every day could be a Sabbath, when work is obsolete, and the prospect of leisure, that abyss of freedom, confronts us? This is freedom at its most dizzying. It is at once a horrifying and challenging future; horrifying because few are ready for leisure and freedom, and challenging because of the promise imminent of a bold leap into as yet unfathomed possibilities of being.

The horror is warranted. Society condemns our "senior citizens" to a residual life sentence of "leisure" as soon as they are sixty-five years old. This liberation from work operates as a rapid death sentence for many. And for still more, release from the experience of feeling useful brings on either the living death of boredom, or the rapid encroachment of gibbering senility in hitherto vigorous men. A friend of mine, a survivor of Hitler's death-camps, visited St. Petersburg one time. The old people he saw shuffling or sitting about the streets reminded him of the "Musselmen" of Auschwitz. They were fatter, to be sure; but the aimless and lifeless expressions of their faces were the same. Next to our prisons and mental hospitals, the retirement centers for those awaiting death are surely American equivalents of concentration camps.

About twenty five hundred years ago, the Greeks lived in a nearly automated society—their work-producing "machines" were slaves and women—and the men produced a flowering of consciousness such as has not existed since. Liberated as they were from the menial chores of producing and distributing goods, men were free to think, imagine, and explore, to perfect themselves in their world. For the Greeks, "original sin" was *lack* of knowledge, not eating from the tree of knowledge. We still have not, today, exhaused all the beginnings they laid down.

Right now, our technology advances inexorably toward near-total automation, and we have responded, not by flights of creative imagination, not by the liberation of our spirits to soar to new heights of possibility, as was true in ancient Greece. We have instead responded by becoming increasingly like our slaves, the machines. We have mechanized more and more our relationships with each other; these become role-bound, boring, far departures from the "swing" of true dialogue. We manipulate ourselves in order to present attractive packages to others. We allow ourselves to be manipulated by advertisers, politicians, salesmen, moviemakers. We routinize our daily round of existence so we will the better fit into timetables for transport from suburb to place of busy-work. We eat, not to nourish and perfect our bodies, but to keep up with Jones, to consume the overproduction of our farms, or to palliate nagging feelings of loneliness. We don't embrace one another in love, despite the liberation permitted by "the Pill"—rather, we fornicate in order to feel, or to feel alive, or to reassure ourselves that we are sexy. We even have our lovemaking scheduled—suburbia on Sunday morning is a place of orgy, after the children are sent off to Sunday school. Our houses are designed for some being other than the human, so little place is there in them for privacy. Every aspect of our lives aims at turning us off, numbing us, so that we will keep our once-born, programmed status in the social system, and not rock boats.

Modern science, in all its specializations, aims at understanding Nature in order to manipulate and control her. This may be fine, for botany, zoology, climatology, physics and chemistry. But the same definition of science, with the same aims, has been extended to the human sciences—especially psychology, but also pedagogy, sociology, political science, economics, and psychiatry. Now no man will consent to be understood, in order to be manipulated and controlled by someone, unless he is mystified and stupefied, so that he doesn't know what is going on. Yet men are being manipulated and controlled daily, and seem unaware that it is going on. Somebody or some institution is playing games with human consciousness, seeking to control it, so that behavior will thereby be controlled, and fit into systems. When man is thus controlled, he has changed in ontological status from person to thing. I submit that this transmutation of man into thing has been going on for a few centuries of western history, but it is continuing today at an accelerated pace.

I'll even indulge a taste for prophecy, and predict that in the next few years, in America, we'll witness a struggle between those who would keep man's consciousness and action to limits that fit a status quo, and those who see in automation the signal for inventing new worlds, for the flowering once again, of human potentialities comparable to the fantastic creativity of ancient Greece. The struggle, as a matter of fact, may be bloody. I hope the champions of human growth in diversity win. I am on that side.

What light might psychology shed on this matter? And what role might schools and universities play in increasing the odds that we will enter a magnificent age of enlightenment rather than an age where each man is even more stringently shaped to roles and statuses that make him useful to the State, but not potentiating of himself in his personal life?

Social Control of Action and Experience

First, a perspective on social systems. These come into being because man cannot live alone. Originally, they are instituted because they seem efficient ways to divide labor, and maximize freedom from want and danger. But then, a struggle for control over goods, wealth and power takes place and some few gain control over the many, by gaining control over wealth and hence the means of socialization. Marx was correct, I believe, in viewing the major institutions of society as means for maintaining the status quo.

The aim of socialization practices, beginning in the rearing of infants, but extending to formal schooling, is so to train people that they will habitually experience and behave in the ways they *must* behave; or so they will be afraid to behave in any way other than those ways which maintain the status quo. Mass media, religion, the law, custom, public opinion, even the healing professions all collude to keep people behaving, and what is even more insidious, experiencing the world in the ways that keep the present social structure intact. Man's highest purpose and duty in America, so it would seem, is to *consume,* so factories won't close down. Advertising insures he will: more money is spent on that means of "shaping" than is spent on education.

If anyone misses being so brainwashed, he is invalidated—encountered with threats and actualities of imprisonment, ostracism, poverty, or hospitalization—unless he is very enlightened, or very cunning.

This is the way societies maintain themselves. This is the way they resist change, whether it be change in national purpose, change in means of production, or changes in class structure.

But when change in the productive base takes place, as is occurring with expanding automation, these ways have become irrelevant and obsolete. A "world" * has truly come to an end, though few realize it.

The "Capsule" We Live In

The world goes on—reality is like a projective test. Man can construe it in myriad ways. The world discloses itself ceaselessly to human consciousnesses, which refract it, and attach meaning to this disclosure in ways that vary from time to time, and place to place. A given world view gains dominance in each society. This is a way to structure the world, to attach value and meaning to it. "Worlds" are structured by projects, or goals and values. Change these and "worlds" collapse, to be replaced by new ones. All this is elementary existential phenomenology.

The "world" most of us in America share is a world that once was haunted by European memories of poverty and material scarcity. The aim was to get rich, and we actually have the productive means available whereby everyone can be rich, at least in a material sense. As au-

---

* The term "world" (in quotes) refers to the world *as experienced* by men or by a particular man.

tomation, powered with nuclear sources of energy proceeds, we can in principle feed, clothe and shelter the world, even a world with a more fully exploded population than the one Malthusian prophets of doom say we now have. Our past and current patterns of childrearing, our aims and methods of schooling, even our ways of playing in leisure hours all gain their relevance and intelligibility from the fact of scarcity —scarcity that long since has ceased to exist. In a way, as we socialize and train to a nonexistent reality, we can say that our very socialization and training is mad. It is akin to training people in the art of stalking, capturing and cooking dinosaurs. The values, skills, ways of relating to others that make up the curriculum of a dinosaur-hunting school somehow lose relevance when there are no dinosaurs to be caught and cooked.

But "worlds" die hard. Each of us lives in a world that I can best liken to an envelope, capsule, or bubble with semi-permeable walls. These walls screen off much of what is, and admit to our consciousness only as much of being as is relevant to our projects. The world beyond the capsule is filled, according to folklore and popular imagination, with bogeymen, cockroaches, slime, and everything hideous. Shatter the membrane, and let this world in, and people become terrified. Rather than face the prospect of posing new projects and values, in order to construct new "worlds," people patch the rents in the walls of their present "world." Seeing becomes a way of being blind, blind to other possibilities that the world embodies.

In America, young people, mature women, and Negroes all are in process of awakening—some with delight, but more with anger, and rage at the dirty joke that has been played upon them. They are breaking out of their capsules. The world is not necessarily what men have told them it is. It has not been ordained by God (if he lives) that Negroes should be stupid, employed in menial tasks, and housed in bedbug infested slums. Nor did God necessarily demand that women should die of boredom and overeating in automated households. And young people—below the age of 18—are wondering if God wants them to put on gray flannel suits to become professional consumers, or to go to Vietnam.

Young people especially, as I encounter them in the halls of training and learning, are beginning to demand inspiration and enlightenment, not stupefaction at the feet of their instructors. They are beginning to look at instructors as *entire men,* not solely as repositories of alienated skill or knowledge, and they are wondering if they want to become like these men. Increasing numbers of young men and women are dropping out. They are finding that the schools and colleges, instead of enlightening them as to how things are now, or turning them on to challenging new projects and possibilities are training them for a slot in professions or corporate enterprise, which support a way of life and experience they find meaningless. And so they turn to marijuana, LSD, and morning-glory seeds for enlightenment, and a kind of travel.

Being Outside the Capsule

There is this to be said for psychedelic drugs—they afford a glimpse to the seeker of the possible world beyond our usual, stripped and de-based image of it. They open Pandora's box. Since we are in it, they let us see outside. They awaken a person's consciousness to possibilities of perceiving, imagining, feeling and remembering that usually lie encrusted under habit, the results of conventional upbringing. Once a person has taken such a "trip," he is never the same.

The drugs seem to work by suspending the "pull" of conventional values and projects upon a person. This is why their widespread use is seen as subversive. This temporary letting go, or detachment yields an ersatz *satori,* or the experience of enlightenment—but with western efficiency. What might have taken an eastern mystic something like 20 years of discipline, asceticism and meditation is achieved in something like 20 minutes, at a cost of 20¢ or $20—truly cheap grace!

But when the drug-traveler returns to home base, he is seldom prepared for what awaits him. The walls of his usual world have been eroded, even rent in places, and more being than he can cope with may be "let in." This may frighten him, if he is unprepared for it. More insidiously, his grip on past projects has been weakened. This may not be such a bad thing, if the projects (like getting rich, or popular, or powerful) are not of his own choosing, but have been inculcated into him. But he usually has no projects, equally compelling, to take the place of those he has lost. And so, he may drift about in a world that explodes with myriad possibilities, none of which feel more important to him than any other. Nothing is worth doing. God (the values of parents) is dead—he was killed with LSD—and boys are left with a man's job: to invest the world with new values and projects when their value-investing apparatus has been rendered anemic by drugs.* And there are no exemplary men around to give witness to the possibility of a challenging, rewarding and meaningful existence guided by projects other than those of becoming a dumping ground for productive output that can't be consumed fast enough.

Psychedelic drugs seem to me to be one of many forms of current protest against the stupefying effect that our socialization has upon man. Man can dissect nature in order the better to control it. He can build machines to work for him. He extends his sense organs and muscles with machinery—but then loses his capacity to see, hear, smell, and move. All these things are done for him, in the name of efficiency, by the very machines he has created.

Not only are the various media—extensions of man, as McLuhan calls them—leaching man of his power; but in order that man might not notice the loss of his wholeness and his creative possibilities, he is stupefied more deliberately. Radio, television, movies, books all help keep man in a stupor. If a person begins to sicken, and suffer boredom, pain, or anxiety—those signs that all is not well in the way he is living his life—the medical profession then steps in with some pharmaceutical product that enables the person to continue living the meaningless life, but without feeling the pain and suffering.

In short, we effect those praxes upon our own consciousness which constrict our world. We repress, distort, close off entire sensory channels, banalize our imaginations, and end up helpless to live in a social and material world we made ourselves, and helpless to change it. We only endure it with the help of booze and tranquilizers.

The use of psychedelic drugs is part of the whole scene. The possibility of an expanded and creative consciousness of the world and ourselves inheres in all of us. But we become alienated from this possi-

---

* Herein lies a challenge for psychological research: What are the conditions and the means by which the *experience* of value arises in a person? What do we know about the parameters of the attribution of value?

bility, in consequence of the way we have been reared. And so we invest drugs and substances with "the power," and the only way we can get this alienated power back is by ingesting 100 micrograms of acid. It's like the joke unenlightened physicians play upon us. They know, or suspect that healing inheres in the organism. Yet they pretend that, without doses of penicillin and assorted wonder drugs, everyone would die shortly after the onset of a sore throat. It's a wonderful way to sell drugs, but probably a debased form of the noble profession of healing (in which medicine holds no true monopoly).

Schools: For Teaching or Training?

The institutions of education are becoming increasingly automated. "Teaching machines" are being incorporated into more schools, as a desperate response to overcrowding and an insufficiency of instructors. Indeed, desperate instructors try to program themselves—their lectures and demonstrations—so that students will be able to blacken the correct spaces on an IBM sheet at the end of a term.

Can you imagine the horror of 5 or 10 thousand people all reading a book in the same way? This is invaluable, if training into pre-set molds and roles is the aim; if individuality, originality and creativity are to be trained out, and uniformity in experience and action is desirable. Indeed, designers of teaching machines could get rich by programming the Bible for a *guaranteed* Methodist, Baptist, Catholic, or Jewish way of reading, and interpreting Scripture.

But this is not education and it is not desirable. Automation will release human energy from the necessity to spend it making goods essential to life. But it will not thereby make life more livable, challenging, and rich in experience. This latter aim calls for *education* —the liberation of human consciousness in its various modes (especially imagination) from the bonds imposed by training. The salvation of man, with the hope he will invent better forms of economic, social, political and interpersonal existence, is education, not training. And education requires teachers, people who awaken and enliven consciousness, not constrain it, like trainers do. Teachers are hard to find. They are as scarce as white whales. Teachers illuminate what is; they are existential explorers, groping for new meanings as they challenge old ones. They are not solely repositories of a skill or corpus of information.

The most powerful psychedelic agent known to man is not lysergic acid, as is so commonly believed. Two more powerful are travel to another land, there to be involved. The other is the awakened consciousness of another human being. Both psychedelic agents may be subversive. This is why travel to some lands is prohibited. And this is why Socrates was given the hemlock and Jesus the cross. Here I'd like to focus upon the self-disclosure of awakened men—teachers. According to this view, a teacher is a man who has been awakened from the illusion that there is only one sane, right and legal way to experience the world and behave in it. He has become "turned on" such that his imagination is vivid. He can perceive the world as others see it, and more: liberated from convention as he is, he sees what others are blind to. The walls of his capsule have been shattered, and rebuilt so that more world is included in his consciousness. He feels, thinks, imagines, and remembers more fully than the average man. He can, perhaps, dance, feel his body, move it and live in it, a Zorba-esque man among nebbishes. Or perhaps he has only a glimmering of other possibilities to which he will be led through his dedication to the beauty that inheres in Latin grammar, or amoebae swimming in slime on a microscope slide (all paths to glory are good).

If such a man, a teacher, discloses the wonder of life as it is for him to pupils, some will indeed "flip." They will be turned on. Their old "world" will explode, or better, implode, when more being is admitted, under the guidance of the teacher.

If this teacher is himself committed to responsibility for some corner of the world—not for money and fame, but for authentic concern and love—then his pupils may be ready to take over when he dies, or extend his vision and responsibility while he still lives.

Where do we find such teachers? How can we disseminate their expanded consciousness of some aspect of the world? It is for the lack of such teachers that young people go to pot or acid. Teachers of this kind are needed more, today, than another cadre of astronauts, or more riot police, psychiatrists, narcotics agents or school counselors.

We are the equals of the Nazis, the communists and the Chinese, at training, mystifying, and stupefying masses of people. We have the possibility, through TV and other media, of getting even better at it. But we also have the possibility of turning on and awakening more people to expanded perspectives on the world, new challenges, possible ways to experience the world and our own embodied being, than has ever been possible before. I don't believe that there is an insoluble educational crisis before us. *I believe rather that we need to sort out our values, to see if we are as serious about educating our population as we have been about training them for the status quo.* If, beginning with the president's office in Washington, a serious dedication to human awakening was awakened, with appropriate budget appended, a fantastic revolution would have thereby been commenced. But such seriousness of dedication would meet incredible opposition from representatives of the status quo—unimaginative and timid men willing to kill in order to avoid the necessity of changing world views. Can you imagine what would happen to advertising, for example— and the firms that use advertising—that art of changing people from men into greedy consumers—if people were awakened? Could you imagine what firms would go bankrupt because an enlightened public would not buy what they produce? Can you imagine which leaders would be voted out of office by an enlightened public? No, we are not, as a nation, serious about education. In fact, we equate training with education, and mistakenly assume that we are giving the people public education when we are really giving them public training.

The Hidden Teachers

There is a scarcity of teachers in the land. Colleges of education do not regularly produce teachers. They produce technicians paid to implement a prescribed syllabus, by prescribed means. This is not bad, because education is a *transcending* project, and there must be something to transcend. But the "turned-on" men—they exist as a kind of underground in every institution that is called educational. The problem is *to induce them to come out of hiding,* for that is what they mainly do. Teachers with an offbeat perspective on the world are punished for their very genius. Teachers who awaken pupils so that they ask embarrassing questions, and challenge existing forms, are frequently fired. And so the youngsters "blow pot" and take "acid" as respite from trainers whom they often feel have "sold out." Or they go through the motions prescribed by the syllabus, get their grades, and escalate themselves as thoroughly programmed men into their place in the professions and business. Indeed, some may actually believe that they are educated, and spout canned attitudes and platitudes as if they were eternal truths, and live lives in the suburbs that are patterned by *Ladies' Home Journal* articles, as if those ways of living were the only thinkable ones. Isn't it curious, that we experiment with nuclear energy, ways to organize a factory, ways to train people, but we do not experiment with ways to live family life, or ways to spend our time.

Universities don't have Departments of Experimental Existence, or Departments of Possible Worlds, or Departments of Human Possibility. Instead, we have subject-matter and instructors thereof, which maintain existential status quos.

I anticipate that, when finally automation reaches full flower, almost every aspect of our daily lives will lose relevance, so oriented is it now to the present ways of producing goods and maintaining the present social and economic structure. Yet, when consuming more goods, getting richer, or getting ahead in the corporation cease to be viable goals, what will be the point of much of our child-training practices—which inspire children to be greedy and bottomless consumers, competitive, false, role dominated, and upwardly mobile? And what will we do with our time? Watch TV? We'll have to learn to enter into dialogue with one another—but there's nobody there.

Living Outside the Capsule

Some of the beatniks and "hippies" who have "opted out" are existential explorers and pioneers. They are risking their time, and considerable money, to see if life is livable outside the usual institutional forms, without the usual hardware of domestic life. Respectable people make it tough on hippies. Indeed, many hippies may be nebbishes. But some I know are serious "opt-outs," serious seekers after ways to live that are more authentic, more meaningful than the prescribed forms of life. *They* may turn out to be our teachers, or teachers of our teachers, when automation expands leisure. Since hippies have no respectability or status to put in jeopardy, many of them are more honest than "squares," at least in love and friendship. Since they work when they feel like it, and play when they feel like it—and moreover, they have someone to play with—many of them are healthier than squares. Indeed, they could be said to be the first enlightened ones to realize our economic-productive system is already quite automated so that one can leave regular employment without starving, and without the economy collapsing. And they are truly experimenting with ways to spend their time, ways for men and women to live together, ways to raise children, etc. They may produce some bungles in such experimentation, but what experiment doesn't, and what kind of experimentation is more important? Be kind to the hippies you see. They have commenced an odyssey of a sort, and you may want them to come home and teach you what they have learned, when you face the emptiness of no productive work (machines do it) and time on your hands. If they are not too bitter over the send-off we gave them, they might teach us how to live life meaningfully and joyfully without recourse to tranquilizers and psychiatry.

Conclusion

The world has shrunk, and there no longer is a category of Them. There is only Us—gropers for challenge, growth, fulfillment and meaning in our lives. Some older, some younger; some enlightened, others mystified and befuddled. Some rich, some poor. Some of us will have to help the rest of the world get as rich as us. Our dilemma is unparalleled in human history. If we are not to die of boredom, or of invasion by the envious, we have two tasks—first, to help the rest of the world solve its material problems, and then to explore how to live, learn and find meaning when there's no work to be done. If colleges and universities are to fulfill their function of education and enlightenment as effectively as they train people into unquestioning conformity, they must encourage teachers to stand forth, and declare themselves in any ways that time, money, versatility, and electronic hardware have made possible. Let teachers disclose, not just the techniques for chemical analysis, or the rules for declining verbs—but also what all this means, how it challenges them in the meaningful pursuit of their lives. Let education approximate to dialogue, and not shaping. Let a college be a community of fellow seekers, not a place where we, the faculty, train *them,* the students. Let the students have contact with heroes with a small "h"—men who are truly seeking enlightenment and wholeness, finding challenges and new values when old ones have worn out. Training will never become obsolete, and we can always find trainers. The social system at large is well protected with safeguards to insure that any change in the fabric of society will be orderly, and not violent or arbitrary. If this is true, and I believe it is, then schools from kindergarten up through university can be places where explorers and trainers cohabit and coexist, where there is a place for learning necessary roles and skills and knowledge, and a place for enlivening and embodying the creative imagination.

16

Society's Need for Respectable "Check-Out Places"

A person needs a place to go when he finds his life unlivable. Society seems to conspire such that there is nowhere to go when you want to be offstage, free from your usual roles, free to discover and define your being-for-yourself. Judges, critics, and commissars are omnipresent. If a man steps out of line and departs from his usual roles, someone is there to remind him of who he is, to define him, and to punish him for daring to define himself. The upshot is many wives and mothers find they cannot face their families another moment without shrieking in protest against the sameness of their unappreciated daily grind. But they stifle the shriek and carry on. Fathers and husbands become bored with their wives, infuriated by their children, and worn out by work that lacks joy—continued only because there is no other work to do, and the bills fall due each month. The children, in turn, cannot get along with each other, or with their parents. Grandparents, aunts, and uncles live a thousand miles away and cannot take the youngsters in for a week or month of respite. And so the trapped ones persist on their joyless, desperate treadmills until physical illness grants them a ticket of admission to a hospital or sickroom. Or they "blow up," have a nervous breakdown, and are treated as "not in their right minds." They may enter a mental hospital, there to be placed in storage until the regime of shock, tranquilizers, and periodic consultations with an overworked psychiatrist brings them "to their senses." But even in the hospitals, there is no respite from roles; patients are cast into new ones and lack the freedom to choose their being. They return to the way of life they lived before, perhaps with the protest in them electroshocked or drugged out of existence.

200

Before this drama reaches its climax in the sickroom or the state hospital, it would be helpful if new alternatives could be provided. What would life in our society be like if we had acceptable "check-out places"? In moments of reverie, I have invented some. Let me describe one such, a healing-house that appeals to me. It is probably healing only for middle-class people.

It is a place where one can enter and find confirmation for *any* way one has chosen to be, or any way that circumstances have brought one to. If a man wishes solitude, he can find it there; and no one will speak to him if he wishes to remain silent. If he wishes congenial and enlivening body-contact, a masseur or masseuse (he can choose which) is available to provide service. If a housewife wants to paint, listen to music, or just sit and meditate, there is a room for her to do so. The place would be like the now outdated retreats and monasteries that once were available for the defeated and the sick in spirit.

Each person would be entitled to a cell with inviolate privacy. There he could go, and stay for a day, a week, a month, or years. No one could enter this little womb without his invitation; and once a person closed the door, no one else could enter.

Routine would be simple and minimal in such a haven. Meals would be spartan. A person could take them communally, in the dining hall, if he wished to socialize, and take part in the preparation and clean-up from the repast. Otherwise, the pantry would be always available, with abundant supplies of fruit, bread, milk, raw vegetables, and similar snacks. A resident could come and go, nibbling as he wished.

If he wished conversation, he could go to the common room, where he could sit; and his presence alone would signify that he would be willing to talk. Or he could invite someone to the privacy of his cell, if he wished to enter into uninterrupted dialogue.

The rule of the house would be freedom for the self, with respect for the freedom of the other.

People who entered would leave their roles at the doorstep. No status, no rank, would interpose itself between the guests—who would have a first name, or a surname, or no name, or a pseudonym, if that was what they chose.

This would be a place where people could quite freely go out of their minds and roles, as these were known outside.

The house would not be solely for those harried, middle-class people who needed a place to go before they broke down. It would also be a place where creative people—writers, painters, dancers, poets—could go to live awhile and present their more tender creations in an accepting, or better, honest milieu, where commercial criteria for judging art and ideas are irrelevant.

This would be a place where one could go to redefine himself, apart from the people "back home," who have a vested interest in keeping the person in the roles by which they knew him, but which were sickening him. The fat ones could slim down, the thin ones increase in girth. The tense and nervous could find surcease and relaxation; the aimless might meet people with aims that could inspire and redirect their lives.

These houses would be the place one went *before* he got sick, or mad. The directors would eschew drugs and medicines. They would heal by letting healing take place. The houses would be places where joy could be experienced, and peace.

These islands or oases could exist in every community. The Howard Johnson- or Holiday Inn-builders could design them cheaply and simply enough—but with more taste, I would hope, than is shown in those rooms designed for everyone and hence no one. The staff of permanent residents could include professional psychotherapists, resident artists, playwrights, dancers, masseurs, writers and teachers, and musicians. Some of these residents might come and go; but all would provide seekers with an atmosphere of spiritual freedom, and examples of the quest for new avenues of being and expression. A workman, professional man, wife or mother, or lonely person could come daily for an hour or so, or weekly, and find relaxation, edification, or companionship. Americanized versions of geisha girls, or geisha men, would be available, not for illicit and illegal prostitution, but for the purpose of inviting a person into the dialogue that leads a man beyond his usual consciousness, even to delight.

I have little doubt that such houses would pay for themselves if they were on a private, pay-as-you-go basis. And I suspect that if they were underwritten by some grant, or by public-health moneys—but with their operation strictly in the hands of the director of each house—they would more than pay for themselves, in the form of physical breakdown that did *not* happen and mental breakdown which would *not* materialize. I suspect that for the people who patronized such a house, intake of drugs and medicines would diminish radically, to the dismay of the pharmaceutical houses. The mass invasion of physicians' clinics and waiting-rooms would be reduced to manageable dimensions. And the waiting lists of practicing psychotherapists would doubtless be less packed with names.

Such houses of retreat and healing will, alas, not become part of every village, town, or city neighborhood. But sensible people will find ways to pool resources so that they can organize them by themselves. Or if they can afford it, they will buy or rent a "pad" on the other side of town, away from family and friends. Perhaps some organizational genius will find the necessary staff, and the capital to invest; and he will become a millionaire by providing what everyone needs, at a price all can afford to pay.

If such places came into being as a normal part of society, I suspect psychotherapists would lose some of their present *raison d'être,* and would have to apply their knowledge of how people sicken and become whole to teaching, and to living fulfilled lives themselves, so that by their being, they would represent viable ways. And I suspect that physicians would find their practices confined to delivering babies, setting broken bones, and stanching the flow of blood. Sales of drugs would diminish, and the directors of pharmaceutical firms would send lobbies to Washington to persuade legislators the houses were subversive and un-American.

17

A Psychology of Transcendent-Behavior[*]

A psychology of transcendent-behavior in man is long overdue. Our present psychology, well-grounded in systematic research, permits us to understand how a man or animal has become as he is now. It can even serve as the basis for prediction of his future condition, action, and experience.

But psychology has thus far treated with only half of man's potentialities for being, the half he shares with animals, objects in nature, and man-made things. Psychologists view man as determined by his structure, his past, or the forces of the present. The thesis is that if these factors are specified, variance in man's action and experience can largely be explained. This approach neglects, even undermines, the other, peculiarly human, and more important half of man's being —his capacity for freedom, his possibility of transcending determiners of all kinds and actualizing projects of his own choosing.

Every goal a man sets *for himself* and sets about achieving—whether it is making something, getting somewhere, or becoming somebody —is a gesture of defiance in the face of forces that make fulfillment of this project improbable. The world has inertia and momentum of its own; so has the human body, as a natural object. The matrix of simultaneously acting determiners will affect man's experience and his action the way a current carries a twig, or as wind and rain sculpture a rocky outcrop. But this is true only if man *chooses to be an object* in the world. This way of being is experienced as "familiar," "habitual," "the path of least resistance," "resignation," etc. It is a choice of being that is available to us at every moment of our existence; but just as man can choose to be shaped, pushed, pulled, or carried

[*] This chapter was first published in *Explorations in human potentialities*, H. A. Otto (ed.), 1966, and is reprinted here with the permission of the Charles Thomas Publishing Co.

by the thrust of past and present forces, so can he transcend this way. He can propose projects that would never come into being if he had not chosen to risk actualizing them. Man's intentionality, his decision to do or be something, is a force in its own right, a force that exists under the sun as surely as do wind, biological pressures, and social norms. If this will is renounced, repressed, or resigned, then behavior will indeed be the resultant of specifiable, natural forces.

Each chosen project transcends specifiable determiners that would make man predictable. If a psychologist could measure the strength and direction of forces which bear upon a person, he *still could not* predict the person's action, experience, or condition unless the individual revealed whether he knew the relevant determiners, and intended to "rise above," or acquiesce to them. If the person's goal were known, the psychologist could weigh forces and make some prediction about the probability of fulfillment. Man's predictability is either proof of the extent to which he has become alienated from his intentional will, or a testimony of the degree to which he has confided his projects to the psychologist.

A psychology of transcendent-behavior is based on a psychology of the will, such as Rank[75] attempted to develop, or a psychology of the *experience* of freedom. It also includes description of *possibilities* of being. The present psychology of man as a determined being portrays man in his most usual way of appearing to others and to himself. A psychology of transcendent-behavior assumes that there are possible levels of experiencing and behaving that *go beyond* the modal level. It postulates that under most conditions of existence, man functions at the level of acquiescence to "forces" and "determiners." From time to time, however, he gets glimmerings from his own experience and that of other people, of other ways of being that are possible for him. He sometimes experiences the world in greater richness, feels upsurges of strength, or accomplishes goals so atypical of him, that even he is shocked. He learns of the amazing accomplishments of others, feats that give proof of apparently superhuman experience, beyond the reach of mere mortals like himself—works of art, music, invention, athletic prowess, and the like, that defy all forces militating against them. These are the focus of a psychology of optimal functioning or transcendence. They are ways of being that call for description, explanation, and specification of the conditions under which they will emerge.

One reason we have no science of transcendent-behavior may lie in the relationship between the individual and the social system. Man, as we encounter him, is fundamentally estranged from much of his possible experience, and from the experience of his possibilities. He has repressed his experience of freedom and renounced his freedom to experience. In order to fit the social systems in which he exists, he feels obliged to conceal much of his experience from others. To conform to sclerosed concepts of himself, he tries to deny dissonant experience.[16] If he conceals too effectively, he finally becomes alienated from his experience. Phenomenologists are discovering that typical human experience is fragmented, serialized, objectified, separated from action—in short, reduced from its earlier promise of richness and wholeness. Indeed, we denigrate as infantile, mentally ill, or primitive[110] those persons who report experience in which fantasy, memory, feeling, perception, conceptualizing, and action are all integrated into a rich syncretic unity. We reward the man whose experience of himself and the world is intellectualized and schematized, like a blueprint. It is such men whom psychologists typically study. Those persons who have transcendent experience are seldom studied because they seem to defy the "laws of behavior." *Thus, the possibility arises that our psychology is only a report of the behavior and experience of human beings who have complied with social and biological pressures* (including pressure from the experimenter[85]) *and have reduced their experience of themselves and their world in order to "play it safe" and conform.* If this is true, there is all the more reason for developing a psychology of transcending.* If man functions typically in the "reduced" state, but has the potentiality for transcending it, then we are called upon to explore the conditions under which such potentiality can be fulfilled. Toward this end, I have explored some attested examples of human functioning

---

* A number of authors' works have contributed to my views on transcendent-behavior. The interested reader might consult Jung (1956, pp. 126–7; 232); Shaw (1966); Frankl (1961); Maslow (1962, Ch. 13); Hora (1961); Laing (1964); Privette (1965); Sartre (1956); Berdyaev (1962).

beyond modal limits and some of the conditions for their emergence. It is hoped that this may provide a beginning of an era where such a special field will not be needed but is instead included in "general psychology." Actually, the study of transcendent-behavior is a misnomer. Man doesn't transcend his real being; he transcends only someone's *concept* of his being—his own concept, or that of an investigator or a witness to his conduct. Man cannot go beyond his ultimate limits. He only reveals powers beyond someone's *concept* of his limits. If modal man's actualizing of possibilities is a feeble hint of what he might be, do, or become; and if man might become what he (or someone) is capable of *imagining* he might become—then wild imagination about human possibilities must be encouraged, both in individuals and in those who function as consulting specialists. Surely it is a sad commentary on the profession of psychology that writers of science fiction, certain leaders, poets, mystics, inspired teachers of the young, all have been more productive of concepts of human possibility than psychologists. They also may know more about the ways of bringing them into being than psychologists presently do.

Some Examples of Transcendent-Behavior

Thinking Transcendentally: Creativity and Originality

There is inertia associated with all forms of human experiencing and behaving. Forces predispose toward continuation of sameness in thinking, feeling, and overt behavioral responses to situations. Freud referred in this connection to a "repetition compulsion" that seems inherent to man. He implied that this "compulsion" is instinctive. Modern behavior theorists are able to show that persistence of behavior is in large measure explainable in terms of reinforcement histories, and schedules of reinforcement. That is, behavior (including perception as well as overt motor responses) tends to persist so long as it is reinforced or rewarded. Sociologists point to constraint on the individual imposed by "agencies of social control." Personality theorists see the self-concept and the need to maintain a sense of identity, as factors in persistent behavior and modes of experiencing the self and the world.

Inventiveness is a departure from the usual. Novel solutions to problems, new ideas in art, literature, and science, all seem improbable at first. They arise in the mind of their creator spontaneously, effortlessly, and sometimes playfully. New ideas seem to crop up when the artist or inventor is *not* trying. Zen Buddhists refer to this experience as "no-mind" (Watts,[105] p. 35). They mean by this, not empty-headedness or stupidity, but rather a cessation of active striving or searching for novelty. The inspired acts of creation seem to occur *after* a person has struggled hard to discover a new truth, a new idea, or the solution to some vexing and pressing problem. Once the new invention has come into being, it carries with it the quality of transcendence. The inventor has transcended his own, and sometimes all mankind's, present limitations (Shaw[94]).

Here we have a hint of a condition for release of transcendent-behavior and experience; namely, the ability to "let oneself be," to "let go," to "stop trying," to let our thoughts play or flow spontaneously, without seeking to guide our thinking process. It goes without saying that novel, original ideas must be criticized and tested for their utility. Not all that is original is immediately useful for human purposes.

Perceiving Transcendentally

Generally, we see the world in its conventional rubrics. We see someone and identify the person as a woman because she has the hair, curves, voice, and gait of women in general. We look at her long enough to assign her to some categories—e.g., pretty or ugly, willing or unwilling, marriageable or not—and then look at her no more. We usually observe the world under the impetus and direction of our needs, values, feelings, and purposes of the moment. Such need-steered perception certainly serves a vital role in our survival and adaptation; but it also tends to blind us to all features of the world that are not immediately relevant to our present hungers, desires, and values. "Desireless" or "undriven" cognition—when we simply open our eyes, ears, noses, taste buds, kinesthetic and organic receptors, and let stimuli play upon them and impress them—seems to be the condition for the enriched mode of perception. Maslow[62] calls this mode of perception "B-cognition," or "cognition of 'Being' "; and Schachtel[90] refers to it as "allocentric" perception. It adds new dimensions to experience;

or, rather, it permits new dimensions to "happen." Colors are seen more vividly; and things, animals, people, or scenes are perceived in their "suchness," in their concrete uniqueness, almost transfigured.*

Moments of such perception are experienced by people as unforgettable. In fact, when people recall the past with vivid imagery, the content of their recollection is almost always the moments when they let the world impress itself upon their senses without selection. They let the world disclose itself to them. When two people fall in love and are truly open and unguarded in their communication with one another, they come to see one another as unique, irreplaceable, quite *unlike* any other human being in the world—certainly not as mere representatives of the classes, men and women. And though it is true that "lovers" who are merely sex-starved, or starved for companionship, are in fact somewhat "blind"—they see in the other only the means of sating present appetites and hungers—it is also true that happy, fulfilled lovers see one another *and the world* more richly and more veridically. In this sense, one can say that people who are in love, people who are open and spontaneous in relation to their loved ones, are *at that time* also more open to their own experiencing, and more perceptive of the real world. Their senses all seem keener; and the world discloses itself more vividly to their eyes, ears, skin and olfactory lobes— to their experience. Their imaginations, too, are released; and their capacity for metaphorical, poetic description is aroused—hence the plethora of poetry on love. Incidentally, it may be that the capacity to think metaphorically is an index of one's access to transcendent powers. Such cognition, then, because it is rare and valued, may be called transcendent perception.

We may well ask, why is it so rare? Why is rubricized perception, perception of things and people as mere members of categories, so common and usual? The answer probably lies in the fact that average people are most often in the midst of many simultaneous conditions of privation, of need; and so their egos, their perceptual apparatus, remain a servant of unfulfilled desires. Here, then, we have a hint

---

* This is the way people report experiencing the world when they have taken lysergic acid (LSD), marijuana, mescaline, and other psychedelic substances. See, for example, Leary, Alpert and Metzner;[58] Blum (1964); and Huxley.[35] See also my account of an experience with LSD in Chapter 13.

for yet another condition for transcendent functioning in general; namely, it may presume the fulfillment or devivifying of most of the person's pressing needs. Once these needs have been met, the person has, as it were, been released from the urgencies of the quest of gratification—he doesn't want to consume the world, or exploit it. He can be content to let it be, and let it impress him with its "suchness."

So far, we have proposed that "letting oneself be" and basic-need gratification are conditions for the release of transcendent experience and behavior in a person. Now, let us explore further.

Remembering Transcendentally

Most people have some difficulty recalling things when they are asked to do so, or when they have some need for information from the past. Like perception, remembering is an act of the total organism; and it is controlled to some extent by the pressure of immediate needs and interests. Hence, one's recall of the past is highly selective, and highly subject to the shaping and distorting influence of present needs, sets, and wishes.[4,69] Sometimes, too, persons have a need *not* to remember selected aspects of past experience; and so they will have large lacunae in their recall of the personal past. These gaps may be filled with fabrications and lies; and at other times, the gaps are experienced as such. It was to explain these failures or inabilities at recollection of the past that Freud proposed his theory of repression. Memories will be actively repressed when their recollection would yield anxiety, shame, or assaults to one's present self-esteem.

Yet, the experience of psychoanalytic therapists, and of hypnotists, has shown that under certain conditions, massive and vividly "imaged" recollection of past events—even of early childhood—is sometimes possible. Certain drugs, viz., sodium pentothal, likewise release vivid and unresisted recall of the past. So do certain sensory triggers—such as an odor, a sound, or, as occurred with Proust, the feeling of an uneven cobblestone under his feet. These *unresisted* acts of remembering occur under special conditions, which we shall explore, since they may throw further light on our quest for the conditions of transcending-behavior in general.

When a patient undergoing psychotherapy finally arrives at a stage where he trusts his therapist utterly, and feels fully accepted by him, he drops his defenses, relaxes, and *lets himself be* while he is in the presence of his therapist. "Letting himself be," in this context, means that he lets his thoughts, his memories, his feeling, and his fantasies unfold *spontaneously*. He does not try to direct or steer the content of his cognitive field. Rather, he lets the process happen. Under these conditions, remembrances will arise that surprise even the patient. He will relate events from his past, with remarkable detail, and then say, with some surprise, "I haven't thought of these things in years." He may be able to recall entire passages of poetry that were learned in grammar school and long since "forgotten"; he may recall scenes in which he and his parents or friends shared some experiences, and be able to narrate entire conversations.

Hypnotists have been able to "regress" their subjects to younger age levels. They are able to suggest to their hypnotic subjects that they are now nine years old, or six. If the subject has truly been cooperating in the hypnotic experiment, he will begin to behave in a manner that resembles that of a child; and he will frequently bring forth, on request, vivid narratives from his own life of events that truly happened in that age-interval.

There must be something in common between the condition of "letting oneself be," that arises in conventional psychotherapy, and responding to a hypnotist's invitation to experience oneself as younger. The similarity appears to lie in the *dropping of defenses;* the relaxation of defenses is in turn a by-product or concomitant of *trust* that has been elicited or earned by the professional person, such that his invitations will be complied with. In addition to the relaxation of defenses and the trust, there appears to be a factor of focusing, of undivided, undistracted, fascinated attention to the flow of one's experience. In everyday, modal living, one can seldom concentrate fully upon any one thing for long. Indeed, to do so invites a stupor akin to, or identical with, a hypnoidal state. Furthermore, the average person has many interests, needs, and wishes simultaneously operative; and no sooner is one need fulfilled than another tension arises. These pressures seem to preclude or prevent the uprush of the past into the present; probably this serves adaptive functions, in that it permits people to live in the present. But the ability fully to recall episodes from the past can also serve adaptive functions in the present, and it can enrich experience. Consequently, an enlarged capacity to recall has value. Novelists and playwrights depend on it for the practice of their art. Transcendent remembering thus is seen to share certain factors in common with transcendent perception; namely, a relaxed, "need-free," undriven, secure present state. Further, in addition to letting be, and need-gratification, we have added *focusing* and *trust* (of another and of the self) to our list of probable factors in transcending.

Learning Transcendentally

The process of learning some skilled performance, or a list of non-sense syllables, or some meaningful verbal material is usually described in psychology textbooks with learning curves. If it is errors that are being plotted against trials, a gradual dropping-off is portrayed. If it is number of correct responses that are being plotted, these are shown to increase up to some maximum level; at this point, the curve becomes horizontal. The person who is seeking to learn something generally experiences considerable effort as he struggles with the demands of the task. If someone addressed a skill to be learned, a poem to be memorized, or a technique to be mastered, and "absorbed" it almost instantly, the learning surely would be marveled at. It could truly be called transcendent learning. "Insight" in learning appears to be a special case of transcendent learning.

Such transcendent learning falls within the experience of most people, but only rarely. The reason, again, is not to be found in the "difficulty" of the task, but rather in the *resistance* to full focusing and attending to the problem at hand. Testimony of persons who have mastered complicated learning assignments with transcendent ease shows that they reach these moments when they have gotten "warmed up." The warm-up process is not unlike a process of "purging"; in this instance, purging one's experience of all thoughts, fantasies, interests, and feelings save *fascination* with the problem (cf. Shaw[94]). The subjective experience of fascination is probably what learning theorists have attempted to explain with the concept of "motivation to learn." But motivation to learn has generally been provided for by rewards and punishments that follow the outcome of the learning process.

When a person has become fascinated by a poem to be memorized, a concert to be played, a technique to be learned (and assuming he has already mastered prerequisite basic skills), he addresses the problem with undivided mind. His very being, from hair to toenails, is focused upon the problem; its solution or mastery comes effortlessly. (See Chapter 10 for a more detailed view of fascination.)

Again, the factor that seems inherent to transcendent learning is that of letting be—in this case, letting oneself become fascinated or absorbed. When one is so absorbed, all else is excluded from awareness, *one "opens up" to the information being disclosed by the problem or task,* and one "lets" one's problem-solving apparatus work by itself.

Another factor that seems inherent to transcendent learning is that the task or problem must have *meaning* and value to the person who is addressing it. It must have meaning in and for itself, as well as meaning in the sense of a means to other ends. Probably, the instrumental value of the learning provides the incentive for selecting the task in the first place. Whether or not the learning that takes place is transcendent depends upon the availability of the fascination response. Thus, we add *value* and *meaning* to our list of factors in transcending.

Transcendent Achievement

Why was Sir Edmund Hillary able to climb to the peak of Mount Everest, when other climbers failed, though they were apparently as well trained, and comparably supported by helpers and technical gadgetry? Why were the Wright Brothers able to get a motor-driven plane off the ground, when others failed? Why does an ordinary football player sometimes make an inspired run that wins a game?

If we assume that such inspired and transcendent actions occur in some people who have been adequately prepared or trained, and not in other people with comparable preparation and training, we are left in a quandary. Presumably, since the remarkable achievement was accomplished, the *capacity* to accomplish it lay dormant in the several contenders for the goal. Why did the successful act emerge from this person rather than that? Let us set aside the factor of luck, although it is important.

The most plausible hypothesis is that the remarkable achievement occurred in the contender who was most fully *committed* to its attainment. Commitment is a curious, and little-understood phenomenon, one to which the term "motivation" hardly does justice.

When one is "committed" to some course of action, some goal, or some mission, one can roughly gauge the degree of commitment in terms of the *price the contender is willing to risk to attain the goal.* The ultimate commitment, of course, is to stake one's life or safety. Before one is willing to expend one's time, energy, or money in pursuit of some mission, one must believe utterly that it is worth it; hence values and meaning are involved. When one's reputation, or one's life, or anything else, is being risked in pursuit of some mission, then the person must believe the goal is worth it in order to be able *to release his inner resources* (viz., inventiveness, resourcefulness, endurance, strength, self-control, etc.) fully for the task. If he only half believes in the worth of the mission, he will hold back. Such commitment, indeed, seems to be one condition for such release. Perhaps here we have another hint of a condition for transcendent achievement—the capacity to see accomplishments as having so much intrinsic importance that they are worth staking everything of value in the attempt to achieve them. This is not to underestimate the importance of making preparations, taking safety measures, having equipment, and downright luck. Rather, the element of commitment seems to induce or inspire the contender to go where others fear to tread, there to find, not danger, but rather, the means to the end. Further, commitment seems to release hitherto latent and unsuspected capacities in the individual. It is an "integrator" of the person, from his glands to his fantasy, such that no muscle works against muscle; and mental processes are synchronized with physical processes.

The one factor which most great achievers saliently share is this capacity to commit themselves, bordering on fanaticism.[31] The absence of self-doubt and the absence of doubt about the worth of the mission seem to be essential to such commitment, while the commitment itself seems to be necessary to the release of inner resources that bring success. Probably, the modal personality is less able to commit himself fully to a given mission, and is obliged by the facts of his life to "spread himself thin"—to make a living, protect his reputation, etc. In fact, he may be committed to some role or status, and this commitment precludes new ones! This is not entirely a bad thing, and it seems necessary to effective living within society. Such division of purposes, however, seems to preclude magnificent achievements.[94]

Transcendent Survival

Another category of transcendent-behavior is sheer physical survival under conditions where death is the best possible estimate of the outcome predisposed by the given conditions.

The successful voyage in 1916 of Sir Ernest Shackleton and his five companions, in an open boat across 1500 miles of Antarctic Sea, with scant rations, skimpy clothing, and subzero temperatures, illustrates transcendent survival, notwithstanding the technical know-how in seamanship of the six men.

Perhaps better illustrations of transcendent survival are provided by the tragic, infinitesimal percentage of Nazi-concentration-camp inmates who managed to live under conditions cruelly designed by the administrators of the camps to hasten death. The horrifying and yet inspiring accounts of Bettelheim,[6] Frankl,[21] and others offer evidence both of wholehearted, dedicated bestiality on the part of captors, and transcendent survival powers on the part of the prisoners who escaped death.

How did the survivors do it? The consensus appears to maintain that survival was contingent, among other things, upon a powerful commitment to life—upon the conviction that survival had purpose and meaning, in spite of the incredible hardships of daily existence. The concentration-camp survivors were persons who were capable of finding new meanings and reasons and purposes for life when the usual purposes and meanings had gone by the wayside. Frankl,[21] who survived the death camps and went on to become a spokesman for the "existential psychiatry," summarized his view of the values which can sustain life, even in death camps, as follows:

> Man has the freedom and responsibility to pursue *creative* values, that is, to work, to make things, to use his energy and resources to produce wealth, or goods. He has the freedom and responsibility to pursue *experiential* values—the good things that life

provides, such as beauty, food, pleasure, etc. When creative and experiential values can no longer be fulfilled, as occurs, for example, under conditions of the death camps, or as occurs when one knows that he will soon die, then man has the freedom and responsibility to fulfill *attitudinal* values. This last term has reference to the attitude with which one faces the certainty of death, or extreme hardship. Ideally, one will face these extremities responsibly, seeking to give them meaning, and seeking to address them at a *human* level rather than at a level of less responsible functioning.

Another type of transcendent survival is illustrated by persons who recover from illnesses or injuries which are diagnosed fatal or incurable. There are many instances of persons who, as it were, defied the best medical opinion and survived cancers thought to be incurable and inoperable. To the best of my understanding, based on available literature, interviews with physicians and nurses, and some contact with patients who displayed this talent for survival, the decisive factor was, again, a strong desire and reason for living, especially loving involvement with others (Bakan[2]). Probably, given such a strong commitment to life, *healing capacities that ordinarily lie dormant are drawn upon, or released.* Doubtless, the maintenance of hope and of determination to live can promote survival; whereas hopelessness and loss of a sense of meaning or purpose for existence can suppress these latent healing reflexes. The capacity of a physician, minister, or relative, or of the patient himself to elicit in him a determination to live, and to maintain hope for a meaningful existence, has been relatively ignored by scientific students of factors in health. In spite of the lack of scientific understanding of the underlying process, any efforts to mobilize hope and a "fighting spirit" in sick people have good promise of tilting the balance of forces in the direction of recovery. We can call this capacity the capacity to inspire, or to "inspirit"; and it seems to be a capacity found in so-called charismatic leaders.

Transcending Personality Organization

This category of transcendent functioning is drawn broadly, to cover such diverse occurrences as the rehabilitation of confirmed criminals to responsible social living; the achievement of Helen Keller at establishing linguistic communication with other people in spite of deafness and blindness; the many instances of people who have risen above environmental forces that predisposed to the development of delinquency, criminality, ignorance, or superstition to attain high standards of achievement, etc.

In all such instances, a common thread may be discerned; namely, a refusal to submit to the apparently overpowering forces of the environment, and to apparent limitations (as defined by somebody) of one's own organism. Some of the "transcendents" were able to release their powers by recourse to prayer or by other religious practices. Still others were inspired or challenged to rise above limitations by another human being who saw potential in them. Still others made the transcendence by sheer faith in their own potentials, when no other human being seemed to share this faith. Perhaps it is at this point that a personal relationship with one's God serves its purpose: the individual feels that, though no human loves him, God does—and, moreover, God expects him to keep trying.

The best therapists of personality likely have this capacity to discern potentials for transcendence in a patient when neither the patient nor others can see such capacities.[94] Further, the effective therapist is able *to communicate this belief in the patient's potentials to the patient.* Finally, the therapist is able to provoke or inspire the patient, not to resign in conformity and acquiescence to the limiting forces of his environment, his past, or his perhaps defective body, but rather to see these apparent limits as *challenges.*

This analysis suggests that the concept which a person has of himself (his self-concept), and the concept of him held by other people in his life, can be factors in transcendence or in the inability to transcend present modes of functioning. If a person *believes* himself to be weak, helpless, or doomed to some fate or other, he will tend to behave or suffer in the way expected. If, on the other hand, he has a concept of himself as a being with much untapped potential to cope with problems and contradictions in his life, then when these arise, he will persist in efforts to cope with them long after someone who sees himself as ineffective and impotent has given up.

When some significant other person, such as a teacher, coach, therapist, or minister, believes he sees potentials for functioning in an individual which the latter cannot presently see in himself, he can sometimes convince or inspire the pupil or patient to efforts that bring success. Under those conditions, the pupil or patient undergoes of necessity a change in self-concept, so as to encompass his perception of new capacities, hitherto not imagined. In fact, there is something in common between an effective hypnotist and an effective teacher, leader, or therapist. A hypnotist is able to capture the attention and confidence of his subject; and through verbal suggestions, he can modify the subject's perceptions of self and the world, and his beliefs about self and the world. Ordinarily, a person cannot lie outstretched between two chairs spaced two feet apart, and then support another person who stands on his body over the space. Under hypnosis, the subject believes he is as rigid as a board; behaves that way; and, indeed, supports the unaccustomed weight. The hypnotist knows that the subject's body has the capacity to support the unusual weight, and he elicits and focuses his subject's strength for the task at hand. A good teacher, therapist, or minister knows (or profoundly believes) that all men have unplumbed capacities for learning, achievement, health, or goodness; and through the relationship with their students or patients, these specialists modify the latters' beliefs about their own potentials, and the consequent performances. If a person will not permit his present concept of self to be shaken, then of course it remains a constraining influence on his behavior; and transcendence will seldom occur in his life.

Review of Factors in Transcendent-Behavior

Let us bring together into one section the factors that seemed to be involved in the emergence of the different examples of transcendent-behavior, and discuss them in a little more detail. Perhaps in the process of so doing, we shall increase our understanding of this valuable mode of functioning and become better able to elicit it in others and in ourselves.

Letting Be

One of the factors which we mentioned in discussing transcendent thinking, or creative endeavor, was the attitude of letting be. This term is difficult to define in abstract terms, for it refers to a mode of experiencing that must be experienced to be known. As close as I can come to defining it is to describe some common occasions when average people are most likely to be in a state of letting themselves be. For example, when one has soaked oneself for half an hour or so in a hot bath, one becomes extremely limp, relaxed, and passive. One's mind, or thoughts, so long as one does not fall asleep, are most likely to drift or play about, without conscious direction. If that is the case, then one is letting himself be. In the state of letting be, the individual does not seek to steer, guide, or direct each thought as it arises, but instead permits it to arise and be followed by whatever thought, image, or memory comes next. If the person who is thus letting himself be has "plugged in" a problem that is to be solved, and has previously exhausted all conscious, logical, methodical efforts at its solution, the probability is increased that the problem will "solve itself" when the man is letting himself be. This will be true, of course, only if the question or problem falls within the realm of solvability by humans.

Letting be, however, cannot be attained so long as a person is in a state of vigilance, anxiety, or conscious *trying* for the attainment of some goal or other. These latter states seem to channel or steer the thinking processes and do not permit the free flow of all kinds of thoughts. Instead, under privation, anxiety, or striving conditions, only those thoughts arise which are directly relevant to unfulfilled needs, or the successful completion of the task in process. Thus, letting be seems most likely to arise only when most pressing problems in existence are *temporarily in abeyance*. Probably, a person who is able, at will, to effectively suppress his ongoing projects so as to permit letting be to arise in himself has more chances of experiencing it, since few people are ever, for long, in a need- and problem-free state.

Openness

A man makes himself open to other men when he reveals to them what he is thinking or feeling—when he discloses his experiencing to the other person. In order to do this fully and freely, the disclosing person must, of course, trust that he is in no danger when he is thus unguarded, defenseless, and open. Yet, as we indicated above, in our discussion of transcendent cognition, when man is that trusting and open, he is also simultaneously in the state when his sense receptors are maximally open to be impressed with what is there to be seen, heard, tasted, smelled, or felt. When a person is guarded and defensive before other men or nature, his sense organs serve a searching function; they are highly selective, seeking sources of danger and safety. This means that the man will be relatively blind to all things that are irrelevant to his present concerns. Thus, a sense of safety and a sense of trust in the goodwill of other people in the situation seem to be essential to openness which, in turn, permits transcendent cognition to take place. Persons who have been competent in coping with their needs and problems and who are interpersonally competent—able to establish safe relationships with others—will be most able to experience moments of openness.

Focusing and Fascination

When one has become fascinated by something—a problem, a person, a book, a scene—then the object of fascination fills a person's experience, and nothing else exists for him. This is the case, for example, in "true dialogue" between persons. The participants in dialogue are "fully there"—their thoughts are not preoccupied with unfinished business, or fantasy that is irrelevant to the ongoing conversation. Under conditions of fascination, when the fascinated person is fully focused upon the problem with which he is dealing, he is at that time wholly *unself-conscious*. He is wholly single-minded (as opposed to two-minded). When a man is thus single-minded, his total organism seems to become integrated or organized into its most efficient mode for full functioning; so it is little wonder that the fascinated person is the one to whom occurs the inspired actions, guesses, solutions, and creative thoughts. But the capacity to become fascinated, and hence fully focused upon some one thing, person, or problem, is not easily regulated. It seems instead to require freedom from customary role-definitions, convention, and habit. It calls for the courage and freedom to get out of one's ego, one's self-concept, and even out of time and space as usually fragmented.

Persons are most likely to display some form of transcendent-behavior in situations where they have the freedom to become fascinated with what truly does fascinate them. Unfortunately, not all things in which people spontaneously become fascinated are of equal social value; indeed, some targets of fascination may endanger a man's reputation or job. Therefore, many people may be ashamed or afraid to pursue their fascinations, and they decrease thereby their opportunities for transcendent functioning.[94]

Commitment and Values

Transcendent-behavior has been shown to occur most usually in persons who are committed to some goal to which they assign high value. Commitment implies price. The more fully a person is committed to some project, problem, or outcome, the more of his time, energy, and personal resources he freely devotes to the quest on which he is launched. The conditions under which people are able to become strongly committed to their work, or to truth, justice, beauty, or goodness, are not as yet fully understood. Since values are created by man, it is most likely that an individual will become committed to some goal, achievement, or task when there have been leaders or predecessors who provide an inspiring example to imitate. Another factor which seems to promote commitment is the promise of large rewards, whether immediate or remote, concrete or symbolic. The persons who become committed to some unpopular cause—who have to fight public opinion, poverty, and even danger to life without support—are more difficult to explain.

Self-Confidence, and a Concept of Self as Transcending

People in whom transcendent behavior is a relatively frequent occurrence likely are persons who trust themselves and have developed some measure of confidence in their powers to cope with situations as they arise. That is, they attribute power to themselves (Heider,[30] pp. 237–242). Self-confidence seems to derive both from a history of graduated successes in coping with increasingly difficult and complex problems, and from the experience of being seen by other people as competent and trustworthy. Lack of self-doubt is often characteristic of explorers, daredevils, and others whose achievements transcend their own previous exploits, as well as the achievements of many of their fellow men. Any experiences which permit average people to diminish their distrust of their own capacities and their own worth, and which permit them to attribute power to themselves, probably would contribute to the frequency with which they transcend their own usual levels of functioning.

The self-concept, which, as we have seen, is a limiting factor in behavior, can also be a freeing factor for transcendent achievement. If it is true, as existential thinkers insist, that man cannot define himself in any fixed way, but is always in process of creating and then re-creating himself, then it follows that the most accurate self-concept is one which permits a man to see himself as a being with relatively unplumbed capacities for all modes of function. One of the conclusions announced by Dr. Elie Cohen,[12] a Dutch physician who survived almost four years imprisonment at the Auschwitz death camp, was that man has powers of survival and adaptation which he had never imagined. The very fact that he and a few others survived conditions calculated to produce death was the evidence for his assertion. It seems likely that *any person who formulates a fixed concept of himself, including a concept of his powers to cope, is doing himself an injustice.* Since man tends to behave in accordance with his concept of himself, then he will not rise to meet a challenge that calls for behavior in conflict with his present self-concept. If a man sees himself as weak, he will not take challenges posed by life, but will instead avoid them. If a man sees himself as always in process of being challenged and "tested" by life, and his capacities as always in process of unfolding, he probably has a self-concept more closely in tune with reality.

Symbols and the Release of Transcendence

Transcendent-behavior has been portrayed as the release of modes of behavior that ordinarily are suppressed by habit. Challenges can release transcendent behavior in a person, but so also can *symbols* like mandalas, and metaphors such as the flag, the Star of David, the name of a cause in which one believes (cf. Jung[46]), or the image of a loved person to whose well-being one has pledged himself. Frankl[21] reported that the image of his wife, which he "saw," or thought about many times during the course of his imprisonment in death camp, helped inspire him to the actions which kept him alive. Doubtless many of the feats of exploration and conquest carried out in the name of King,

Country, or the Glorious Cause all illustrate the release of transcendent functioning in the persons who pursued those exploits. The fascinating question for research is, "*How* do symbols release energies, resourcefulness, and the other requisites to transcendent functioning?" According to conventional psychological terminology, such symbols function as motive-arousers; but the psycho-physiological mechanisms by means of which this comes about are poorly understood. Indeed, excessive analysis and intellectualizing about symbols seem to rob them of their inspiring (or, at times, dispiriting and depressing) powers. They can only be meditated upon, revealing thereby new possibilities of meaning. Symbols are a variety of metaphor; and metaphor, not rational words, may be the idiom of man's self in process of transcending itself. Symbols and metaphors are experienced as irresistible images of possibility, and we need to learn more about them.

Challenge and Transcending

The concept of "challenge" has been mentioned throughout the foregoing discussion of transcendent-behavior, and it will be useful for us to examine this phenomenon in more detail. To be challenged—by a person, by God, by a possibility that has been imagined, by a problem, or by a crisis—means that an individual *cannot* ignore the situation at hand and devote his attention elsewhere. Challenges, almost by definition, are attention-grabbing. A challenge is similar to a call for help. It entices, or demands, a full focusing of attention and resources to the matter at hand. Effective leaders, teachers, and personality therapists are all exceedingly forthright in challenging others (and themselves) to transcend present levels of functioning.

The individual who responds to problems and crises as challenges to be addressed rather than as threats to be avoided is likely to display transcendence with higher than average frequency. Deeply religious people report that they experience God as a Being who perpetually challenges them; and under the instigation of this challenge, they continually bring forth from themselves achievements and feats of endurance which might be impossible for persons less challenged. It may be proposed as a hypothesis that challenge, however brought about, is a highly important condition for some types of transcendent-behavior.

Transcendent-Behavior and Healthy Personality

The foregoing sketch of transcendent-behavior and conditions for its emergence is intended to provide a glimpse of potentials for functioning that lie beyond the average or usual levels, and some hints as to means of releasing them. Since all the classes of such behavior have occurred in some few people, the promise is implicit that they can occur in more people, more of the time. One of the aims of the field of personality hygiene, beyond that of preventing mental illness, should be to understand and master the conditions for transcendent-behavior, so that, ultimately, the average personality will be not a mere non-candidate for a psychiatric hospital, but instead a being who can release his capacities for transcendent functioning as needed. Therapists of personality then would not be experts at restoring those with neurosis or psychosis to "normal" levels of function; rather, they would be more like those few inspired and inspiring teachers who are able to elicit transcendent performance from their students, to the surprise and delight of all.[94]

Perhaps the element of mystery, surprise, or unpredictability that seems associated with most of the examples of transcendence implies that man, to function most fully, must transcend the programming and shaping of his behavior and become less predictable and controllable. This is not to glorify caprice in human affairs. Rather, it is a suggestion that, when man reaches impasses in his existence and becomes ill, perhaps the solution lies not in seeking to train him so he will become "better adjusted" and more predictable. Instead, the solution may lie in so supporting and challenging him that he acquires a greater ease in entering himself and releasing the unpremeditated, spontaneous action which we have called transcendence.

Some Experiments in Transcending

There is already a great deal of work being done daily by a class of people that I shall call "transcendence experts." With or without their knowledge, they are capitalizing on the efforts of predecessors who have groped for centuries to transcend "the ego"—their own, or the egos of the thinkers of their time—viz., the Yogis, the Zen Buddhists, the Hindu mystics, the Chassidim, the alchemists, the Sufis, and others.

The transcendence experts whose work I have observed (but not evaluated in any systematic way) are "teachers" of various kinds. First, let me mention the work of Roy Hart, a voice teacher in London. This man has a clientele composed mostly of people in the performing arts—singers and actors. By a series of progressive exercises, he is able to get persons to vocalize through a continuum from a heavily vibrating basso to a piping soprano, but with true tone. I listened to a quartet at his studio in which two women sang the bass and baritone, and two manly men sang soprano, with beautiful effect. I saw persons utter unearthly (transcendent) grunts, shrieks, and cries—using their voices for expression that goes well beyond that which is customary in polite, middle-class society. The persons who took part in these exercises and performances told me they derived considerable personal, psychotherapeutic benefit from extending of the use of their voices.

Now, let me report on some observations made in a morning visit at a mental hospital near Paris, where the physiotherapy program enjoys an importance in the rehabilitation of psychotics that is equal to the psychotherapeutic program. Patients are introduced to a program of exercises and games and movements which literally get them back into their bodies. They are given massages, they take part in games which permit them to regress to early levels of childhood; they make bodily movements which go beyond the movements which typified their pre-hospital existences. They are touched by others, and they touch others' bodies in a natural way, as part of the games, and as part of everyday discourse. These patients literally are brought back into their skins, and become less afraid to feel and use their bodies, as in psychotherapy they become less afraid to acknowledge and admit their feelings, fantasies, and memories. It seems fair for me to state that, through the physiotherapeutic program, the patients transcend their concepts of their own bodies, and come to re-experience their bodies and to integrate them into human relationships in ways that permit ongoing growth of self to occur.

A deliberate exercise in transcending-behavior has been carried on in the Peace Corps' "outwardbound" training camp in Puerto Rico (cf. Jourard[40]). There, trainees are exposed to a variety of challenges that most of them have never encountered before, viz., rock-climbing, "drown-proof" procedures that permit them to stay relaxed in water for hours on end, childhood games that call on them to let go their "adult" demeanor and play patty-cake with gusto, five-day treks through the jungle with only a 4-ounce piece of salt codfish and a tea bag for provisions. The trainees discover, to their amazement, that they can meet these challenges that go beyond their previous, comfort-ridden American life-styles, and beyond their concepts of their own capabilities. In many ways, the successful Peace Corps Volunteer is an embodiment of the potentialities of young (and not so young) Americans to transcend both their own upbringing, and the concepts of the "typical American" which are endemic in host countries abroad.

If we add to this list brief mention of the coaches of people who produce magnificent performances in sports and in the musical, dancing, and other performing arts, we have an impressive source of possible information about the conditions of transcendence. There is no reason to suspect that the champions or the superb performers on stage, platform, or screen are a special breed of human beings. Rather, they are persons who committed themselves to an avenue of self-expression and presented themselves to teachers or coaches. The latter presumably shared the contender's images of possibility and set about releasing and actualizing these. I suspect that our heroes of the playing field, of the cultural arena, of the study, or of the laboratory are persons whose fulfillment is a proof or pledge of hidden potentiality *in the broad mass of the population*. Too few people have any idea of their latent possibilities. Perhaps their concepts of their powers are false, and perhaps they are false because our educational procedures indoctrinate people with a view of themselves as beings with sclerosed possibility. If it is possible for a multibillion-dollar education program to train people to see themselves as limited beings, it should also be possible for that program to encourage people to see themselves as embodiments of the capacity to transcend their present concepts of themselves and their powers.[70]

An Epilogue

Throughout this chapter, we have implied that transcendent-behavior transcends, not human possibility, but rather someone's *theory* or *concept* of possibility. We have also suggested that the theories of the investigator may be self-fulfilling, because of the peculiar balance of power that obtains in a typical setting where research into human behavior is carried on—the investigator, with a theory to test (prove), invites and often gets behavioral collusion from the low-status people who are the subjects in his study (see Chapters 2, 4). This notion, if valid, implies that investigators with daring theories about human possibility may well be able to invite or elicit astounding performances from subjects as well as they elicit behavior that proves their hypotheses about determiners of human limits.

Indeed, a "compleat psychologist" of the future will resemble the "incompleat psychologist" of the present in one respect. He will continue to seek to specify the determiners of man's condition, his behavior, and his experience, as befits a scientist committed to the assumption of a deterministic universe. But he will also be committed to freedom and respect for man's capacities for transcending, and fuller functioning. Consequently, as each new determiner is discovered and studied, he will seek ways by which the "thrust" of this determiner's impact on man can be subverted, neutralized, surmounted, or enlisted in the support of individual man's freely chosen projects, his intentional will. As things now stand, it is only the psychotherapists who seek to learn about man's "thrownness" in its myriad dimensions, in order to help him transcend it. Research psychologists must take some responsibility for the uses to which their demonstrations of "lawfulness" are put. They can show men how to beat these laws by transcending them, lest other men capitalize on the predictability that psychology reveals. They can, indeed, seek to learn more about helping man to experience his will and to eschew resignation to the thrust of determining forces. They can explore the path to those possibilities for optimal functioning that lie buried beneath habit and socialized being, so that more can realize the experience of liberation, satori, awakening, or the attainment of selfhood.

Summary

This chapter is devoted to discussion of transcendent-behavior; that is, behavior that transcends the usual or expected behavior shown by a person. Examples of transcendent-behavior were taken from the realms of thinking, perception, remembering, learning, achievement, survival, and personality reorganization.

The following factors were proposed as conditions for the emergence of transcendent-behavior in an individual: letting be, openness, focusing and fascination, commitment and values, self-confidence and a concept of self as transcendent, symbols, and challenge.

18

Epilogue: Humanistic Psychology and the Disclosure of Man

I have shown some directions I have taken, over the past ten years or so, in my efforts to make psychology more relevant to the fuller development and individuation of *persons*. These have been groping efforts, usually my response to the direction in which the main corpus of psychology was going. For a long time I felt like some kind of "outsider," with attendant feelings of self-doubt; but it soon became apparent that there were many psychologists who likewise were dissatisfied with the mainstream of psychological endeavor, and these organized into an interest group—the American Association for Humanistic Psychology. This group is singular, I think, in that it seeks no power, but seeks only to champion the view of man as a free human being. The aim is not to destroy the accomplishments of psychology to date, but to enlarge and to build upon the partial foundation that already has been laboriously constructed. The humanistic breed of psychologist seeks to find new ways to do research, to invite man to disclose himself, and to utilize findings that will further free man from stagnant images of his possibilities. We seek ways to maximize growth and to discover the social conditions that make such self-actualization possible for more people.

I will again indulge my taste for prophecy at this point, and forecast psychology in the future—perhaps to help bring this image of possibility into being. I do think that scientific psychology has served the social system well, in helping to make the process of socialization more manageable and comprehensible. We have earned whatever "salt" that government and business agencies have shaken our way. But it is time now to serve a new master, namely, the little man that Reich[79] described—and try to help him become less little. And, as

230 DISCLOSING MAN TO HIMSELF

more people are liberated from wage-earning drudgery by automation, this becomes a matter of dire urgency. As people's worlds of possibility expand, it is vital that they be able to respond to the heady wine of freedom with growth, and not terror or madness. We are truly at a time when there must be either a humanistic revolution in all branches of human enterprise and collaboration—or else we shall find that a counterreaction will take place, leading to totalitarianism of the radical right or left. Already, in places like California, where there is more of everything that exists, one finds thrusts in the direction of exploring human potentialities on all fronts—and there is likewise the potential there for fanatical, anti-humanistic repression.

I would like to see more research-psychologists exploring the frontiers of human capacities, learning ways to invite more little men into new dimensions of development. I would like to see more psychotherapists functioning as gurus and counselors for transcendence (Shaw[94]), rather than as skilled spokesmen for, and reinforcers of, the social status quo. I would like to see more psychologists functioning as protectors of human freedom and enlightenment, as disclosers of man to himself, to balance the efforts of those of us whose work has served as guidance for industrial, business, political, and institutional leaders in ways to direct masses of little men.

I would like to see psychology leading psychiatry in the arts of evoking potentials for health and full functioning, rather than following psychiatry in its search for pockets of pathology. In fact, as Szasz'[99] view that mental illness is a myth gains universal currency, psychiatry may prove to be an obsolete discipline; and a new profession of growth-guides and counselors will have to spring into being. Perhaps psychology can take the initiative in this direction. Certainly, mental hospitals, as they now exist, should be obliterated, and replaced if at all by acceptable houses of retreat and meditation—but that is gradually happening anyway. The speed might be accelerated, however.

I think that the concern for human possibilities that marks a humanistic psychologist makes him an important resource person to such agencies as the Office of Education, offering guidance and suggestions as to means for enriching our present institutions of learning, so that they educate and liberate people as well as presently they indoctrinate and socialize them. Whether this happens, of course, depends upon the initiative, resourcefulness, and vitality of humanistically oriented psychologists, as it does upon the goodwill of responsible officialdom.

We are on the brink of new leaps in the evolution of man—because of the fantastic development of technology. We must welcome this possibility, and those of us who study man can help our fellows and ourselves to find our ways and our possibilities in an unprecedented era. It is either that, or be soul-less pedants, furiously busy with irrelevant issues in the backwaters, not the mainstream, of the human course.

Bibliography

1. Bakan, D. A reconsideration of the problem of introspection. *Psychol. Bull.*, 1954, *51*, 105–118.
2. Bakan, D. *Duality in human existence*. Chicago: World Book Pub. Co., 1966.
3. Barron, F. Freedom as feeling. *J. humanistic Psychol.*, 1961, *1*, 91–100.
4. Bartlett, F. C. *Remembering*. Cambridge: Cambridge Univ. Press, 1932.
5. Berdyaev, N. *The meaning of the creative act*. New York: Collier, 1962.
6. Bettelheim, B. *The informed heart*. Glencoe: The Free Press, 1960.
7. Blum, A., *et al. Utopiates. The uses and users of LSD-25* New York: Atherton, 1965.
8. Braatøy, T. *Fundamentals of psychoanalytic technique*. New York: Wiley, 1958.
9. Buber, M. *I and thou*. New York: Scribners, 1958.
10. Buber, M. *Between man and man*. Boston: Beacon Press, 1955.
11. Bugental, J. F. T. *The search for authenticity: An existential-analytic approach to psychotherapy*. New York: Holt Rinehart & Winston, 1966.
12. Cohen, E. *Human behavior in the concentration camp*. New York: Grosset and Dunlap, 1960.
13. Deikman, A. J. Experimental meditation. *J. nerv. ment. Dis.*, 1963, *136*, 329–343.
14. Edwards, A. L. *The social desirability variable in personality assessment and research*. New York: Dryden, 1957.
15. Ellis, A. *Reason and emotion in psychotherapy*. New York: Lyle Stuart, 1962.
16. Festinger, L. *A theory of cognitive dissonance*. Evanston: Row, 1957.
17. Fiedler, F. A comparison of therapeutic relationships in psychoanalytic, nondirective and Adlerian therapy. *J. Consult. Psychol.*, 1950, *14*, 436–445.

233

18. Fisher, S., and Cleveland, S. P. *Body-image and personality*. Princeton: Van Nostrand, 1958.
19. Frank, J. D. *Persuasion and healing*. Baltimore: Johns Hopkins Press, 1961.
20. Frank, L. K. Tactile communication. *Etc. Rev. gen. Semant.*, 1958, *16*, 31–79.
21. Frankl, V. E. *From death camp to existentialism*. Boston: Beacon Press, 1959. Also published in paperback under the title, *Man's search for meaning*. New York: Washington Square Press, 1963.
22. Frankl, V. E. Dynamics, existence and values. *J. existent. Psychiat.*, 1961, *2*, 5–16.
23. Fromm, E. *The forgotten language*. New York: Rinehart, 1951.
24. Gendlin, E. T. *Experiencing and the creation of meaning*. Glencoe: The Free Press, 1962.
25. Gendlin, E. T. A theory of personality change. In Worchel, P., and Byrne, D., *Personality change*. New York: Wiley, 1964.
26. Goffman, E. *The presentation of self in everyday life*. New York: Doubleday, 1959.
27. Goffman, E. *Asylums, Essays on the social situation of mental patients and other inmates*. New York: Doubleday, 1961.
28. Harlow, H. The nature of love. *Amer. Psychol.*, 1958, *13*, 673–685.
29. Heidegger, M. *Being and time*. London: SCM Press, 1962.
30. Heider, F. *The psychology of interpersonal relations*. New York: Wiley, 1958.
31. Hoffer, E. *The true believer*. New York: Harper, 1951.
32. Hora, T. The process of existential psychotherapy. *Psychiat. Quart.*, 1960, *34*, 495–504.
33. Hora, T. Transcendence and healing. *J. existent. Psychiat.*, 1961, *1*, 501–511.
34. Husserl, E. *Ideas: General introduction to pure phenomenology*. London: Allen & Unwin, 1931.
35. Huxley, A. *The doors of perception, and heaven and hell*. New York: Harper, 1954.
36. James, W. *The varieties of religious experience*. New York: Modern Library, 1944.
37. Jourard, S. M. Self-disclosure and other-cathexis. *J. abnorm. soc. Psychol.*, 1959, *59*, 428–431.
38. Jourard, S. M. Age and self-disclosure. *Merrill-Palmer Quart. Beh. Dev.*, 1961, *7*, 191–197.
39. Jourard, S. M. *Personal adjustment*. An approach through the study of healthy personality. New York: MacMillan, 1963 (2nd ed.) (a).
40. Jourard, S. M. *Some observations by a psychologist of the Peace*

Corps' "outward bound" training program at Camp Crozier, Puerto Rico. Washington, D. C.: Peace Corps, 1963(b).
41. Jourard, S. M. The transparent self. Princeton: Van Nostrand, 1964.
42. Jourard, S. M., and Landsman, M. J. Cognition, cathexis, and the 'dyadic effect' in men's self-disclosing behavior. Merrill-Palmer Quart. Behav. Dev., 1960, 6, 178–186.
43. Jourard, S. M., and Remy, R. M. Perceived parental attitudes, the self, and security. J. consult, Psychol., 1955, 19, 364–366.
44. Jourard, S. M., and Secord, P. F. Body-cathexis and personality. Brit. J. Psychol., 1956, 46, 130–138.
45. Jung, C. G. Two essays on analytical psychology. New York: Meridian Books, 1956.
46. Jung, C. G. Symbol formation In Coll. Works, Vol. 8, pp. 45–61.
47. Kazantzakis, N. The Odyssey, a modern sequel. New York: Simon and Schuster, 1958.
48. Kelly, G. The psychology of personal constructs. New York: Norton, 1955.
49. Kesey, K. One flew over the cuckoo's nest. New York: Signet, 1963.
50. Kessen, W., and Mandler, G. Anxiety, pain, and the inhibition of distress. Psychol. Rev., 1961, 68, 396–404.
51. Kretschmer, W. Die meditativen Verfahren in der Psychotherapie. Zeit. f. Psychother. u. Med. Psychol., 1951, 1, No. 3.
52. Laing, R. D. Transcendental experience in relation to religion and psychosis. In The politics of experience and the bird of paradise. London: Penguin, 1967.
53. Laing, R. D. The self and others. London: Tavistock Institute Press, 1962.
54. Laing, R. D. The 'divided' self. London: Tavistock, 1960.
55. Laing R. D., and Cooper, D. Reason and violence. London: Tavistock, 1964.
56. Laing, R. D., and Esterson, A. Sanity, madness and the family. London: Tavistock, 1964.
57. Laing, R. D., Phillipson, H., and Lee, R. Interpersonal perception. A theory and a method of research. London: Tavistock, 1966.
58. Leary, T., Alpert, R., and Metzner. The psychedelic experience.
59. Luijpen, W. A. Existential phenomenology. Pittsburgh: Duquesne Univ. Press, 1963.
60. Lyons, J. Psychology and the measure of man. New York: Free Press, 1965.
61. Maher, B. A. Progress in experimental psychology. New York: Academic Press, 1964.

62. Maslow, A. H. *Toward a psychology of being*. Princeton: Van Nostrand, 1962.
63. Maupin, E., Individual differences in response to a Zen meditation exercise. *J. consult. Psychol.*, 1965.
64. May, R. Intentionality, the heart of human will. *J. Humanistic Psychol.*, 1965, 5, 202–209.
65. Merleau-Ponty, M. *The phenomenology of perception*. London: Routledge and Kegan Paul, 1962.
66. Miller, H. *The air-conditioned nightmare*. New York: New Directions, 1945.
67. Mowrer, O. H. *The crisis in psychiatry and religion*. Princeton: Van Nostrand, 1961.
68. Mowrer, O. H. *The new group therapy*. Princeton: Van Nostrand, 1964.
69. Murphy, G. *Personality, a biosocial approach to origins and structure*. New York: Harper, 1947.
70. Murphy, G. *Human potentialities*. New York: Basic Books, 1958.
71. Orne, M. T. The social psychology of the psychological experiment: with particular reference to demand characteristics and their implications. *Amer. Psychol.*, 1962, 17, 776–783.
72. Polanyi, M. *Personal knowledge. Towards a post-critical philosophy*. New York: Harper and Row, 1964.
73. Powell, Jr., W. J. A comparison of the reinforcing effects of three types of experimenter response on two classes of verbal behavior in an experimental interview. Unpub. Ph. D. dissertation, Univ. of Florida, 1963.
74. Privette, Gayle. Some factors in transcendent behavior. *Teachers College Record*, 1965, 66.
75. Rank, O. *Will therapy*, New York: Knopf, 1947.
76. Rapaport, D., Gill, M., and Schafer, R. *Diagnostic psychological testing:* the theory, statistical evaluation, and diagnostic application of a battery of tests. Chicago: Year Book Publishers, 1946.
77. Reich, W. *Character analysis*. New York: Orgone Institute Press, 1949.
78. Reich, W. *The murder of Christ*. New York: Orgone Institute Press, 1953.
79. Reich, W. *Listen, little man*. New York: Orgone Institute Press, 1948.
80. Reifel, Lee. Unpublished research, University of Florida, 1965.
81. Reitan, H. and Lackey, L. Unpublished research, University of Florida, 1966.
82. Ribble, Margaret, *The rights of infants*. New York: Columbia Univ. Press, 1943.

83. Rivenbark III, W. R. Unpublished research, University of Florida, 1963, 1964.
84. Rogers, C. *Counseling and psychotherapy*. Boston: Houghton Mifflin, 1942.
85. Rosenthal, R. The effect of the experimenter on the results of psychological research. In B. A. Maher (Ed.), *Progress in experimental personality research*. New York: Academic Press, 1964, 79–114. Also *Experimenter effects in behavioral research*. New York: Appleton-Century-Crofts, 1967.
86. Sartre, J. P. *Being and nothingness*. An essay on phenomenological ontology. London: Methuen, 1956.
87. Sartre, J. P. *La critique de la raison dialectique*. Paris: Librairie Gallimard, 1960.
88. Sartre, J. P. *The psychology of imagination*. New York: Citadel Press, 1961.
89. Sartre, J. P. *The problem of method*. London: Methuen, 1963.
90. Schachtel, E. G. *Metamorphosis*. New York: Basic Books, 1961.
91. Scheff, T. *Being mentally ill*. Chicago: Aldine, 1966.
92. Secord, P. F., and Jourard, S. M. The appraisal of body-cathexis: Body-cathexis and the self. *J. consult. Psychol.*, 1953, *17*, 343–347.
93. Secord, P. F., and Backman, C. *Social psychology*. New York: McGraw-Hill, 1965.
94. Shaw, F. J. *Reconciliation:* A theory of man transcending. Jourard, S. M. and Overlade, D. C. (eds.) Princeton: Van Nostrand, 1966.
95. Sivadon, P., and Gantheret, F. *Rééducation corporelle des fonctions mentales*. Paris: Éditions Sociales Françaises, 1966 (in press).
96. Spitz, R. *"Hospitalism," in Psychoanalyt. Stud. Child. I.* New York: International Univ. Press, 1945.
97. Stratil, M. Unpublished research, 1966.
98. Sulzer, J. Chiropractic as psychotherapy. *Psychotherapy: theory, research and practice.* 1964, 2.
99. Szasz, T. *Pain and pleasure. A study of bodily feelings.* New York: Basic Books, 1957.
100. Szasz, T. *The myth of mental illness.* New York: Harper, 1961.
101. Tawney, R. H. *Religion and the rise of capitalism.*
102. Time-Life. *The drug takers.* New York: Time, Inc., 1965.
103. Trocchi, A. A revolutionary proposal. In *City Lights Journal, No. 2.* San Francisco: City Lights, 1964, 14–36.
104. Van Kaam, A. *Existential foundations of psychology.* Pittsburgh: Duquesne Univ. Press, 1966.
105. Watts, A. W. *The way of Zen.* New York: Mentor, 1959.

106. Watts, A. W. *Nature, man, and woman.* New York: Mentor, 1960.
107. Watts, A. W. *The joyous cosmology.* New York: Vintage, 1965.
108. Webb, W. B. The choice of the problem. *Amer. Psychol.,* 1961, *16,* 223–227.
109. Weber, M. *The Protestant ethic.* New York: Scribner, 1948.
110. Werner, H. *The comparative psychology of mental development.* Chicago: Follett, 1948.
111. Whitaker, C., and Malone, J. P. *The roots of psychotherapy.* New York: Blakiston, 1953.
112. Wilson, C. *The outsider.* London: Gollancz, 1956. (Paperback edition: London, Pan Books, 1963.)

Name Index

239

Subject Index